The Art of BEing... HUman

Olusanya Bey

OlusanyaBey

Copyright

Copyright © 15,110 (2024) by Olusanya Bey
All rights reserved.
No portion of this book may be reproduced in any form without written permission from the publisher or author, except as permitted by U.S. copyright law.
This publication is designed to provide accurate and authoritative information regarding the subject matter covered. It is sold with the understanding that neither the author nor the publisher provides legal, counseling, investment, accounting, or other professional services. While the publisher and author have used their best efforts in preparing this book, they make no representations or warranties with respect to the accuracy or completeness of the contents of this book and specifically disclaim any implied warranties of merchantability or fitness for a particular purpose. No warranty may be created or extended by sales representatives or written sales materials. The advice and strategies contained herein may not be suitable for your situation. You should consult with a professional when appropriate. Neither the publisher nor the author shall be liable for any loss of profit or any other commercial damages, including but not limited to special, incidental, consequential, personal, or other damages.
Book Cover by Olusanya Bey
Charts & Tables by Olusanya Bey
First edition 15,110 (2024)

DEDICATION

This book is dedicated to the Mothers of my humanity, first and foremost to Akuaya Eyo- the Mother of ALL Creation, the Divine compeer of- Oyaluode, it is through Her that we may come to know God, to my Mother- Ruth Springer Gill- who ushered me into existence from a state of triple darkness, into the light of life, to my Great Aunt- Ruth Springer- who pulled me through the fire into the circle of my Ancestors... to chastise and guide me, before sending me back to heal and fulfill my destiny, to my maternal Grand Mother- Gladys Russell Springer- who taught me the power of refinement, to my paternal Grand Mother- Doris Andes Gill- who fed my love for words and reading, to my daughter- Cypris Sky Warr- for continually helping to raise her father to manhood, to her Mother- Robin (Omiladun) Morton- she who healed me physically, mentally and spiritually, and to ALL WOMEN who demonstrate the Creator's ability to conceive and create (both mentally and physically) and represent the Divine Feminine aspect of Absolute BEing . Those who, from the beginning of time, have conceived, delivered and nurtured a Universe, despite opposition from a cultural mindset hell-bent on denying the "truth" of who you are, and what you represent.
I LOVE YOU DEARLY!!!

(Poetic Interlude)

The Measure of Me

And the evening and the morning were the first day" Genesis 1
ever wondered why the... scriptures... phrase it that way?
what exactly were the... prophets... trying to say?
perhaps the measure of time... did not begin with the sun...
instead...
it's mother... is the moon, it is She... who gives birth thru her...
night...
nurturing him... in the darkness of her... womb... giving him...
dee'light.
hmmm... what are we to assume?
while contemplating this metaphor her... image came to mind...
aaaah! this! is what i... met her for... so she and i can...
come... together... a love divine... giving birth to... the cycles of...
time.
i bow to her... the sun sets and She... ascends to her... heavenly
throne...
we... give birth to a... Universe and... call it... home!
O nwo Olodumare l'oju l'oju (looking at god in heaven)
O nwo ara aye l'enu. (looking at humans on earth)
Isoro Orun, e wa ba mi t'oro yii se, Isoro Orun. (heavenly spirits, descend and make this ritual a success for me, heavenly spirits)
Isoro Orun, e wa ba wa tun oro yii se, Isoro Orun. (heavenly spirits, descend and make this ritual a success for us, heavenly spirits)
mother... earth... she... yin.
the rhythm of your movement... your biological... and celestial...
nature...
it is... in you i... find... the womb... to give birth...
to the space... to a place... for... some time... to begin...
time to intone the... beautiful phrases ... to invoke the energy of
all! ...your beautiful...phases... the magical ways... in which you
express...

Olusanya Bey

the many faces... the facets... the multiplicity... of this... ALL! i see...
this always changing, never-ending... creation...
while you... forever... remain the same...
and! maintain... the celestial cycle of the creative spirit...
in your rhythm... mmmm! that rhythm...
that wavelike rhythm of your... buttocks...
as they rock... keeping time... like... tick... tock
back and forth... while you walk... in a wavelike... wavelike... like...
my mother's hips?...
water...
omi-gbuu (the deep splashing water)
ojo-gbuu (the deep splashing rain)
omi, aribu-sola (water, one who makes the deep a place of honor)
abiyamo-afidi-soju-ona (one whose vagina is a road of passage)
abiyamo-abirin-welewele (the nursing mother of gentle strides)
yeah! my mother walks... and talks... with a rhythm... like the ocean
ogudu gbada... ogudu gbada... ogudu gbada... (the sound of sea waves)
yes!... my mother's hips are... wavelike... in motion.
and your honey breath... as you inhale... and exhale...
it whispers in my ear... as i seek to move in harmony...
with the rise and fall.. of your life's cycle, the beat...
of your pulsing... heart... in tune... or... in time... with you.
because i realize your rhythm... mmmm!
that rhythm... izzzz... giving motion to the cycles of eternity,
and harmony with you... is the true... measure of a man.
i mean... speaking... my word... my bond... my life... my measure...
as a man...
it is important that when i... measure. my time...
it has been... well spent... in harmonious movement with the mother...
the earth... she... yin... balance to my yang...
the sacred synchronization of sun and moon... heavenly bodies on a horizontal plane...

5

OlusanyaBey

The Art of BEing HUman

moving in tune... shall come... wait! Go slow... not too soon...
AUMMM... KRIIMMM... BIG BANG!
liiiiyeee! poppy... yeah! ...and you mommy...
are the high priest and high priestess of... this! most sacred alignment...
we set the tone... the tune... the sun... the moon...
the heavenly rhythm... hmmmm! we set a Universe in motion
yeah!... earth... she... yin... my... sacred womb(man)...
i want to spend some quality... time... with you...
so that you... can measure the man... that... i am...
as i move in harmony to your rhythm... to your... motion...
to the undulating waves... of your ocean...
ogudu gbada... ogudu gbada... ogudu gbada...
that rhythm... mmmm! that rhythm...
Iya mi Osun ati Isoro Orun, e wa ba mi t'oro yii se, Iya mi Osun ati Isoro Orun.
Ase... Ase... Ase...
Toh... Toh... Toh...

PREFACE

**In the Name Of Allah, The Almighty, The Merciful.
All Praise Is Due Allah, The Rabb[1] of All the Worlds.**

La ilaha illa Allahu.

There is nothing to worship, there is only Allah.

~Muhammad, Surah 47:19

The Art of BEing... HUman... is a poem in progress, written by the invisible hand of the author of this UnIverse. That would be... She. It is a semi-autobiographical work of non-fiction penned by the God'Us.
In my UnIverse the Grand Architect is a single mother/nature

---

[1] The compositional qualities denoted by the Names comprising existence (Rububiyyah). Everything that exists in the UnIverse is a composition of consciousness + energy. The primary source of power that drives all actions in this dimension is no other than the qualities pertaining to the supremacy of Rububiyyah.
Our Rabb is nothing other than the Name composition/Divine qualities comprising our essence. However, these Divine names express themselves through us in the form of compositions, and this compositional structure is our unique constitution as an individual.
In respect to our 'compositional constitution', the names comprising our essence and their specific proportions, we are servants of our 'Rabb'. In consideration of the attributes of our being and our absolute essence we are not different to or separate from Allah.
Once we get to know our essence and our attributes, we will see that all of the meanings that manifest through us are the results of the Divine names, and that's when the path to knowing ourselves will be opened to us. Then we will begin to know ourselves in terms of our essential being and as the various forms and meanings in existence. Indeed! We ALL come in the name of ... Allah.

7

The Art of BEing HUman

raising Suns and daughters (who resemble full Moons and other stellar, heavenly bodies) in her image, teaching them to sing a song of creation, so that they may engender never-ending cycles of... time, with nothing, but love to spend. That's right! The first song in this UnIverse was a hymn[him]... sung into BEing by... Her. Polar opposites, complimentary in their opposition, magnetically attracted, vibrating in harmony... moving in a... rhythm... a dance!

This BEing of Light... the perSun called Olusanya is also a poem in progress... a Divine Utterance. Her word... made flesh. God-in-Person. The Creator's finest idea made complete, given autonomy to experience creation from a God's-eye point of view! In my moments of solitude, I've come to realize that I'm just a messenger... trying to stay out of the way of a message that only I have been preordained to deliver, and it seems I can only fulfill this task successfully if I surrender my will to Hers. I am not the author of this poem. I am the pen and the paper... the subject observing, the object BEing observed. I am... Eve's 'Atom'... the creative spark of Her genius, typed in genetic codes called DNA, AND... inscribed on bones, hidden in plain sight, for open minds to see. It is not within my capacity to claim authorship, but I am made in her image and claim the copy-rights & lefts for the story I am born to tell.

And so it begins... Imagine if you will... a man impregnated with the seed of awareness, from SHE... Blessed to nourish this germ of life as it gestates into a living being... a "divine" example of inter-being... a massive conglomeration of elements. The mental artifacts and constructs... of a man molded by his family, environment, time, and... circumstances... his interactions with the UnIverse. The emptiness of space... filled with... everything and... nothing... illusory... like thoughts, here one second, gone the next.

This book is only here to attract your attention for a moment. If I get your 'full' attention in the "now", then I will have it forever. Iqra! (Read!)

The Art of BEing HUman

Olusanya Bey

I would be remiss if I let the reader begin to read without first advising them to approach the information shared with your "child-mind". Suspend everything you 'believe' to be true and approach this book with a sense of wonder and excitement about what you are about to discover! Beliefs are nothing more than self-confining theories that cannot be proven true. Read this work with an open "third eye". You will transform onto a higher plane of consciousness and push your BEing, beyond belief to actuality, to the direct experience of higher creative forms and vibrations.

Noble Drew Ali, the founder of the Moorish Divine National Movement stated, "In order to change a people, you must change their literature." This book is my demonstration. An invite to my brotHers and siStars to embrace change, to embrace Sankofa... to go back and fetch it (our Ancestral traditions and technologies), put them in today's context, so that we may create the beautiful world we all know is possible, but seem to have difficulty manifesting.

This book will not introduce you to anything you do not already know, or to information you have not already been exposed to. This is a book about 'open secrets'. Open secrets are those that are obviously visible, accessible to everyone, but their substance remains hidden because most people do not know or understand the significance behind the symbols in their lives, or because the truth is often camouflaged from the masses, so that they can continue to be shepherded... like sheeple, by false prophets, pseudo-religions, lies and deceit. Signs and symbols are not just for marketing, traffic signs, ornamentation, or arbitrary pointless impressions with no objective purpose. Signs and symbols have actual, unique and explicit meanings, they offer us goals and provide us with guidance. Some can be very simple messages, like a "STOP" sign, however failure to heed this sign may cause an "accident", possibly affecting many lives, beyond those involved in the crash. Signs also identify what direction you are traveling ("91 S" or "84 E"), or what you can do on your way ("Restaurants

Ahead," or "Basketball Hall of Fame, next exit"). The astronomical signs and symbols are also generic, but are recognizable ONLY IF YOU KNOW the meaning behind them. The letters of the alphabet, as well as numbers are signs and symbols, so the act of reading is not only the act of deciphering symbols, but also interpreting them correctly so that you can extract their entire meaning and the truth contained within them. The same can be said for mathematics. Dear Reader, don't just decipher the words in this book. Analyze them, digest them, assimilate them, reflect on their effects upon your person. These are not just words... they are vibrations/frequencies, some will resonate with you and some won't. All of them are going to affect you, so you might as well pay attention.

> *"And Hu it is who spread out the earth, placed firm mountains and rivers on it, and made two of every kind of fruit. He draws the veil of night over the day. Indeed, there are signs in these matters for a people who reflect."*

~Ar 'Rad, Surah 13:3

One of the greatest open secrets of America that has been concealed for far too long is the "identity theft" of this continent's original inhabitants. We currently find our nation embroiled in conflicts over what has been labeled "identity politics". However, this is not something new or recent in terms of American history or world history. The Greeks are often referred to as the "fathers of Western civilization, yet when you read the historical accounts written by the Ancient Greeks themselves, they consistently point to Kemet/Ancient Egypt as the source of their knowledge and learning. Why have the majority of so-called historians ignored this fact and given the Greeks credit for something they never took credit for themselves? Although we may accurately accuse the Greeks of "cultural appropriation" it is clear from their own historical accounts that they were not trying to claim Kemet's

Olusanya Bey

identity, in fact, would often give credit where credit was due.

America, however is another story. The hybrid-European colonists, fully aware of the identity of this continent's original inhabitants implemented a plan, through the power of the pen, to co-opt/appropriate/steal their identity. Why?

In international law identity and land go hand in hand. One's identity is derived from one's land of origin. The hybrid-European colonists, having expatriated themselves from England or their land of origin via the creation of the first Continental Congress, Declaration of Independence and revolutionary war, needed a new identity that was not tied to Great Britain. No one ever asks how the colonists were able to arm themselves and fight a war against the nation that, up until their rebellion, provided them with most of their needs. Some historians may mention the alliances formed with the continent's original inhabitants, but never go into detail about the basis of these agreements/treaties, or the scope of their obligations. If they had it would reveal the diabolical degrees of their betrayal to the indigenous people. The colonists did not just give themselves a new identity that linked them to the natives and their land, they also changed the native's identity. In reality there is no such thing as a "native American" because the natives of Central, North and South America never identified themselves as "Americans" OR THEIR CONTINENTS AS THE "AMERICAS". That was an identity given to them by *"individuals having a particular racial, religious, ethnic, social, or cultural identity seeking to promote their own specific interests or concerns without regard to the interests or concerns of any larger political group"* (i.e., The original people of North, Central and South America). That is the literal meaning of identity politics according to Noah Webster. First the colonists renamed the land, then they mislabeled the original people by calling them Indian, Black, Negro and Colored. Is it any wonder that the so-called colored people of America have such a difficult time identifying themselves? Our current state of affairs is the natural result of a long-standing practice of identity politics which, like all endeavors founded upon fiction or falsehood, must eventually come to a head and respond to natural law which cannot be dismissed by ideologies and dogma.

Identity:[2]

1. a: sameness of essential or generic character in different instances
   b: sameness in all that constitutes the objective reality of a thing : oneness

1. a: the distinguishing character or personality of an individual : individuality
   b: the relation established by psychological identification

Good Ol' Noah Webster, widely known as the "father of American English, in his 1828 dictionary defined American as: noun "a term originally applied to the aboriginals, or copper-colored races, found here by the Europeans; but now applied to the descendants of Europeans born in America; A native of America". America's entire identity is a product of escheat and hypothecation, cultural appropriation in its purest form. Who were these copper-colored people, how did they identify themselves, when did they become "red", and why did the colonists choose to label them American, later label them Indian, Negro, Colored and Black, instead of naming them by their chosen appellations? Until we correctly identify the original inhabitants, and the reason a term was

---

[2] It is the author's premise that what we are dealing with as a culture when it comes to so-called identity politics goes much deeper than the average dialogues about the subject. Most of the discussions center on aspects of identity that deal with personality and an individuals psychological identity. These are subjective aspects of identity, are open to interpretation. However, it is a fact that human beings share an essential oneness or generic character, a sameness in all that constitutes their objective reality as a species, and as individuals (in different instances). As in all existent things, identity has an objective aspect and a subjective aspect.

[3] American Dictionary of the English Language, Noah Webster 1828

Olusanya Bey

"applied" to them instead of "identifying" them by their chosen names, no American identity is safe from erasure. As much as I am tempted to go into detail on this subject, it is not the purpose of this book. However, in order to put the system I am introducing in its proper context we will have to discuss America's habit of misappropriation, attempted erasure, and total fabrication of identities to some extent. After all, sans my inherent racist social conditioning, it wasn't difficult for me to track down the origin of the Tzulkin system (generally known as playing cards) even though numerous authors before me allowed themselves to fall into the trap of inherent bias and either could not, or would not, follow the trail of bread crumbs to the loaf of bread or to the bakers themselves. Individuals in America who identify themselves as white (and black) have a great deal of difficulty overcoming their social-conditioning and recognizing historical facts, in particular; 1) how far back into antiquity the history of so-called "black" people actually reaches, 2) that we established the foundations of civilization and a monolithic, "pyramid culture/network" that began in the Americas and spanned the globe. Again, as much as I am tempted to go into greater detail, that is not the purpose of this book. I just want to present this calendar/divination system I am sharing in its proper historical context so that we may restore it to its original form and function and learn to use this ancient technology to solve our modern-day woes. We can discuss America's fictional history and fabrication of world history at a later date. I merely want to point out that many of our issues as a nation are a result of mis-taken identities. We have forfeited our identities as children of the Most High for a

---

[4] The author is using the term "pyramid culture" to identify those cultures that built "monoliths" to demonstrate their understanding of, and alignment with, "Universal forces and powers. Although many of these monoliths were pyramids, they remain the most well-known, we also have standing stone structures like Stonehenge, the Gate of the Sun/Calendar Gate in Tiahuanaco, Bolivia, or the observatory of Xochicalco, in the Mexican state of Morelos where a vertical opening in this artificial cave produces in the dark chamber a perfectly perpendicular beam of light, when the sun is passing through the local zenith.

myriad of pseudo-identities that only serve to move us further away from our essential nature and Oneness.

Occasionally I will provide definitions of certain words because I want to be clear about what I am presenting. I have come to realize that, as a society, we have fallen into a bad habit of redefining words that have been agreed upon throughout history. Today we live in a nation where words are redefined or simply made up out of thin air so that individuals can validate their thoughts and feelings, in the face of actual facts and realities they find too uncomfortable or difficult to deal with.

The oldest calendar system in history was created by a people known as the Tutul-Xi, more commonly referred to as the Olmecs. There is a direct connection between the Tutul-Xi and the continent commonly known as Africa but that is a discussion for another time and place. The Mayans inherited the calendar systems of the Xi, who through their precise, accurate, scientific observations were able to formulate their astronomical calendars and apply their knowledge of these laws and norms to arrive at a profound understanding of biological-celestial mechanics, of which we HUman BEings play a part. Thomas Morrell, in his work entitled "The Ancient Book of Time, the Lost Mayan Time Codes" vols. 1-3 was the first contemporary Cardologists I had found in my studies to make the connection between the playing cards and the Mayan calendar systems, this connection has also been explored and expounded upon by Dr. Ali Muhammad and the Aboriginal University.

Incidentally, if you are a religious person who is easily offended by anything that may challenge your religious beliefs then this may not be the book for you. Although I may use references from different religious scriptures/traditions or so-called Holy books I am sharing what I have identified as a "Sacred Science" and "way of living", based upon actual facts and natural law, not "beliefs". This Tao has been expressed throughout the ages in metaphor, within

The Art of BEing HUman

Olusanya Bey

ALL of the Sacred Scriptures, and was simply known as the religion of the Stars. Throughout the course of history these "Sun" books or astronomical documents have been co-opted by the different religious authorities and converted into mysticism, superstition and dogma, used as a means to control and mislead the masses. If we can suspend our beliefs and look at the history of our planet objectively, it is an undeniable fact that the greatest atrocities that have been perpetuated throughout history have been in the name of the different religions. Humanities most infamous and atrocious crimes have all been perpetrated by "believers". For the sake of this book the term "believer" is defined as; *an individual or group of individuals who accept things on face value, from an emotional basis, that they cannot prove to be true or factual.* When I use the term "religion" I am referring to *an organized system of beliefs, centered around an iconic individual, a cult of personality used to shepherd the masses.* It is important to understand ALL religious teachings in the context of their human historical, cultural and social development in order for us to promote greater understanding and continue to advance humanity. Keep in mind that the etymology of the word religion identifies its Latin root as "religere/religare". Relegere, according to Cicero, means to "go through again" (in reading or in thought), from re- "again" + legere "read". However, etymology among the later ancients (Servius, Lactantius, Augustine) and the interpretation of many modern writers connect it with religare "to bind fast" or to "bind again/back" by virtue of the notion "place an obligation on," or "bond between humans and their Creator." Therefore, religion in its true sense would be *a system of thought or beliefs designed to re-connect/bind HUmans back to their Creator.* Religion is the practice of "re-alignment", a way for us to restore our connection to the Divine, open ourselves to its guidance, and develop our full potential as "children of that which is Most High".

Contrary to the beliefs of many there is absolutely nothing irreligious or atheistic in the employment of astronomical emblems to describe and illustrate the nature and attributes of

Absolute BEing/Divinity. If so, the writers of the Bible have been very naughty, because that sacred volume is full of solar and astronomical references to the Creator. (Numbers 24:17[5]; Psalm 19:1-4[6]; Matthew 2:1-2[7]; Daniel 12:3[8]; Revelation 22:16[9]). In fact, the first words found in the Bible introduce us to the Creator of all things through astronomy when it states, "In the beginning God created the Heavens and the Earth".

There are basic questions that human beings have been asking themselves for centuries but modern man still seems to have no answers: What is the Universe, who am I, what is my relation to the Universe? Even though countless philosophers, scientists and mystics have been explaining these topics in their own capacity, they have not been able to offer holistic answers to the world of thought that has satisfied everyone. Or have they? It is the

---

[5] "I saw him and not from now, and at the end and it is not near; the star shall shine from Yaquuv and the Prince shall arise from Israel, and he shall destroy the mighty men of Moab and he shall subject all the sons of Shayth."
Aramaic Bible in Plain English.

[6] Heaven makes heard the glory of God and the firmament shows the work of his hands.
Day unto day pours forth speech; night unto night shows knowledge.
There is no speech nor words whose voice will not be heard.
Their Gospel went forth into all the Earth, and their words into the end of the world; in them he pitched his tabernacle for the sun.
Aramaic Bible in Plain English

[7] 1. Now when Yeshua was born in Bethlehem of Judaea, in the days of Herodus the King, The Magi came from The East to Jerusalem. 2. And they were saying, "Where is The King of the Judaeans who has been born?" For we have seen his star in The East and we have come to worship him.
Aramaic Bible in Plain English

[8] And doers of good and the intelligent shall shine as the light of the heavenly sphere, and those who declare the many righteous shall be shining brightly and remaining like the stars for eternity, and to the eternity of eternities.
Aramaic Bible in Plain English

[9] I, Yeshua, have sent my Angel to testify these things among you before the assemblies. I AM THE LIVING GOD, The Root and The Offspring of David, and his Companion, and The Bright Morning Star.
Aramaic Bible in Plain English

Olusanya Bey

author's assertion that what we know and perceive as the Cosmos/Universe is the manifestation and expression of ONE Infinite energy/BEing, that is "Divine" in Nature, and within which everything we see (and don't see) has it's BEing.

The western religious traditions are ancient allegories/metaphors of the yearly passage of the 'personified' Sun among the twelve polarities of the Zodiac and are founded upon a system of astronomical symbols and emblems employed for the purpose of teaching and illustrating two truths; 1. the existence of ONE spiritual, invisible, omnipresent, omniscient, and omnipotent BEing, and the immortality of the HUman soul, and 2. that these two doctrines were also originally taught in all of the ancient mystery schools, by the use of the same astronomical metaphors and symbols. Astro-logics* and the Tzulkin (in their proper form) retain these truths, while the different religions have, for the most part, either degenerated into corrupt systems of poorly-disguised sun worship, or dogma designed to mislead and control the masses. The sun, originally intended to be a 'symbol' of Absolute BEing, was, over time, confused with the anthropomorphic 'personification of God' and itself worshiped as a 'God'. Our destinies... as HUmans BEing do not require worship of any being/thing, it simply requires us to contemplate the nature of our BEing in relationship to Absolute BEing/Divinity, to express this Absolute BEing through our own unique composition or energy matrix, or as the Quran points out, our unique "disposition".

Say, "Each does according to his disposition, Your Lord knows best

---

[10] I am using the term astro-logics as a way to differentiate between the science of biological and celestial mechanics (the reasoning that supports its application) practiced by our Ancestors and contemporary Astrology. The Tzulkin/Card system and Astrology share some of the same biological and celestial mechanics, but they are two very different systems in terms of methodology. The author has observed that many Cardologists have superimposed numerous contemporary Astrology practices upon the Tzulkin/Cards and have missed out on the simplicity and beauty of the system's "astro-logics".

The Art of BEing HUman

who is better guided in the way."

~Quran Surah 17:84

Now... having said all of that, what if there are means for us to decipher these signs and symbols, to know our unique composition, our individual energy matrix or life purpose? The playing cards, the system widely known as the Destiny Cards is exactly that... a key to decoding the "symbols of our destiny"! How ironic... a key to unlocking the Divine potential within every human being was created in the so-called Americas, by the Ancestors of people who have had their "human" potential put into question by cultural appropriation, misinformation and outright lies. It is not the 'only' means for us to receive guidance. Our Indigenous ancestors around the world have developed many systems of divination that allow us to tap into our "essential BEing" and communicate with the Divine.

We have reached a point in our evolution as a species where our physical sciences have finally developed to the point where we have begun to decode and verify the 'spiritual science' hidden in the metaphors of our Ancestors and Ascended Elders. We have also reached a period in our nation's history where access to information has allowed "original people" to bypass their "gatekeepers" and obtain historical information that has not been whitewashed, watered down by voluntary assimilation and an unhealthy desire to "fit-in" and be "accepted". Individuals, especially the descendants of the First/Old World people, will now be able to openly encounter the Universe and their experience of it without intermediaries (parasites, politicians, priests, pundits, so-called intellectuals) forcing social, religious, or ethical categories upon us.

This book is a challenge to let go of and transcend everything you believe to be true, so that you can begin to insperience/experience your "Divine" BEing, and KNOW that to be true. Your BEing, OUR

The Art of BEing HUman

Olusanya Bey

BEing, ALL BEing is an intelligent expression of Unity and Love made manifest by this Creative Energy/BEing more commonly referred to as God. This book is a gift from our Most Ancient Ancestor, a way to "READ" the system, the Book of Movement and Measure put in motion by Absolute BEing, and to understand our BEing in relationship to it, each other, and EVERY other form of BEing in our UnIverse!

"HU is the Originator of the heavens and the earth, and when HU wills to create a thing, HU only says to it: 'BE', and it is."
~Quran Surah 2:117

To know the truth, to have one's 'self-awareness' raised, not by recognizing a political philosophy, but by knowing what the simple signs and symbols of everyday life mean, a person can choose. She/He can choose (that's freedom!) to participate... or not... in the good, bad or indifferent aspects of our society, government, religion, and commerce. Having the ability to choose, to make conscious and not socially-conditioned or manipulated choices, is true freedom based on knowledge, wisdom and understanding.

The science shared in this book is a gift from the Most High, passed down from time immemorial by our Tutul-Xi, Kamitic, Moorish, "African" Ancestors and transmitted through me... to you.

Accept it or reject it. The truth needs no champion. It is what it is, doesn't care how you feel.

"In him we live, and move, and have our being; as certain also of your own poets have said, for we are also his offspring."

~Acts 17:28 (KJV)

OlusanyaBey

The Art of BEing HUman

(Poetic Interlude)

The Common Denominator

from gil-scot heron to common...
the denominator...
that remains the same...
is the name "Original People"...
the god and the goddess...
the church and the steeple...
the mother and father..."" come as ONE
ALL things being equal... their seed... the sequel...
gives birth to another ONE... another sun...
not cuz your mine... because you shine...
radiating light from the "Divine"...
we are ALL! thoughts...
from the original mind...
the breath of life...
to inspire and expire...
to inhale and exhale...
life is a rhythm...
a rhyme... a dance with seven veils...
like... hip! hop! tick...'"" tock..."" you can't stop!...
the movements and measures of time...
the code of mathematics scales...
from zero to nine, the cipher to be Born...
the natural order of elevation...
so why are we in... decline?
kinky is just another word for spiral..."" G!
it's your nature to wind...
to get wound and spring forth... resound...
blaze through summer...
then fall... rewind in winter, then..."" rebound.
in the beginning was the word...
a movement in sound...
a tone becomes a verb...

The Art of BEing HUman

Olusanya Bey

the movement is the music...
the ways and actions are the measure...
ya heard!
and yet I'm still disturbed...
by the amount of our people...
who refuse to hear... the song of the caged bird...
when it enters their... inner ear...
whose wingtips pound their... "inner" ear drum...
it sings songs of free [the] dom...
flips the script...
so that blind, deaf, and... dumb...
means that we have BEcome...
enlightened people, no longer medieval...
we see no.. hear no... speak no evil...
in just one moment... I believe we will...
dance to the music of the original drummer...
the beat of the original ONE...'"' love is god- god is love- the
HEART!... is the original drum
Can u feel it? Can u feel it? Our funky sensation!

INTRODUCTION

THOU ART... DIVINE!

1. A psalm committed to Aspah. God standeth in the assembly of gods: he judgeth among gods.
2. How long will you judge unjustly, and accept the persons of the wicked? Selah
3. Do right to the poor and the fatherless: do justice to the poor and needy.
4. Deliver the poor and needy: save them from the hand of the wicked.
5. They know not and understand nothing: they walk in darkness, albeit all the foundations of the earth be moved.
6. I have said, "Ye are gods, and all ye are children of the Most High.
7. But ye shall die as a man, and ye princes, shall fall like others."
8. O God, arise, therefore judge thou the earth: for thou shalt inherit all.

~The Geneva Bible- Psalms 82:1-8

Absolutely nothing happens by chance or accident. As a young god growing up in the desert of Queens, New York I would often play the game Othello with the other young brothers and sisters in the community. It was one of our favorite games. Our generation were sirius gamers, but most of our games were played on boards or with a deck of playing cards. We didn't have the benefit of video technology (we also had no idea about the technology we were holding in our hands while playing our card games).

Othello is a very easy game to learn, but it is a difficult game to master. You can take a minute to learn the rules and then spend a lifetime playing, mastering the strategy, and enjoying the game. Also, like chess and many other games... Othello is a great metaphor for the game of life. It's played with 64 reversible/two-sided disks", on an eight-by-eight square board. The disks are black on one side and white on the reverse. Each player starts with two of their disks on the board, in a perfect metaphor of the interaction of yin/yang, the four elements, and the 4 letters in the language of genetics. Black move first, seeks to capture the white players pieces by surrounding them on two sides by his pieces and reversing them to his color. White then takes their turn with the same goal in mind. Play proceeds until all of the players pieces have been placed on the board, the players then add up the pieces of their color to determine the winner.

What I am naming the Art of Human BEing is similar to Othello. Contrary to popular programming and social-conditioning the game of life has very simple rules that are not difficult to learn. However, you are most likely going to spend the rest of your life striving to master the game... your destiny.

What is the "art of HUman BEing"?
Let's break it down, build from the foundation. After all, at this stage of the game it has been a ridiculously long time since we fell from God, it is high time we rise up from Devil.

---

[1] There are 64 different codons in the genetic code. Codons are three letter genetic words and the language of genes use 4 letters. The three-letter nature of codons means that the four nucleotides found in mRNA — A, U, G, and C — can produce a total of 64 different combinations (4*4*4 = 64. Of these 64 codons, 61 represent amino acids, and the remaining three represent stop signals, which trigger the end of protein synthesis. There are also 64 Hexagrams in the I Ching system of Divination.
The two sides of the disks represent the binary nature of ALL manifestation, the cycle of birth and destruction. There are no inconsequential actions, they are either constructive or destructive, 'life-affirming' or 'life-negating' (61of the genetic codons produce amino acids, 3 serve as stop signals).
During the course of this book the author will point out the mathematics that he sees as the underlying order of ALL Universal phenomenon.
[2] Conscious use of skill and creative imagination in the expression of the state or quality of our being (artful or not), based upon the study and observation of our nature (knowledge of self), and representative of our essential nature.

ART
1. skill acquired by experience, study, or observation.
2. the conscious use of skill and creative imagination especially in the production of aesthetic objects the quality or 'state' of "being" artful
1. of a high quality or 'state' of execution.

HUman
1. a culture-bearing primate classified in the genus Homo, especially the species H. sapiens. Human beings are anatomically similar and related to the great apes but are distinguished by a more highly developed brain and a resultant capacity for articulate speech and abstract reasoning. In addition, human beings display a marked erectness of body carriage that frees the hands for use as manipulative members.
2. of, relating to, or characteristic of humans.
3. representative of or susceptible to the sympathies and frailties of human nature.

BEing
1. the quality or state of having existence.
2. something that is conceivable and hence capable of existing.
3. the qualities that constitute an existent thing.

A quality of my existence that I sometimes practice in the state of my being artful is poetry, so... I have acquired a skill - by study and observation, in the meaning and use of words to communicate (through articulate speech) abstract reasoning, ideas in a rhythmic and poetic manner. What I have just described is just one of the ways I practice what, for the purpose of this book, I am defining as the "art of BEing HUman". Here is a more formal definition: "the conscious use of skill and creative imagination in the expression of the state or quality of our being (artful or not), which is based upon the study and observation of our being (knowledge of self), and representative of our 'essential' nature which is... Divine." In other words... through the conscious/mindful use of creative visualization I govern my being in a manner representative of my essential nature and the laws of its being, which are... Divine! I am... God-In-Person! There is a flip side to this. When we do not develop this capacity within our being the result is, seemingly opposite in nature, we become... Devil.

As you read this definition keep in mind that it does not just give meaning to "the art of HUman BEing... it gives it form and function! It gives it a form and function that is Divine by design and replicated throughout creation!

In its most basic terms, the "art of BEing Human" underpins two very basic truths;

1. There is no mysterious "god out there" managing our existence from some distant place called heaven. There is only the One Absolute BEing, that for the purpose of this book I am identifying by the name Allah. It is this BEing which comprises our essential reality, whose knowledge, wisdom and understanding we should be striving to acquire.
2. Human Beings - in terms the Names (Al Asma al Husna) and qualities of Allah comprising our essence... are immortal. Therefore, we should align our lives in accordance with our inherent endless potential within and seek to fully embody them so that we may represent that which is Most High.

Poetry is just one of the mediums or modes of expression I use in "my" art of HUman BEing. However, it is more of a byproduct of my major practices which are Divination, Contemplation, Implementation and Observation... over time, using the Tzulkin system of divination. Imagine that! With a deck of cards, I can read the blueprint of my being from womb to tomb and map out my life's journey so that I may successfully navigate the murky waters of this flesh! Simply put, this is a book about how I use an ancient divination system, the Tzulkin, and a quintessential perception of the cycles of time to navigate my life experiences. The Tzulkin is a tradition that comes from the oldest roots of Amaru Khan culture.

Let me clarify my intent by stating that I am, by no means, an authority on the card system being presented in this book. I claim authority on only one thing, that is the HUman...BEing... denoted by the name Olusanya Bey. I know what keeps my boat afloat and how to navigate it appropriately. I know what turns me on and what turns me off, how to function at the peak of my abilities, when I'm doing so, and also when I am not and why. I choose to identify the system, popularly known as Destiny Cards, as the "Kitab Al'Qadr (The Book of Destiny)/The Unbound Book of Movement and Measure", named the Tzulkin by its makers - the Tutul-Xi, more commonly known as the Olmecs. It is one of the tools that has enabled me to follow the most sacred maxim of the Ancient Masters - Temet Nosce [Know Thyself], empowering me to obtain knowledge and understanding of my... Soul's incarnation [Individualized BEing]. Self-knowledge and self-realization are the necessary preludes to 'God-realization.' I am not writing this book because I am a self-proclaimed "master of the system". I don't even claim mastery of myself... yet! However, I do use the system on a fairly regular basis as it applies to my life experiences, so I have practical knowledge and actual experience of the system's inner/outer workings. I have also done extensive research into the cards and what I believe to be the working principles behind the system, this book is my "sharing" of said principles. It will shed light on what I deem to be the proper understanding and use of the Tzulkin calendar system.

In essence, I navigate my earthly vessel in the same manner as my Ancient Ancestors, via the 'heavenly/celestial bodies', only today I use a deck of cards instead of an astrolabe or sextant. According to my research and understanding the greatest possible application of cartomancy (card divination) is to gain self-awareness, spiritual

Olusanya Bey

insight. By reading the cards as the blueprint/microcosm of our lives we gain objective insight into our own reality, needs, habits, desires, and paths (open, closed, or otherwise). I recognize that many cardologists use the cards in a predictive/fortune-telling capacity, however my experience is that "reading" the cards is best when they are used to gain spiritual insight and perspective into difficult matters and to aid one's spiritual growth and development. In other words, there is an actual and factual roadmap of your destiny. It would behoove you to learn how to "read and interpret" it! Again, I don't claim to be a master, that's why I practice. I am sharing my understanding so that you may apply your knowledge and wisdom and arrive at your own understanding. I encourage the reader to research all aspects of this system and its techniques in order to find out what works for them. It is vital to understand that throughout all of our spiritual studies that there is no one 'right' technique, there is only the technique that is 'right-for-you'. No system has ALL of the answers, once the HUman element is added (to the science, the methods, or rules used to arrive at the material one is reading) the process turns into an 'art'.

My personal introduction to this system is a result of research into my Ancestral heritage in the Americas and the ancient, so-called "Meso-American" calendar systems, it has been enhanced through the many books written by individuals who have helped to lay a solid foundation for the study and practice of "card divination". My particular approach to the cards has been strongly influenced by the books of Ali Muhammad, Thomas Morrell and Iain McClaren-Owens. The work of these authors enabled me to make the connection between the ancient "Meso-American" calendar systems (the oldest calendar systems in existence) and the system more commonly known as Destiny cards, filling in the blanks left by many of the books on Cardology. This book is a distillation of that outer knowledge and research combined with the mindful insperience and direct experience of the energies identified by my cards. The cards, ancient symbols of knowledge and wisdom, become more than academic studies, they are sacred portals for deepening our intuition and attunement. A transformative shift unfolds as seekers transition from external inquiry to immersive communion, embracing the cards with a newly aroused reverence. The Tzulkin's components serve as vessels, not to compel us, but to allow us to channel these profound energies. Their strength arises not from historical authority, but from the immediacy of personal experience.

Within the framework of meaning lies the boundless expanse of personal revelation, the essence of creative energy—an unorthodox voyage into a system that reveals the deepest essence of existence. Divination dances away from rigidity, rejecting the dogmatic, authoritative worldview, and instead flows toward the infinite potential of our human creativity. Any insights that may nourish this vital creative river, preventing it from stagnation and the illusion of absolute truth, is priceless.

No faith/religion reigns higher than truth, and truth is a tapestry woven by the open-hearted. The Tzulkin mirrors this ideology— ever-evolving, flowing with the currents of change, yet preserving its timeless essence. Anything unable to adapt and evolve within shifting landscapes, while retaining its core, will wither into a lifeless husk, devoid of vitality. Set-in-stone systems are, more often than not, constructs of control that stifle creative revelation and the vibrant spirit of existence. The principles of the Tzulkin have not been set in stone, instead they have been set in motion by the author of this Universe and can clearly be seen in the movement and measure of everything in existence.

The techniques I am sharing are a means of describing and using this experience. They are not—and can never be—a substitute for your direct experience. Their strength derives not from some long-established authority, but from present experience. Because of this essential interaction, the personal nature of the Tzulkin makes it an ever-evolving, dynamic process. Within the basic framework of meanings, there is the freedom of our own personal experience. This is the epitome of the creative force.

America as a nation, the world as a "collective consciousness", is fixated on the idea of "ownership". This notion comes from a lack of understanding the true nature of the "Mind", as well as an extremely materialistic view of ownership. It is this misconstrued idea of ownership/copyright that I believe has led to many of the inconsistencies you will find when reading books by different "Cardology" authors. Individuals have felt a need to put their "unique stamp" on the science of the cards, while unconsciously maintaining socially-conditioned myths, in doing so have created a certain degree of misunderstanding in regards to the science of the Tzulkin calendar. I did not author this system, so I cannot claim ownership of it in any sense of the word, nor will I seek to add to something that is already complete in and of itself. What I will share is my "understanding of" and "approach to" the cards, their form, function and practical application. I will also share my understanding of the origins of the Tzulkin system, in order to begin setting the historical record of its origin and America straight, so that we can receive the full benefits of the system.

Olney Richmond, who many see as the individual most responsible for introducing the science of the cards, in his "Mystic Test Book" states, *"Reader, do not be misled by any of the so-called occult works upon the subject. They are very numerous and all quote and re-quote from each other, but it is the old story of the "blind leading the blind," and we can see without glasses, behind all of this dust-throwing, the secret hand of the great enemy of our order, and the enemy of science."* This was my initial experience of Cardology. You have many individuals claiming to be masters/authorities on this system, while offering misleading techniques and information. Having said this, I have no doubt that my book may raise some of the same questions within readers that I had, but it is my sincere hope that it will also provide valid explanations for what may appear to be its inconsistencies.

The Art of BEing HUman

During the course of my study, I often found myself wanting 'one' book that reconciled the inconsistencies I was discovering, while teaching me the underlying principles and techniques of the Tzulkin's methodology. At this point I want to mention a few of the authors that provided the keys for me, Alexander Dunlop, Ali Muhammad, Thomas Morrell, and Iain McLaren-Owens. All of theses authors opened my eyes to different aspects of the inner-workings of the Tzulkin, but I still desired that 'one' book that brought everything together in one place. One book, that would allow any reader to develop their own understanding of the systems inner-workings, as well as developing their own 'practical application' for "living and interpreting" this beautiful 'orderliness'. It has been said that in order to know correctly the very foundations on which anything is based, we need to DIG UNDER the foundation on which it STANDS. Only then can we arrive at a true understanding of the subject. I have put in an earnest effort to do exactly that. I believe the knowledge this book provides makes available, to the person who wants to know, the open secrets of the Tzulkin.

This book is a vade mecum, a primer, a beginning point for those who choose to study the Tzulkin. It is not a textbook as much as it is personal musings upon information I have gathered, the knowledge gained through my practical application. It is my hope that this work will at least aid in encouraging a greater dialogue among 'cardologists' about the origins, mechanics, methodology of the science we practice, and the true meaning of its application. I do not anticipate that all readers will accept or adopt the views I advocate; it is more likely that many will emphatically disagree with them, probably even oppose them. I'm comfortable with that, but if those who disagree with me are, at the very least, inspired to take a more extensive look at the subject than they previously have, and if in their opinion I am wrong in my points of view, will strive to discover the truth for themselves, I'm definitely cool with that too! If I am wrong and have not uncovered the basic truths of

Olusanya Bey

this system, but by writing this book inspire others to do so, I'll be very grateful and look forward to them sharing their knowledge, wisdom and understanding!

> *"The 'Black*[a]*' mind establishes a network of equivalencies between all things by means of a system of symbols that involve practical and theoretical metaphysics which, on one hand explains the Universe, thus responding to the innate need to understand, and on the other hand, forms the spiritual framework of men's lives."* (The Pale Fox).

I have used the above quotation, taken from the book "The Pale Fox" by anthropologist M. Griaule & G. Dieterlen, because they identify what they are referring to as the "black mind". What they are identifying as the black mind is, in fact, a "cosmology" or universal view that was shared across major portions of this planet by ancient cultures. Cultures that were founded by human beings who, by today's standards, would be identified as "black". Griaule and Dieterlen were astounded by the cosmological view of the Dogon people, their deep understanding of celestial movement previous to the discovery of telescopes. Of course, this was a result of their cultural bias and the campaign that had already been set in place to reconstruct history, especially the history of the "original people".

I am defining cosmology as- the science, theory, or study of the Universe as an orderly system and of the laws that govern it. In modern cosmology the cosmologist, in effect, pretends to be an incorporeal spirit who stands outside the cosmos. The quest is to achieve "objectivity," but no attempt is ever made to grasp the

---

[a] Although the author understands Griaule's use of the term "Black" to mean "Indigenous/Original" for the purposes of this book the term "black", unless otherwise specified is a legal term used to designate "chattel" and to replace the legal status of the indigenous peoples from that of "Landlord" to "tenant" and "property". The more accurate description would be "melanated mind".

nature of the inescapable subject who is needed in order for the object to be known. According to my Ancestors all presumption to disembodied, "objective" knowledge must be set aside. Knowing the subject that knows is all important, true knowledge of the cosmos/our Creator is inaccessible without true knowledge of the self. It should be obvious to anyone that what we as subjects can know about the cosmos depends to a large degree on our starting point (our point of orientation), and this goes back to who we are. Of course, it is also true that the tools and methods that we use in our investigations determine what we will discover, the same as the mesh of our net determines what kind of fish we will pull from the sea. Nonetheless, more than anything else, the investigator herself is the net. Any understanding of the world begins somewhere, and the where of the beginning determines the where of the journey and the ultimate destination.

There is a Zen allegory about a man and a horse. The horse is galloping swiftly, and the rider appears to be heading somewhere important. An eyewitness along the road cries out, "Where are you going?" and the rider replies, "I have no idea! Ask the horse!" Far too many of us are like the man on the horse, this is our life's story. We are riding the horse, but we don't know where we're going and we can't stop. The horse… is our social-conditioning and habit-energy. These two forces of habit can be relentless as they continuously push & pull us. Often, we are unaware of them, if we are… feel powerless to change. Through our use of the Tzulkin we can take hold of the reins, if we add the practice of mindfulness to our 'reading' we can rein in the horse and begin directing our lives accordingly.

When I finally surrendered to the fact that this book was a portion of my "measure", I knew it had to be "Moor". Meaning - It had to come from a point of view that was distinctly "Moroccan", so that it may "rock boats", shake individuals out of their socialized doldrums, also serve to correct some of the historical record of this continent, commonly known as America. For most Americans and especially so-called African Americans, the study of their origins has been approached from a skewed Hybrid-Eurocentric worldview (many so-called black scholars are still guilty of this). The effect of this worldview on the African-Americans has been the development of mistaken identities, mental slavery and for those who identify themselves as "white" a false sense of superiority and privilege. My research brings with it a worldview that also dismisses the very existence of the biological racism that European science has established to control behavior. I am anchoring my approach in rhythm with Neely Fuller Jr's views on the so-called victims of racisms priorities:

Each and every victim of racism should minimize the time and effort spent doing anything other than, thinking, speaking, and acting in a manner that helps to eliminate racism, and establish justice (balance between people). Each and every person should seek to do this, every day, in every area of activity including Economics, Education, Entertainment, Law, Politics, Religion, Sex, War, and Counter-War.[ii]

The European mind has always struggled to reconcile the origins of civilization with a people it has been conditioned and trained to see as inferior, so the origins of the cards has been left to theories or obscurity. Most Cardology authors would rather attribute the origin of the cards to the lost-city of Atlantis than to acknowledge the antediluvian presence of the original people, especially in the Americas. This refusal to admit to the pre-historical presence of highly-melanated people, particularly on this continent is a major cause of the lack of understanding regarding the impact of so-called "black" people on our country's historical development. However, once this system was re-introduced to the descendants of its originators the phenomenal energies of the cards asserted themselves from a deeper, spiritual, level. The foundation of

---

[ii] pg. ix - The United Independent Compensatory Code/System/Concept A Compensatory Counter-Racist Code, 2016 Neely Fuller Jr.

racially-biased academic studies on the cards acted as an entry-point for those who had a deeper, biological and spiritual connection with this time-honored divination system. The change came when indigenous people began to work the techniques experientially rather than to study them externally—to encounter them in direct, numinous, revelatory ways.

Some may read the above and say I have a chip on my shoulder. My response: "It's not a chip, it's the entire world and my Ancestors and I have been holding it up since time immemorial!"

The Art of BEing HUman

Olusanya Bey

(Poetic Interlude)

Speaker For the Dead

i seek...
to point out patterns in life thru...
poetry that is written in-between the lines and'"
off of the paper, still...
clearly represented in the words...
presented by a presence seen and...
unseen... the author is an... Ausar...
omni-present... ALL-I SEEING...
pyramid of matter, multi-dimensional...
BEing... liquid... solid... vapor...
my... trans[ce]-mission is to... trans[ce]-end...
the mindset of the... original earth... raper...
[that's... mutha fucka for all... giants still... "sleeping"]
the god... hard... steps becuz... the devil's...
still creeping... thru cracks in your...
mental constructs... where he... conducts...
cognitive manipulations so we won't...
MAN UP... and... build a... just and free nation...
"word is bond"... the enemy is not a...
"white movement"... it is a... "indigenous stagnation"...
realize! there is nothing that can stop...
a people filled with the... spirit of their Ancestors...
and determination...
if these signals are... not clearly received then...
adjust your... mental station...
tune in... to a different reality...
as long as u live life longing...
for the life lived by another...
u can never be free.
did we... or did we not... give birth to civilization?
when do we return to BEing...
original people, and...

OlusanyaBey

The Art of BEing HUman

stop living lives of... imitation?
the Ancestors say...
speak! but...
i don't think your hearing me.

PREREQUISITES

"The Principles of Truth are Seven; he who knows this, understandingly, possesses the Magic Key before whose touch all the doors of the Temple fly open."

-Kybalion

The Ancestors taught that the Universe has ground rules. These rules were handed down from antediluvian times by the chief law-giver of Kmt (pronounced Kemet)/Ancient Egypt by Tehuti, known to the Greeks as Hermes or Thoth. These Tehutian principles provided humanity with a comprehensive analysis of the nature of creation and of the Universe. However, Western history makes no mention of pre-Adamic/antediluvian times outside of biblical reference, and often treats this period of history as if it were mythological. Of course, this skewed perspective of this portion of history leaves huge gaps in our ancestral cultural legacy that now must be remedied if humanity wants to continue to evolve past its current fascination with self-destruction.

1 As human beings began to multiply and spread across the surface of the earth as God commanded, they had lovely daughters.

2 The sons of God saw how beautiful the humans' daughters were, and they decided to take any daughters they wanted as their wives.

Eternal One: My life-giving Spirit will not sustain human beings forever because they are, after all, made of flesh. Therefore, I will put a limit on their lifespan of about 120 years.

4 Now at that time and for some time to come, a great warrior race"[15] lived on the earth. Whenever the sons of God would have

---
[15] Hebrew, *Nephilim*

sex with the humans' daughters, the women bore them children who became mighty warriors. In the days of old, they became famous heroes, the kind people tell stories about."[*]

Western academics have a long-standing habit of... standing on the outside of what they examine, believing somehow that they can create an experience without actual involvement. This has been their mode of operation from the outset of Greek civilization and continues to this day. It is important to note that this pattern regarding the Western mindset, inherited from the ancient Greeks was identified a long time ago by Imhotep (known to the Greeks as Asclepius), a student of Tehuti, who many historians advocate was Hippocrates teacher:

"For the Greeks have empty speeches . . . that are energetic only in what they demonstrate, and this is the philosophy of the Greeks, an inane foolosophy of speeches. We [the ancient Egyptians], by contrast, use not speeches but sounds that are full of action." [17]

As a mindfulness instructor I have experienced this mindset firsthand. I have been asked to guide mindfulness classes with the caveat that I had to limit my "talk" about mindfulness because the attendees want to have an "experience". My response was, "how will they know if they had the experience of mindfulness if they don't know what mindfulness is?" The western mind is full of assumptions that often interfere with the individual's capacity to receive information, even when the desire to do so is very real. It is similar to a scene from the movie "2012" where a young monk is seeking answers from an elder monk. While he is standing in front of his elder rambling about impending doom the monk is pouring tea into an overflowing cup. After finally noticing what is going on the youth points out the overflowing cup, the monk responds, "That is you. You come seeking answers, but your cup is already

---

[*] Genesis 6:1-4 The Voice (VOICE) Translation
[17] Brian P. Copenhaver, Hermetica (London: Cambridge University Press, 1992), p. 58

full. How will you receive them?" It is this same mindset that produces a world FULL of religions and spiritual traditions that speak about morals and character, yet somehow fail to develop them in the majority of its adherents. I am not saying these traditions have no merit. I am simply saying that without the adherent's full immersion in the principles being espoused in their holy books... it is superficial at best, and... still waters... run deep. Not one of the prophets left behind a "belief" system. They all espoused a "way of living" that led to the unfoldment of man's divinity, now it is up to her to embody that way of life and give birth to some "heaven on earth". Suspend your beliefs, empty your cup, enjoy the tea about to be spilled!

Although I am not going to go into depth on these principles, they lay the foundation for everything in this book and I encourage the reader to make it a priority to understand these principles and apply them to their daily lives. Practicing anything with technical know-how but without philosophical understanding is worse than impractical - it can be dangerous. If I know how to use a hammer, but don't know why and when a hammer should be used... what could possibly go wrong? I might use it to open a window, as a nut cracker, swat flies, or to deliver love taps. The most practical knowledge is why to use a thing. Only then is it truly useful to know how to use that thing. These principles are very much the foundation of the conscious use of our skill and creative imagination in the expression of the state/quality of our being (artful or not), which is the art of BEing Human. They are the ground rules of this entire book! At their core, they emphasize the interconnectedness of all things and seek to understand the nature of reality through seven fundamental principles. These principles serve as guiding concepts for individuals seeking self-discovery, personal transformation, and spiritual growth within the Kemetic philosophy.

The Tehutian principles or laws are seven in number. In the Supreme Mathematics of the 5% Nation of Islam the number seven represents God/The Creator, or to be more precise... one who is in flow/alignment with the Divine. Seven is not a random figure, it is a powerful and highly significant symbol of divine or universal connection that penetrates to the very core of existence. The following observations illustrate this point:

1. There are Seven Days in a week and Fifty-two Weeks in a year (5 + 2 = 7).
2. There are Seven Cardinal Colors in the solar spectrum.
3. There are Seven Key Notes in the musical scale.
4. There are Seven Continents and Seven Seas.
5. Originally, there are Seven Visible Planets, called the Seven Governors by the ancients, also referred to as the Seven Angels/Seven Thunders in the Christian Bible.
6. There are Seven Holes that lead into the human body – ears, nostrils, mouth, anus, and vaginal or penile openings. *
7. There are Seven Chakras

There are more, but I think you get the point. It is also important that I tell you that this is not limited to the number seven. All numbers, mathematics as a science, demonstrate the unity/connectivity of all things in nature. We will touch upon this a little more when we get to the chapter on numbers.

The Seven Tehutian Principles

1. The Principle of Mentalism

"The All is Mind; The Universe is Mental"

Through this principle, it's believed that our Creator is pure consciousness, or thought, and the Universe is a manifestation of the mind of the Creator. This principle of asserts that mental

---

* Ancient Future (The Teachings and Prophetic Wisdom of the Seven Hermetic Laws of Ancient Egypt), by Wayne B. Chandler

processes are foundational to our experience of reality. This principle resonates with modern cognitive science research, which suggests that our thoughts influence not only how we perceive external events but also how we respond to them. Our beliefs, attitudes, and expectations shape our experiences and can either limit or expand our potential for personal growth. This concept highlights the power of the mind in shaping our perception and understanding of the world around us. In other words, our thoughts shape reality.

KEY: Using this law, we, too, can harness the power of our minds to create the life we want.

2. The Principle of Correspondence

"As above, so below; as below, so above. As within, so without, as without, so within."

Closely related to the first principle of mentalism this principle states that what we hold in our thoughts and mind will become our reality. It explains the many dimensions and planes of existence, including those of lower and higher vibrational frequencies and how they are connected. What this means is that our external world is a reflection of our inner world. Our external world is 360-degree mirror, everywhere we look we are seeing ourselves reflected back to us. Wherever you go, there you are. Our outer world merely expresses our thoughts, beliefs, feelings, attitudes, etc. * Therefore, if we can change our inner world, we can also change what is happening on the outside. HUmans are a micro-cosmos, a small reproduction of our entire cosmos, in body and mind, so we respond to the same Universal laws. Astro-logics

---

[*] "And to Allah belongs the east (the place of birth and origin) and the west (setting-disappearance-death). So wherever you turn there is the face of Allah (you are face to face with the manifestation of Allah's Names). Indeed, Allah is all-encompassing and Knowing."
Surah 2:115, Decoding the Quran, Ahmed Hulusi

is the study these laws and all the analogical celestial correspondences between macro-cosmos (UnIverse) and micro-cosmos (HUmans).

KEY: Applying this law is all about understanding your connection to our Creator, the world around you and how you're showing up for yourself and the Universe through your thoughts, and actions. When we have a firm grasp on how, why we're interacting with life and how it's affecting us, we can recognize and break patterns, live in alignment with our highest good, and experience harmony with everything there is.

3. The Principle of Vibration

"Nothing rests; everything moves; everything vibrates."

The principle of vibration states that all things, both physical matter and spiritual energy, hold a certain vibration. Science tells us atoms are in constant motion, as is the UnIverse itself. Even our hearts, as they beat, give off different vibrations depending on our emotional state. By aligning with positive vibrations and raising one's energetic frequency, individuals can attract harmonious experiences and manifest desired outcomes. This principle suggests that our thoughts, emotions, and actions have a direct impact on the reality we create for ourselves. When we're "vibing high," we're able to avoid low-level frequencies that don't serve us, this includes disease (dis-ease).

KEY: With this principle, we acknowledge that we have the power to control our vibration rather than our vibration controlling us. Application of the first two principles will help us to do this. You want to do things and think thoughts that allow you to maintain a state of inner peace/ease, where our bodies are vibrating at high frequencies/positive levels. We also want to surround ourselves with individuals and things with like vibrations, making it that much easier for us to maintain our chosen level of vibration.

4. The Principle of Polarity

"Everything is dual; everything has poles; everything has its pair of opposites; like and unlike are the same; opposites are identical in nature, but different in degree; extremes meet; all truths are but half-truths; all paradoxes may be reconciled."

This principle explains that seemingly opposite things are actually one and the same at varying degrees. A simple example of this is hot and cold. Cold is just the absence of heat, and they're both one thing: temperature. We can also apply these seeming opposites to water and produce a solid- ice, and a gas- steam. Again, seemingly opposite in nature, but both- water. Physical matter and spiritual energy are the same thing, with spiritual energy vibrating at a much higher level, such that it can't be perceived by our senses. Love and hate are two ways of experiencing the same thing, a relationship toward something. This is the foundation of alchemy, or the ability to "transmute" your experiences at will. In the electromagnetic world this law appears as positive and negative; in the chemical world as acid and alkaline; in the atomic as electron and proton; in the biological world as male and female. In nature we see polarity expressed in various ways:

- Man/Woman
- Left/Right
- Up/Down
- Hot/Cold
- Life/Death
- Yin/Yang
- Joy/Pain
- Love/Hate
- Rich/Poor

KEY: Applying the principle of polarity takes a certain degree of mental stamina and involves shifting the way you look at something, potentially turning it completely on its head. When a lower vibrational emotion is bringing you down, can you recognize it, feel it, and transform it to a more positive one? Understanding polarity helps individuals navigate life's challenges by recognizing that difficult times are often opportunities for growth and transformation. By embracing both positive and negative aspects of existence, we can cultivate greater harmony within ourselves and in our relationships with others.

5. The Principle of Rhythm

"Everything flows, out and in; everything has its tides; all things rise and fall; the pendulum-swing manifests in everything; the measure of the swing to the right is the measure of the swing to the left; rhythm compensates."

Closely related to the principle of polarity, the fifth principle states that between the opposing poles, there exists an inherent rhythm. The tides move in and out. We inhale and exhale. Everything is in motion. Nature has its cycles and seasons, so do we. Understanding this principle allows us to recognize our life's— and the Universe's—natural rhythms, so we can actually work with them rather than having them working against us. Modern science, through its observation of the microscopical manifestations of nature, has discovered that all cells of living matter, and all crystals of nonliving matter, have varying periods of rhythmic motion beginning with their birth and controlling the process of development to maturity, and guiding the evolutionary steps preceding the process of breaking down or reproducing others of their own kind. It has been found that the cycles which distinguish the rhythm of each of these species or classifications of matter is harmoniously related to the cycles observable in the movements of the planets and the effects of 'rhythm' on the tides of the waters of the earth, and the growth of all plant life and animal life as well. Even in the functioning of our bodies, such as our breathing, the beat of our heart and similar movements contributing to the maintenance of life, there is a definite rhythm closely resembling, and having a harmonic relationship to, the larger and more pronounced rhythms of the energy of Absolute BEing.

KEY: Know that nothing lasts forever, and things are always and forever changing. By embracing rhythmic cycles such as rest after activity or introspection after external engagement, individuals can optimize their personal growth journey. Recognizing the ebb and flow inherent in life allows us to adapt more effectively to changing circumstances while maintaining inner stability. As you get deeper into working with this law, you'll be able to work with your own mental and emotional states to avoid dramatic pendulum swings in your thoughts and feelings. Become more aware of your emotional state and using polarity (principle 4) and rhythm to start getting more comfortable with the natural flux of your life.

6. The Principle of Cause and Effect

"Every cause has its effect; every effect has its cause; everything happens according to law; chance is but a name for law not recognized; there are many planes of causation, but nothing escapes the law."

Everything is connected through the principle of cause and effect, for each cause of one thing is merely the effect of something else, going back to the very beginning. In order to understand why the events in our lives happen we must look at causation. In our physical Universe the Sun and the planets in our Solar system are the primary initiators of causation. They impact the Earth's magnetic field, this field is the medium or field of growth in which we live. The Earth's magnetic field also provides us with an atmosphere, as well as the most vital thing we need for our HUman existence... the air we breathe. This principle is all about acknowledging the effects of our thoughts and behavior and how we may change them to bring about greater effects. This concept prompts self-reflection regarding one's motivations behind actions taken throughout life. By taking responsibility for our choices and considering potential consequences before acting, we become active participants in shaping our own destiny rather than passive recipients of our circumstances. Divination allows us to identify causes and effects that we may be missing. Thus, as we self-reflect on the potential consequences of our actions, we may make better choices that will insure better outcomes.

KEY: When something doesn't go as planned or you find yourself feeling unhappy, ask yourself, what was the cause? Often times, we find ourselves reacting to the world around us, trapped in the back-and-forth of reacting to our circumstances rather than advancing our own path. When we take action (become the 'cause') to get the effect we want, we move from 'feeling' like a victim to 'being' empowered.

7. The Principle of Gender

"Gender is in everything; everything has its masculine and feminine principles; gender manifests on all planes."

The seventh principle states that all things have masculine and feminine qualities. The two sexes can be thought of as a physical manifestation of this principle, but make no mistake, on an internal level, all of us hold both energies. (think left and right brain). Do not get it twisted... males and females are both clever mixes of masculine and feminine energies. Masculine and feminine energies do not only exist on the physical plane they dwell on the mental and spiritual planes as well. The concept of Gender within Tehutian philosophy extends beyond biological gender to encompass energetic principles. It recognizes that everything possesses masculine and feminine qualities, regardless of physical form. These qualities represent active and receptive forces in all areas of existence. Understanding the interplay between these forces helps individuals cultivate balance within themselves and their relationships. By embracing both assertive action (masculine) and intuitive receptivity (feminine), individuals can tap into their full potential for personal growth and creative expression. The unity of these two energies is essential for creation, and when one has a healthy balance of both, they're better able to apply all of the principles together for maximum benefit.

KEY: Accept all the parts of yourself, and understand that balance in all is key for self-mastery. Western culture has seriously misunderstood this principle, as a result we have a society of individuals struggling to accept themselves for who and what they are, and how to present or express themselves to their fellow humans being. Understanding this principle is the key for the balance between the physical, material, and masculine plane and the feminine, subtle, and spiritual plane to emerge, so that we can reach the harmony and completeness that are so essential for life.

These seven Kemetic principles provide a comprehensive framework for understanding reality, consciousness, spirituality, and personal transformation within the context of Tehutian philosophy. Each principle offers unique insights into the nature of existence, guiding individuals on a path towards self-discovery and spiritual growth.

By recognizing the power of our thoughts (Mentalism), seeking connections between different aspects of life (Correspondence), aligning with positive vibrations (Vibration), embracing duality while seeking balance (Polarity), attuning to rhythmic cycles (Rhythm), taking responsibility for our actions (Cause & Effect), and embracing both active and receptive energies within ourselves (Gender), we can navigate life with greater wisdom, purpose, and harmony.

The Art of BEing Human invites individuals to explore these principles as tools for inner transformation – allowing them to shape their reality consciously rather than being passively influenced by external circumstances. Through dedicated practice and application of these principles in daily life, one can strive towards greater self-awareness, spiritual awakening, and fulfillment on their unique HUman journey.

As you learn these principles and begin to practice them you will realize that all of these principles are interwoven, run incredibly deep, and may take a long time to fully understand and embody (remember our Othello analogy!). Each time you come back to them, you will understand them in a new way, or on a deeper level. Given time, these principles can help you master your own mind and your life as a whole.

Now, let's begin to explore Tzulkin mechanics, so that we can see how the seven laws may be applied to greater understanding and mastery of our lives and destinies.

Olusanya Bey

THE KITAB AL' QADR

Sura Ash-Shams (Sura 91:1-10)

By the sun and its heat and radiant brightness[20],
and by the moon as it follows it;
and by the day when it manifests it,
and by the night when it covers it;
and by the sky and HU who built it;
and by the earth, and HU who spread it,
and by the soul and HU who proportioned it,
and inspired it to understand what is wrong for it, and what is right for it!
Indeed, he succeeds who purifies it.
And indeed, he fails who corrupts it.

In the course of our BEing HUman we navigate a multitude of internal and external energies, on a daily basis, that are determining factors in the development of our character, and the development of our behavioral tendencies. These tendencies are, for the purposes of this book, the 'proportion/disposition' that the BEing denoted by the name Allah[21] gives each human being as

---

[20] The word *duha* (dad-ha-ya) as used in the original Arabic applies both to the light of the sun and to its heat. Although in Arabic its well known meaning is the time between sunrise and meridian when the sun has risen high, at its height it does not only give light but heat as well. Therefore, when the word *duha* is attributed to the sun, its full meaning can be expressed more appropriately by its "radiant brightness" than by its light, or by the time of day that it is. It also implies the "radiant/wavelike" nature of UnIversal energy.

[21] The common use of the term God suggests the existence of a deity beyond the individual. A deity that grants the wishes of individuals in exchange for being praised, and exalted (worshipped). Muhammad, who articulated the Quran, taught that there is a System present within life, by which those who fail to comply, are led to suffer the consequences of their actions.
Servitude (as opposed to worship) is the output of activity by individual manifestations, based on the creation program given to them by Absolute BEing. That is, when individuals live (move) according to their natural

The Art of BEing HUman

their 'measure'. The more we can become aware of these energies and how they interact with each other and our BEing, the greater the chance that we can navigate them successfully and realize the true nature/potential/reality of our BEing... HU²man.

Olney Richmond, who many regard as the individual responsible for introducing the little book of Seven Thunders, called by most-playing cards, as the "Religion of the Stars". In my 'spiritual' studies I have come to realize that ALL of the s0-called 'sacred' scriptures when properly decoded are astronomical documents. Therefore, there will be occasions over the course of this book where I will refer to the Quran and other scriptures to illustrate this point. These references are not, in any form or fashion, an endorsement of any of the religious institutions that may be attached to them. The author is an advocate of "Sacred Science" and the cultivation of one's spirit through its practice, or "way/tao" of living.

We currently are living in a period where science is finally capable of proving what many spiritual traditions have alluded to throughout time. Erwin Schrodinger, the Nobel Prize Austrian physicist, often referred to as the father of quantum physics, compared the unity and continuity of Vedanta to the unity and continuity of the wave function observed at the quantum level. In

---

disposition (measure), they are serving the purpose of their creation (destiny). ALL activities of all individuals can be thought of as servitude. Submission and rebellion are different types of servitude. The BEing inferred by the author's use of the name Allah is the One Giver of ALL Movement and Measure, and is known by many names depending upon one's culture and spiritual tradition.

[*] When we speak of Allah/Absolute BEing in the third person the proper pronoun to use is HU. Many translators of the Quran use the pronoun HE. However, as pronouns take the place of a person, place, or thing and nothing can take the place of Allah this is an error. Also, Allah is beyond gender. In ancient times the word man was used to express both genders (male as well as female), that is why I choose to use HUman to signify our individualized manifestations of Absolute BEing.

an autobiographical essay he explains that his discovery of quantum mechanics came as a result of his attempts to give form to the central ideas of Vedanta.

For the purposes of this book, we'll define Vedanta as the basic Vedic teachings concerning the ultimate identity of the "individual soul" (HUman BEing) with the "Supreme Soul/Absolute-Consciousness/Atman". Some would say "God-consciousness". The author, however, does not bear witness to the notion of a "God", prefers Absolute/Divine BEing in relationship to HUman BEing. The goal of Vedanta is for each of us to have the direct experience of our true nature, and it is held that each and every one of us is qualified to have that experience/highest illumination, if we are willing to put forth sincere effort. In fact, it is our "destiny" to experience the "Divine" nature of our BEing!

Schrodinger wrote, "This life of yours which you are living is not merely a piece of this entire existence, but in a certain sense the whole; only this whole is not so constituted that it can be surveyed in one single glance. This, as we know, is what the Brahmins express in that sacred, mystic formula which is yet really so simple and so clear: Tat Tvam Asi, Thou art That. Or, again, in such words as "I am in the east and the west, I am above and below, I am this entire world."

When a human being is born at a particular time and in a particular place on the surface of the Earth he is surrounded on all sides by celestial bodies, either visible in the sky or invisible below the horizon. In the science of the Tzulkin/Cardology [23], the positions (angles) of these celestial bodies are related to the newly incarnated individual and, if this relationship is properly interpreted, define the basic structural character of this child's biological, psychic and spiritual organism, as well as the manner

---

[23] The Tzulkin has come to be known by many names, during the course of this book I will be using them interchangeably so that the reader may become familiar with all of them.

in which her potential at birth will/should be actualized through the numerous cycles of their personal experiences. For each of us, time begins on the day we are born and ends on the day we die.

In the Tzulkin system each playing card represents a day of the year, carries its own energy signature through the elements/suits, planets, and numbers. Not only does your birth card identify your life path and unique predisposition/characteristics, but since the cards are linked, they also interact with each other. Knowing another individual's card can tell you a lot about their personality as well, will also provide you with accurate information about the type of relationship you could possibly have with them. Working with the Tzulkin enables you to reach different levels of understanding yourself, as well as allowing you to perceive and tap into different dimensions, vibrations of energy. Although the Tzulkin integrates concepts/principles with the spiritual sciences of Astrology, Geometry and Numerology it is a Meta-Symbolic science and divination system that stands on its own. I like to refer to it as the Unchanged, Ever-changing Book of Universal Law. The Quran refers to it as the Umm al' Kitaab or "Mother of Books."

In the words of Olney Richmond - *Any book written in a language other than symbolic must in the course of time become nearly non-understandable through changes of language and meanings of words, to say nothing of loss through translations, etc. But symbols are the same in all tongues and among all peoples.* [34]

The Tzulkin (Playing Cards) is therefore an unbound book of symbols revealing the unchanged laws of our Universe, as it expresses the Oneness of Absolute BEing, through the infinite diversity of the Universe and our "individualized" HUman BEing. It is a "person-centered" metasymbolic system of biological-celestial mechanics which assists the individual in the solution of their personal and interpersonal problems, especially in the

---

[34] The Mystic Test Book or The Magic of the Cards, Olney Richmond, pg. 19

Olusanya Bey

development of their self-awareness, fully actualizing their birth-potential.

It involves the relationship between the larger Universe outside you and the personal Universe within (there's that law of correspondence!). The same energies that function in your personal Universe function in the larger one 'out there.' The blueprint we call the Life Spread, or the Life Path, outlines the energies that flow in your magnetic field. At the moment of your birth you took into your body, with your first breath (Ruh), the electromagnetic vibrations manifesting on that day and time, at that particular spot, on earth. This basic energy pattern constitutes your behavioral characteristics and tendencies, that unfold cyclically throughout your entire life. These cycles are determined by the movements of our planetary bodies and have been encoded in the deck of playing cards. The deck of playing cards that we use

52 Cards in a Deck	52 Weeks in a Year
12 Count Cards	12 Months in a Year
13 Cards in each Suit	13 Weeks in each Season
	13 28-day Lunar cycles in each Year
	12 Polarities with the Sun as a center point
4 Suits	4 Seasons (Spring, Summer, Fall, Winter)
	4 Stages of Evolution (Creation, Growth, Harvest, Completion)
	4 Elements (Water, Air, Earth, Fire)
	4 Cardinal Directions (North, East, West, South)
	4 Stages of Matter (Solid, Liquid, Gas, Plasma)
Numerical Value of Cards = 364, plus the Value of the Joker as 1.25 = 365.25	A Solar Year is 365.25 Days

for games to entertain ourselves is, in fact, a symbolic representation of our solar and lunar year. The above correlations relate to a cycle of one year. However, the nature of time is linear, circular, cyclical and proportional. In general, the majority of books written about the cards only go over the 91-year Life cycle, the 7-year cycle, and the 365-day yearly cycle, while offering no explanation as to the nature of their origin (with the exception of the yearly cycle, which is obvious to anyone who observes the correspondences stated above). Our yearly cycle is, of course, based upon the Earth's orbit around the Sun. What is the basis of the 91-year cycle, or the 7-year cycle? In his book "The God Clock" Thomas Morrell reveals the astronomical foundations for these cycles.

> *"Approximately every 7 years, the planet Saturn, transiting around the Zodiac, makes or forms a hard aspect, or angle to its location in one's Astrological Natal Chart (a chart to display in a graphic format a picture of the heavens above at the moment a person was born) it creates a square (90 degrees), opposition (180 degrees), another square (90 degrees) and finally a conjunction (0 degrees, known as the Saturn Return.) The 7-year cycle then, is simply a quarter, or Season of Saturn's motion."* [25]

Once we understand the 7 years cycle our new-found comprehension allows us to unveil a larger 28-year Saturn cycle within the book of movement and measure. So, the planet Saturn (fittingly known as 'Chronos' or 'Father Time') is a key to understanding, unlocking the code of time/the Tzulkin, and the basis of the various spreads.

Every year we experience four 91-day seasons, which give us an indication as to what the 91-year Cycle really is – it is a seasonal increase of a larger cycle of time... a 364-year cycle. What is extremely intriguing about this larger cycle of time is that when it is divided into the 7 planetary periods, each period is 52 years in length. In his book "The Ancient Book of Time" Morrell states that

---

[25] The God Clock A New Look at the Passage of Time, Thomas Morrell, pgs.11-12

Olusanya Bey

in the fall of 1966 he made a discovery that revealed to him the mathematical/planetary code on which the method of motion, or progression of this system is rooted. He states that his discovery revealed that the periods of progression in the Tzulkin are based on the motion of specific planets, seasons of those motions, and correspond exactly to the natural planetary cycles and seasons we experience as HUman BEings on Earth. Morrell not only succeeded in uncovering the basis of the three well-known cycles (91 year, 7-year, and yearly), but he also revealed 5 more (previously unknown) cycles - the 364-year, the 28-year Saturn, the 91-day Seasonal, the 28-day Lunar and the accurate 7-day weekly cycles. Over the course of our lives we will experience:

364, 91-day seasons in 91 years	Seasons: $4 \times 91 = 364$
364, 28-day Lunar cycles in 28 years	Lunar cycles: $13 \times 28 = 364$
364, 7-day weeks in 7 years	Weeks: $52 \times 7 = 364$

Each of these cycles represents time unfolding and they are closely tied to the natural cycles and seasons we experience on our planet, especially in relationship to 3 specific celestial bodies, the Sun, the Moon and the planet Saturn.

As I mentioned earlier, the science of the cards was introduced by Olney Richmond in his "Mystic Test Book" (1893), and was further developed in two other books by Edith Randall ("Sacred Symbols of the Ancients" 1974) and "What's Your Card?" by Arne Lein (1978). Robert Camp, probably the most well-known Cardology author, has written several books that also explore this system. All of these books provide decent introductions on how this system of 'reading the cards' works, but as I also mentioned earlier, they contain errors in understanding and therefore methodology. Morrell, in my opinion, has corrected many of the errors that have been perpetuated within the Cardology community. However, I believe that he has also fallen victim to cultural-conditioning, did not follow his theories to their natural conclusion.

The Art of BEing HUman

In the book "Nuggets From King Solomon's Mine" by John Schmalz (published in 1908) the author gives a detailed illustration of the 52 playing cards and demonstrates correlations between the dimensions of the deck of cards and astronomical measurements. He also introduces the ancient idea of 'Quadration' (The Squaring of the Circle), explains how it has been encoded in the Cards and the Great Pyramid of Kemet (Egypt). The square and circle shapes are related in Euclid's 47th problem of "Squaring The Circle," known to be the primary goal of the Masonic craft. Squaring the circle, however, does not in this case refer to a mathematical problem: it is a spiritual reference to a human being's instinctive quest to harmonize their physical and spiritual natures. The Square & Circle symbolize our human state as 'an eternal soul manifesting in a temporary body'. The circle is our spiritual side that cannot be seen, heard, touched, tasted, or smelled (our 'spirit' cannot be perceived by our five senses). It is our true, inner, and perfect Self, the part we feel when we close our eyes and think "me". The circle, however, is bound by the Square; our circle/spirit is bound by our body. Stop here, for a moment, think of a four-sided square, and of how we have previously demonstrated Humans BEing experience Nature in "fours":

- Four Cardinal Points (North, South, East, West)
- Four Seasons (Winter, Spring, Summer, Fall)
- Four Elements (Earth, Air, Water, Fire)
- Four States of Matter (Solid, Liquid, Gas, Plasma)
- Four Stages of Evolution (Creation, Growth, Harvest, Completion)

Since ancient times, the square has been a symbol of the physical body. The circle, on the other hand, has always represented the soul. The metaphysical idea of 'Spirit' and a spirit traveling from one body to another is exemplified by the mathematical concept of 'Infinite'. Infinite/Infinity can be described as a recursive loop or something that recurs over and over again; continuing indefinitely (a never-ending circle of 360 degrees). The concept of a spirit and

Olusanya Bey

"placing a spirit" (or anything in the realm of the infinite) into a body (or anything physical and finite) has always been known in the Western occult world as "Squaring the Circle" or... Quadration. In other words, <u>the quadration of the cards into the 90 quadrates/spreads symbolically demonstrates the process of Creation</u>, the fractal nature of our Universe and the distillation of Spirit/Mind into Flesh/Individualized BEing. Morrell also mentions the "squaring of the circle" in "The God Clock", while mathematically demonstrating quadration/the "scattering of the cards into the four winds/the 4 directions".

In the "Mystic Test Book" Olney informs us that all symbolism is founded in mathematics and geometry. He introduces what he refers to as the "Sacred Number" 142857 (consisting of 2x7... 4x7... 8x7 plus 1 which represents the Ego). According to him the Ancient Magi reasoned that the number 1 followed by an infinite number of zeros/circles would be an accurate representation of the infinite. Now, if we take 1 and add any number of zeros, from one to infinity, and divide that number by 7 (the "Mystic" number that represents the Soul in nature) we end up with the Sacred Number.

$10 \div 7 = 1.42857142857$
$100 \div 7 = 14.2857142857$
$1,000,000 \div 7 = 142,857.142857$

Here's where it gets more interesting, more intriguing! Morrell also demonstrates how quadration/the scattering of the cards to the 4 winds relates to the "squaring of the circle". In doing so he uses a circle with a diameter of 7 (the Soul Number) and a circumference of 22. This ratio (7/22) is known as the "simple approximation" of "pi" (the relationship between a circle's diameter and its circumference). When we divide the circle's circumference by its diameter (22 ÷ 7) the result is 3.142857142857 (the numeral 3 followed by the Sacred Number). Morrell goes on to explain that *"when a circle's diameter is quadrated, or in Indigenous Native terms, thrown to the 4 directions, it creates a square that perfectly envelopes the circle. This square would have a measurement of 7 on each of the 4 sides."* So, in mathematical terms, the squaring of a circle is calculating a square that would have the same area as a corresponding circle. The quadrature of this circle is accomplished easily by creating a square that encompasses the circle, with each side being the same length as the circle's diameter [7]. I also want to point out that when we divide our calendar year (365 days) by 7

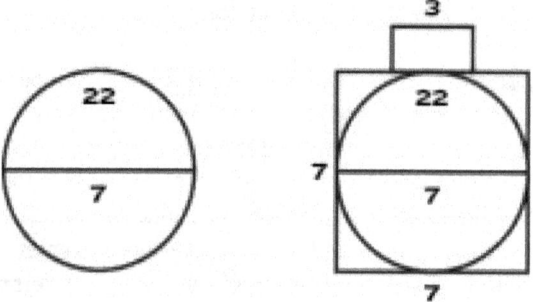

we get 52, with 142857 (the sacred number) as a remainder.

When using the Tzulkin we take a deck of cards in perfect order (from the Ace of Hearts to King of Spades) and quadrate it (through a mathematical shuffling), then we lay the cards out in 7 columns and 7 rows with the last 3 cards placed on top, centered. As we can see the mathematical process for circling the square also demonstrates the layout of the 91 Quadrations in the Book of Time. Those who believe this to be simply a coincidence lack a proper understanding of synchronicity and the order of operations governing our Universe. The elements of quadrature - the dominating feature of the Great Pyramids - are likewise the dominating feature of the playing cards. These correspondences unmistakably link the cards with the Great Pyramid (and others), as they are the only structures on our planet that are based upon and repeatedly emphasize, in their construction, the ancient

---

* The God Clock A New Look at the Passage of Time, Thomas Morrell, pg. 92

formula of quadration - the basis/foundation of all phenomena in nature; terrestrial AND cosmic. The Great Pyramid clearly symbolizes this approach. Built in 2480 BC on the points of the compass, with its passages aligned to the stars, its base and height fit the "squared circle" of the Earth and Moon. All phenomena are based on exact proportion; there is no chance or accidents anywhere to be found in our Universe. All is in harmony, under mathematical rule, therefore nothing can be altered. HUmans BEing, Creation's highest ideal made complete, stand on the same mathematical platform as the lowest/tiniest creature that exists. The Universe plays no favorites! All is evolving, slowly but surely, from the simple to the complex, up the same evolutionary ladder, rung by rung, each step measured and weighed by the same right and exact unchanging laws that give everyone the highest justice.

From the surface of the Earth, the Sun and Moon appear to be the same size. Our Ancestors recognized this as just another proof positive of the perfection of creation, as this relationship only exists if they are viewed from the Earth's surface. The size of the Moon when compared to the Earth is 3 to 11. This means if we bring the Moon down to Earth and draw a circle through the center of the Moon its circumference will be equal to the perimeter of a square enclosing the Earth. The Earth and Moon in proper size relation are also embodied in the cross section of the Great Pyramid. A circle squaring is implied in its construction: the square surrounding Earth has the same perimeter as the circle intersecting the center of the Moon. This relationship is demonstrated in the following figure. Notice its similarities with the quadration diagram provided by Thomas Morrell.

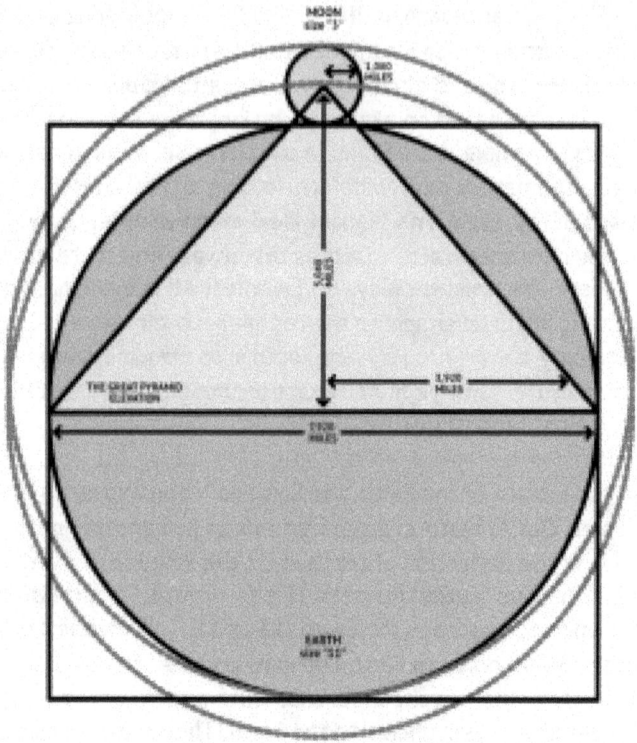

Radius of Moon - 1,080 miles = 3x360
Diameter of Moon = 2,160 miles = 6x360 = 18x1x2x3x4x5
Radius of Earth = 3,960 Miles = 11x360 = 33x1x2x3x4x5
Radius of Earth + Radius of Moon = 5,040 Miles
= 1x2x3x4x5x6x7 = 7x8x9x10
Diameter of Earth = 7,920 Miles = 8x9x10x11
There are 5,280 feet in a Mile
= (10x11x12x13) - (9x10x11x12)

I am pointing all of this out to say that NOW is the time for us to a consider a more intelligent consideration of the playing cards, their symbolism, as well as their true nature and purpose. This symbolism (according to Olney) consists of a union and harmonizing of the symbols of time, numbers, human relationships, spirituality, geometry and astronomy.

In Vedic Astrology there is a concept called "Kālapuruṣa" (the embodiment of time/Cosmic Being). Using the law of correspondence the structure of our galaxy can be viewed as an individual body, an entity with a personality! This galactic structure, that we call 'The Milky way', is actually a living unit, a life form. This Cosmic Being is known as Kala Puruṣa. Just as human beings have consciousness, so does the earth. The structure that we refer to as the 'earth' also possesses consciousness that is specific to it. Just as the earth has consciousness, so does the sun, and just as the sun is conscious, so is our galaxy! The consciousness of the sun, in comparison to the galactic consciousness, is like the consciousness of a single cell in our body, in contrast to our consciousness. Our galaxy subsists in the Universe as a conscious individual being, among millions of other such galaxies! Milton Pottenger, in his book "Symbolism" (1905) wrote, "as the body of the individual is the medium, or vehicle through which the individual mind or spirit expresses itself, so the Universe in its entirety is the body or medium through which the universal mind or spirit of God finds expression". But what is consciousness/mind?

Our Ascended Elders were trying to explain this similar intelligence through the non-material fields that in their language/terminology formed the 'Water field', the 'Air field', the 'Earth field' and the 'Fire field'. These electromagnetic/radiant wave/vibratory fields are what possibly sit behind our collective unconscious and are also responsible for our higher awareness. This same view is now being proposed by scientists, who advocate that "consciousness/the mind" is a localized electromagnetic field[27],

---

[27] J. McFadden, Synchronous firing and its influence on the brain's electromagnetic field: evidence for an electromagnetic theory of consciousness. Journal of Consciousness Studies 9 (4) 23 - 50, 2002

specifically our Earth's magnetic field. In other words, what we refer to as "our minds" are localized electromagnetic fields designed to receive and transmit the integral energy of the Cosmos. We are the piece with the magnetic! In many indigenous cultures around the planet this magnetic field is referred to as the "World Tree", symbolizes the axis mundi (the axis of the earth between the celestial poles). It supports the heavens and connects them to the earth, as well as the underworld via its roots, while its branches reach out in the four cardinal directions. The Tutul-Xi called this World Tree the Yax'che, in Norse mythology it's Yggdrasil, Iroko in the Yoruba tradition, Irminsul in Germanic traditions, and Ashvattha in Hindu mythology. We'll explore the Earth's magnetic field and its effects upon our persons more in our chapter on the planets.

This flowing vibratory symphony of our solar system can be taken as analogous in its intelligence to that of the wave-function observed by scientists in quantum particles. This incarnated vibratory intelligence of our galaxy not only can transcend the space-time barrier it can guide humans unconsciously through the four elemental fields of Water, Air, Earth and Fire. The highest consciousness literally duplicates itself in every possible aspect of nature: as in the structure of the Universe or our individual self. As above, So Below... On Earth, as it is in Heaven (the Law of Correspondence). We live in a "holographic/fractal" Universe! It is this unseen wave structure of planets and all matter, which through their subtle influence and natural resonance tie into the quantum vibratory fields observed within our brain cells and forms the non-local and the collective unconscious basis of the human mind, as well as the human heart.

Compared to the electromagnetic field produced by the brain, the electrical component of the heart's field is about 60 times greater in amplitude, and permeates every cell in our body. The magnetic component is approximately 5000 times stronger than the brain's magnetic field and can be detected several feet away from the body. Our nervous system acts as a "receiving station", an "antenna," which is tuned to and responds to the electromagnetic fields produced throughout our galaxy via the Sun and Moon, the planets, as well as the hearts and minds of other individuals. Our 'card spreads' act as our "tuner's dials", allow us to 'dial-in'/'tune-in' to our personalized frequencies with more clarity!

Speaking as a person playing a Nine of Hearts birth card, I think that this capacity for exchange of energetic information, particularly by the heart's electromagnetic field, is an innate (often dormant) ability that heightens awareness and mediates important aspects of true empathy and sensitivity to others. I also propose that through "reading" and playing our cards correctly that this energetic communication ability can be intentionally increased, producing a much deeper level of nonverbal communication, understanding, and connection between people (a "UnIversal Love" if you will!).

In essence, what science is alluding to now and the Tzulkin/Kitab Al'Qadr demonstrates quite effectively, is that we can celebrate life either by orienting and navigating our brain towards our uniqueness, individuality, ego, reasoning ability, judgment and lower-self or we can celebrate life by training a shift towards the infinite creativity embedded in our UnIverse, our "indwelling intelligence"/Higher/Essential Self.

There are two types of consciousness. The first is the manifestation of the Names[28] as a whole, to observe itself through

---

[28] Every chapter of the Quran, with the exception of one, begins with "In the Name of Allah, The Almighty, The Merciful.
 A 'name' is only used as a reference to an object or quality. A name does not explain what it references in totality, but merely implies an identity, or an attribute of an identity. Sometimes, a name is used only to direct the attention to multiple qualities, without revealing anything about the identity. The Asma al' Husna (Beautiful Names of Allah) are references made to the 'creational' properties of Allah through which the entire known UnIverse and everything in it becomes manifest from nothingness into a holographic existence.

the appearance of individualized compositions/BEings. This is the Universal Pure Consciousness. The second kind is the individual consciousness of each manifestation, formed by genetic inheritances, environmental conditionings and astrological influences. For the purpose of clarity in this book, we will refer to the second kind as 'consciousness' to avoid confusion. Consciousness is an output of the brain and hence confines itself to comprise only the body (humanoid). Consciousness uses the mind to evaluate ideas and to live accordingly. But the mind, pressured by the body's biological make-up, often malfunctions. As such, it is near impossible for the mind to find the Reality all on its own. Furthermore, the mind makes judgments based on sensory perception. This is why the mind is invited to 'believe', to have 'faith' in what lies beyond its area of perception. For, the reality 'beyond' matter encompasses matter.

When HUmans BEing, who are manifestations of Universal Pure Consciousness, begin to experience themselves as individualized conscious beings in this physical body, the struggle of this relationship with their 'partner' (body) and the battle to go back to their essential reality begins. The observing One, the one being observed, the observation, are all ONE!

The "Cosmic Consciousness" acts as a mirror to humans. Or, to be more precise, humans are like mirrors that reflect the qualities of the Absolute One. HUmans can reflect and exhibit the qualities pertaining to the cosmic consciousness to the degree to which they can discover and know their 'true selves'. Thy kingdom come, thy will be done when humans BEing learn to embody their inner Divinity and begin expressing themselves accordingly. If you want to experience that BEing/UnIversal Energy commonly referred to

---

"And to Allah belongs the most Beautiful Names, so turn to Him through the meanings of His names. And leave the company of those who practice deviation concerning His Names. They will be rewarded for what they have been doing." (Quran 7:180)

as... God then you must embody its Divine principles and order of operations.

Our personal Book of Time, through the metasymbology of the playing cards, is our Kalapurusa, our "embodiment of Time", our Kitab Al'Qadr/Book of Destiny". It allows us to be conscious/aware/mindful of how Cosmic Consciousness/Supreme Soul manifests itself through our "localized" consciousness/minds and hearts and to govern ourselves accordingly (if we choose to!). Your personality is new but not the soul. The soul is the unit of evolution. The personality is the unit of incarnation. When you become conscious of who you truly are—an Infinite Soul using a personality through which to function—you will remember!

By learning how to interpret the energies of the Cards we were born to play, and how to better incorporate them into our daily lives we allow ourselves to attune our personal elemental, electromagnetic energies to Absolute BEing/Universal Force and Power (what some, including the author, might call the Creator) and once again offer ourselves (and each other) the opportunity to become the 'co-Creators of Life' that all of the Sacred scriptures have told us we are meant to BE! So you see Dear Reader, the cards are not a fortune-telling device, instead they are a tool for developing self-awareness so that we may become the Divine Beings, the God'Us we were born to BE!

"If you want to find out the secrets of the Universe, think in terms of energy, frequency, and vibration."

~Nikola Tesla

"If we are persuaded that not only external fields of solar and cosmic origins but also human attention and emotion can directly affect the physical world and the mental and emotional states of others (consciousness), it broadens our view of what interconnectedness

means and how it can be intentionally utilized to shape the future of the world we live in. It implies that our attitudes, emotions, and intentions matter and that coherent, cooperative intent can have positive effects."

~The Global Coherence Initiative

"Intuition makes us look at unrelated facts and then think about them until they can all be brought under one law. To look for 'related' facts means holding onto what one has instead of searching for new facts."

~Albert Einstein

The first part of Tzulkin calendar study involves the use of your memory. The Polarities and the Planets that rule them must be memorized and visualized. Contemplating the Card symbols, their Elements and Numerology, reflecting upon their meanings, meditating on their energies, will bring you in contact with the power behind them. Keep in mind: any knowledge gained through outer study can only take you as far as your conscious mind. There is a Higher/Absolute/Supreme Mind beyond that, where you can gain direct experience/knowledge from the source of your BEing. That part of you already IS Knowledge - IS Wisdom - IS Understanding... and may be 'insperienced' NOW. The Kitab Al'Qadr is a time-tested, proved means of knowing that SELF. So... let the journey begin!

Time is a factor of Matter and the Present... is Eternity!

The Art of BEing HUman

Olusanya Bey

(Poetic Interlude)

p

while... conversating with trees...
I watched as...
they got drunk from... wine-colored leaves...
I... sipped on... sunlight...
transformed by... melanin...
half-baked I... receive...
revelations! thru my skin...
visions altering realities... perceptions...
synchronicities unveiling mankind's... deceptions...
quantumly strung on...
solar charged... organic hallucinogens...
I'M HIGH! on this... Life!
so... where other poems end...
this U.N.I. verse only begins...
to show and... tell a reality of... revolution...
be careful, keep up! our Mother Earth spins...
for a reason...
do the knowledge... for everything in life...
there is a... time and a... season...
FOR REAL Y'ALL... the time for...
boycotts... marches... and sit-ins...
is... OVER!
no time... left for protests... only solutions.
the HER...ricanes are the... prelude
now... HIM... HE... [ME?]... that SUN U see...
is about to go... SUPERNOVA!
Ameri...ka... ka... ka must pay for its... sins.
so I... spit... fire thru... words that burn...
if we stop... "giving away" our power, and...
"take" responsibility... our world will take a... turn...
for the... bette!
but until it does...

OlusanyaBey

The Art of BEing HUman

HIS words will get... hotter, and HER storms...
more wet... "we've only just... begun"...
to put and end... to the...
"divided and conquered" mindset...
and "A"... return to the... ONE!
this little diddy... called "P" for "poem"...
is so U don't... forget...
if "we" dont "do it"... it aint gonna get "done"...

YEAH!... ALL of THAT!... I just said...
from a little drink of...
SUN!

CHEERS! here's to... FREEDOM

The Art of BEing HUman

THE FOUR SUITS

We'll begin with the card Suits as they represent part of the fundamental blueprint, or foundation upon which the entire system is built. They also demonstrate how we experience life on our planet. In life timing is everything, the Bible says, *"For everything that happens in life—there is a season, a right time for everything under heaven."*[29] The 4 card suits represent, among other things, the four seasons: Spring, Summer, Fall and Winter. Morrell in his book "The Ancient Book of Time" points out that all of the progressions in this system are based on a specific planetary motion, or a 'season' of a planetary motion. Just as there are specific cycles and seasons related from the Sun to our Earth, we also experience our own personal/biological cycles and seasons within the system. These cycles are; creation (first quarter/Spring), growth (second quarter/Summer), harvest (third quarter, Autumn) and completion (fourth quarter/Winter). We can use these cycles to better understand the influence of specific charts and their timing.

"Earth was the female element and water the male element, and from the fire and ether they received their spirits, and Nature produced bodies after the species and shapes of men."[30]

Ancient Egyptian texts state that the Goddess Nun represented the primordial waters—the pre-creation chaos— possessed characteristics that were identified with four pairs of primordial powers/forces. Each pair represents the primeval dual-gendered twins—the masculine/feminine aspects.
The Universe and everything within was formed from 4

---

[29] Ecclesiastes 3:1
[30] *Poimandres* (The Divine Vision), Corpus Hermeticum. Originally written in Greek, the title was formerly understood to mean "Man-Shepherd" from the words ποιμήν (shepherd) and ἀνήρ (man/human), but recent studies on its etymology assert that it is actually derived from the Kemetic phrase p'eim·ôntè-rè meaning "Knowledge of Re" or "Understanding of Re".

ingredients. The fabric of existence is woven from these elements, scientists have confirmed through their research that we are indeed made up of the very fabric of the Universe. Accordingly, the Yoruba people of Nigeria refer to the Creator of humanity as Oba'tala (the King of the White Cloth), the Universe is his tapestry. These ingredients are present in the stars, the matter that composes the Universe and the 4 elements. These elements are Water, Air, Earth and Fire.

A Greek philosopher named Empedocles is credited with the cosmogenic theory of these four elements being the root of all existing matter. However, we know through our research that the Ancient Kamitic civilization used these same elements, the early Greek philosophers more likely than not learned this system from them.

The four elements—Fire, Earth, Air, and Water—each represent a basic kind of energy and consciousness that operates within everyone. Each person is consciously more attuned to some types of energy than others.

Abu 'Ali al-Husayn ibn Sina, better known as Avicenna, defines elements as simple substances which provide the primary components of the human body. These are symbolic expressions. Because all the elements recognized so far exceeding 100 should correspond to any of these four elements which virtually encompass all the known elements of today. The four elements have also been assigned four temperamental qualities; hot, cold, moist and dry.

The element of any card that is emphasized in a spread (by suit, significant planetary placement in/aspect to a polarity, line, or column) demonstrates a specific type of consciousness and method of perception to which the individual is strongly attuned. Keep in mind that, although I provide keyword meanings for the respective elements, it is important that you understand the importance of working with the elements so that you can realize how they manifest themselves within your BEing, as well as the Universe. Remember, "As Above, So Below - As Within, So Without".

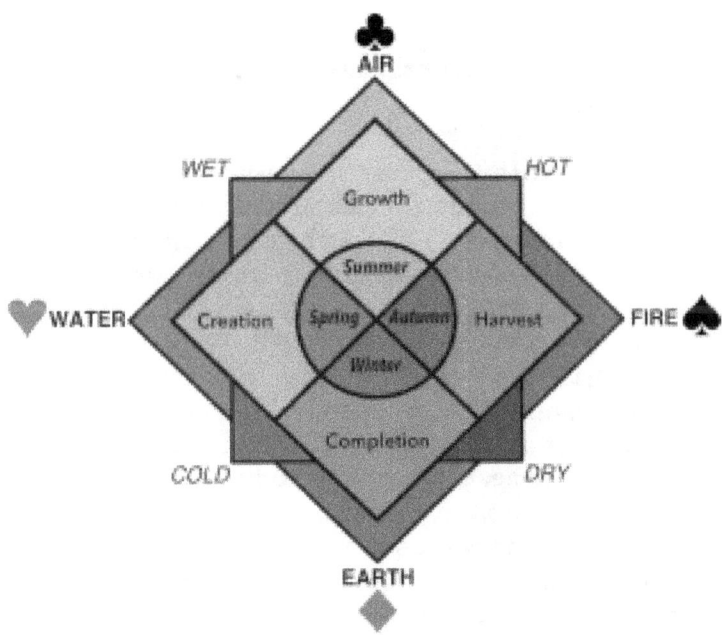

WATER | HEARTS | CUPS ♥:

Water can be refreshing, like a cool stream or it can be dark and mysterious like the depths of the ocean. Water that is contained is easy to deal with, like swimming pool, water that is un-contained and out of control can do great damage, like a tsunami. Water cards represent the intuition and emotional aspects because it flows and it's liquid or it could be solid like ice, it can evaporate into air and turn into clouds. Water is complex and a paradox it is everywhere and can be almost anything. Water is the sum— the composite principle of fire, earth and air. Water is also a substance over and above them. These concepts were expressed in the

Ancient Egyptian texts as Nu/Nun, the primeval (liquid) water that contains all elements of the Universe. Plutarch confirmed that in his Moralia Vol. V:

"For the nature of water, being the source and origin of all things, created out of itself three primal material substances: Earth, Air, and Fire."

It is for this reason that the author acknowledges water as the element of Hearts (as opposed to some cardologists who claim fire as the elements of Hearts). Water cards are the most emotional of all cards, they flow down deep and search out crevasses and cracks to explore, symbolic of the unknown emotions of the human psyche. Not only is water essential to life and covers the whole globe, but water makes up the largest percentage of all living things. Since water is found in everything everywhere, water card people have an affinity for dealing with others, they can see into other people, they understand the motives and needs of other people and to sum it all up, they are borderline psychics and the most in-tune with the people around them. This makes them empathetic, caring and helpful but they are often overly sensitive and can be easily hurt by others who do not acknowledge the sacrifices that have been made and how deeply involved they really are.

Water Cards symbolize the cooling, healing principle of sensitivity, feeling response, and empathy with others. Water is a simple substance whose position in nature is exterior to the sphere of the earth and interior to that of air. Water is cold and moist in temperament, although only slightly so. Water is easily dispersed and assumes any shape without permanency. It is this characteristic that Bruce Lee, the creator of Jeet Kune Do, refers to when he says, "Be like water." In the construction of "things," the addition of water allows the possibility of their being shaped and molded and spread out. Shapes can readily be made from it, and just as easily dispersed. Moisture dispels dryness, the latter being

Olusanya Bey

overruled by the former. Moisture protects dryness from crumbling (as moist earth, or mud), and likewise, dryness prevents moisture from dispersing. Thus the two elements of earth and water are interacting and interdependent. Water is, of course, absolutely essential to life.

As previously mentioned, water traditionally relates to the emotions – rushing streams, calm and tranquil lagoons, the hard, violent pelting of rain, and the crisp iciness of frost. Like water, we can 'reach boiling point' or 'let off steam,' or 'chill out.' Water has softness to it, yet with time and persistence, has the capability of shifting the contours of jagged rock into gentle smoothness. Water relates to change and adaptation, especially emotionally. The element of water has magnetic properties; it nurtures and sustains.

Individuals who are Hearts suit usually possess sensitive yet strong emotions. They can beautify life with their ability to give love and support or show affection and compassion. Caring and sensual, they can be the most loving partners and loyal friends. Their natural charm and excellent people skills imply that they can succeed in careers dealing with the public or working in the community. Alternatively, they can express themselves through their innate talents, creativity, and idealism. Those who belong to the Hearts suit need to learn how to best utilize their emotions and recognize that with the power of love they can achieve great results. The challenge of the Hearts suit is not to succumb to emotional impulsiveness or fears that can evoke negative feelings such as selfishness, hatred, or jealousy.

Positive qualities: understanding, placidity, mildness, trusting nature, devotion, mercy, forgiveness, modesty, compassion, fervor, pliancy, meditativeness, internalization.

Negative qualities: indifference, heartlessness, laziness, indolence, rigidity, lack of daring, lack of concern, unstableness, dejection.

AIR | CLUBS | SWORDS ♣:

Air is the element that you can't touch or see, but strangely it can be contained, like when we blow up a balloon. When it is contained in this way, it either somehow escapes or it becomes stale. Air people are free and cannot be contained or this same thing will happen to them. Air is uncertain and unpredictable; it can generate a thunderstorm with violent winds. Air cards are also volatile in this manner, they are unpredictable and eccentric. Air is the most necessary element, being necessary to fire, earth and water. Air people live in their mind. They are oftentimes caught up in their thoughts which may elevate them to new levels where no other element can reach, like the upper atmosphere. Here they can formulate theories, solve problems clearly and see the world below. Air people are said to regularly be out of touch with reality, but they are also very advanced in thinking. They are very mental-oriented individuals having a knack for intelligence but possibly also lacking emotional depth.

Air Cards are correlated with the mind's sensation, perception, and expression, especially related to personal interaction and to geometrical thought forms and abstract ideas.

The temperament of air is hot and moist, and its purpose in nature is to make things finer, lighter, and more delicate and thus more able to ascend into higher spheres. Air is also the agent by which breath moves in and out of the body and causes/makes possible the involuntary movements of the body. Air can represent the heavens, where the Creator spirits live. Generally, air relates to the mind, the intellect and quickness of thought. A predominance of air cards may indicate that you are too much 'up in the clouds' and not grounded or in touch with reality. Or it may suggest things are happening very quickly in your life; your intuition is heightened with insights and an enhanced awareness – possibly more hunches or synchronicities than usual. Air relates to the spirit world (as does fire). Air is a detaching element and enables coexistence of the two main elements, fire and water.

Clubs people are usually rational and intelligent, with an inquisitive or curious mind. If they pay attention to their inner voice, they can also develop their intuitive abilities. Mentally quick and often enthusiastic about their favorite subjects, they usually succeed when they recognize that their intellectual power is their principal asset. Often freethinking and communicative, these individuals are eager to acquire knowledge, express their thoughts, or join debates and discussions. A tendency to talk rather than listen may also instigate their tendency to argue. Nevertheless, astute and well informed, they can benefit greatly from early education or special training. They often choose work that requires mental agility, such as commerce, administration, law, or teaching and counseling. Alternatively, a natural gift of the gab may lead them to sales and promotion. They can also express their mental creativity through writing, problem-solving and designing.

Positive qualities: vigilance, care-freedom, kind-heartedness, trusting nature, clarity, lightness, independency, dexterity, optimism, diligence, acuity, joy, smiling.

Negative qualities: lack of perseverance, dishonesty, gossipy, cunningness, backbiting, garrulousness, inconstancy, touchiness, prodigality.

EARTH | DIAMONDS | PENTACLES ♦:

Earth is real, you can see it, hold it, smell it. Suitably so, earth signs are very "down to earth" and real. Earth is the foundation on which everything is built. Earth people are solid and stable and composed of many diverse parts. They are multi-faceted people, like the many mineral compounds that compose the earth. There is nothing wishy-washy about these people, they do not have their head in the clouds, nor do they sit on the fence. They are dependable, you know they will always be there and they are stable. Most of the time, tend to be more stable than the other elements. Earth does not change. It stays there and allows whatever is growing to continue to grow and progress. Earth people are not fond of change, they like stability and regular life that can grow upon and develop. Why start something new if what is already there is fine? Earth people are the most materialistic and possessive of all the cards. Earth people are also concerned with what's on the surface and never really dig deep to get to the bottom of it, they are happy with what's on the surface. As a result, in a superficial culture such as ours, Diamonds can be too easily relegated to money and finances, instead of values and resources, which are the basic principles of true economics. Economics is the equitable distribution of your resources, whether it is among your family, community, state or nation. The chief resource being your people... human capital. Human energy is the only true currency or "energy of exchange". It was this understanding, along with mastering the currents of the sea/oceans which allowed our Moorish Ancestors to conduct trade and become the first masters of international commerce. The author would also argue that they lost sight of these principles, eventually became corrupt, as a result their empire crumbled.

Earth Cards reveal a harmonization with the world of physical forms and a practical ability to utilize and improve the material world. Earth is an element usually situated at the center of our existence. In its nature it is at rest, and because of its inherent weight, all other elements gravitate toward it, however far away they may be. It is cold and dry in nature, and it appears so to sight and touch, so long as it is not changed by any other elements. It is by means of the earth element that the parts of our bodies are fixed and held in place; thus the outward form of the body is due to the earth element.

Earth traditionally represents a sense of being grounded, or connected with nature. Being 'down-to-earth' and 'having one's feet on the ground' are earth expressions. A predominance of earth symbols can highlight an already existing affinity with the earth, or a need to get out in nature more to feel the dirt between your toes – to be "grounded" or material. Earth relates to physical manifestation, abundance and the cycles of life. The element of earth binds fire, water and air in various proportions, which makes possible the formation of materials with different properties. Earth cards can bring people (the other cards) together in the same manner.

Diamonds represent practicality, sensation, money, and the ability to evaluate. In highly developed Diamonds individuals this ability to evaluate goes beyond money, as they can assess personality qualities or spiritual values intelligently. In the less developed person, however, a Diamonds card places much more emphasis on materialism. Nevertheless, most Diamonds cards have a shrewd assessment of material opportunities that usually works well for them. It helps them understand how to commercialize their skills and talents or those of others. More importantly, it provides a strong inner system to understand life. Every experience and every piece of new information is evaluated as to whether it is useful. Although at first this evaluation system is used to merely obtain money, property, or material security, eventually a Diamonds values become clearer as to what produces happiness. Positive Diamonds individuals work on themselves by constantly updating and upgrading their value systems. This leads them to want to obtain wealth so they can become more generous and philanthropic.

Positive qualities: consistency, conscientiousness, perseverance, punctuality, caution, resistance, responsibility, carefulness, firmness, reliability, sobriety, ambition, respectfulness, matter-of-factness.

Negative qualities: stuffiness, superficiality, laziness, indifference, cumbersomeness, touchiness, lack of conscientiousness, irregularity, timidity, scornfulness.

FIRE | SPADES | WANDS ♠:

Fire can do good, like cooking food to eat and keeping us warm or it can do great harm, like burning down a house or an entire forest. fire is a combustible, unpredictable element, a chemical reaction that can go off easily and quickly go from a small flame to a raging fire. Fire cards can ignite easily too, they are very temperamental however if managed properly, they can be very beneficial. in fact, fire cards must be managed and under control in order to be of benefit. Fire people can be emotionally volatile yet they are very passionate. fire can change its course in an instant, those born as fire cards are very dynamic, like the spreading fire, are the first to set out into the unknown and take initiative. Fire is more than just a physical thing, it is quite mystical and fire people apprehend the world through their intuition, they trust their gut (or they should anyway) because it rarely ever leads them wrong. Fire people have a strong sense of self just like fire which has no regard over anything in its path, fire people are quite self-centered but they are moving so fast that they never get stuck on themselves, fire needs to spread and explore. Fire people tend to be impulsive and like fire spreading, often leap before they look.

Fire Cards express the warming, radiant, energizing life principle which can manifest as enthusiasm, confidence, encouragement, and the drive to express oneself. Fire is hot and dry in temperament, and its role in nature is to rarefy, refine, transform and intermingle things. Fire has the power to penetrate and can ride through the element of air. It has the capacity to overcome the coldness of the two cold elements, earth and water, and so it can create and maintain harmony among the other elements. A predominance of fire cards may represent a strong spiritual focus in your life (you feel enthusiastic and 'fired up'!) Fire brings transformation, and can indicate changes in your personal world that totally turn your world around. From the ashes of the fire, regeneration. The element of fire has electrical and creative properties.

Spades represent the need to work to make theories a reality and thus produce wisdom. A highly developed Spades individual is self-disciplined and productive, with the ability to sacrifice for the greater good of all. If working on themselves Spades people are willing to discipline themselves for self-improvement. Through their experiences and self-mastery they often become students of highly specialized knowledge or even disciples of mystery schools or so-called secret societies, where they can further develop their acute insights. They should learn to offer their services to humanity and relinquish personal ambition. If functioning negatively, however, they may force discipline and their strong will onto others through misuse of personal power, often becoming bullies.

Positive qualities: vigorousness, zeal, enthusiasm, courage, decisiveness, power of creativity, daring, diligence, dedication.

Negative qualities: quarrelsomeness, irritability, urge to destroy everything, passion, immoderation, jealousy, voraciousness, vindictiveness, violence, hate, anger, sudden ebullition.

The terms Earth, Water, Air, and Fire do not literally mean clods of dirt, buckets of water, etcetera. The four elements are sometimes referred to as "primary matter;" which, when combined, gives rise to the various forms of material existence such as mountains and rivers. Likewise, the burning fire that we see is not the element fire, which is really the potentiality of fire within the substance. For example, green wood has the element of fire within, but this may or may not be brought forth as flames, depending on whether it is ever ignited. In fact, all of the elements bear this relationship between their capacity within and the reality of their form.

As we can see, all of the concrete objects of this world--from the

most immense mountain to the minuscule forms of sub-microscopic life are related by these four elements. It is also through these same four primary elements that all earthly objects are related to (and influenced by) the planets and their polarities (which also have primary qualities within them).
The movement of these four elements is continually taking place, so that change is a continuous process within the human body. This change is both cyclical and progressive, can be measured by discriminating individuals who choose to use their intellects and ability to reason.

He gives wisdom (the system by which the qualities of the Names are manifested) to whoever He wills, and whoever has been given wisdom has certainly been given much benefit. And none will be mindful `of this` except those with intellect and deep contemplative skills.

Al' Quran Surah 2: Ayat 269

The Art of BEing HUman

(Poetic Interlude)

Straight up... No chaser

"we are people of the mighty... mighty people of the sun,
in our hearts lie all the answers to a...
virus we can't run from".
that's right! we can't run, nor can we hide from a...
dis-ease that lives... inside.
these were the words my egun, my auso, my ascended elders
used to wake me this morning to greet the mourning...
of a brand nu'being day... in the u.s. of a.
"wake up son", greet the sun remember how to shine
in relationship to the one.
too much time denying divinity, "humanizing" your flaws,
now, is the time... to give birth to eternity, no fear... no pause
yes, it's... time! to get...sirius, so i...
hop on the coltrane to interstellar space enter my...
retreat, to my 'looks-within' place.
where everything intersects, and all roads... lead to my essence,
where every insperience comes with a lesson... followed by a
blessing
for those who see the signs!
requests from my egungun should never be ignored,
so i woke up, began writing while most people still snored.
"wake up everybody no more sleeping in bed,
no more backwards thinking... time for thinking ahead"
know what else they said?
"there's no dietary choice that can save us from these...
chickens come home to roost, nothing better than the sun
to give your immune system a boost, and... oh yeah!
there's no such thing as immunity from... nature's laws!"
so i... salute! the sun... and it's twin!
flip the script, like... dominique dawes, turn my attention within
pay it to the piper... HU... breathed life into. my person,

OlusanyaBey

The Art of BEing HUman

so this life i love could begin.
quiet as its kept... its beginning was where its end began
we're all going to die one day that was... always the plan,
i'll be damned... oh wait! too late... i was born "black" in america,
so i guess i already am. still...
i'll be damned... if i "choose"... to live my life in fear,
if i do, i pray... the Almighty take me... the hell out of here!
there's absolutely no cause that will cause me to place myself... in captivity?
i've already been a participant in amerikkka's prison industrial complex,
there will be none of that shit for... moi,
i don't give a fuck how unpopular that may make me...
with the herd.
you heard?
you can call it self-quarantine if it makes you feel better,
but that's not what i'm seeing.
i see a nation, once again, being herded by its fears,
losing its faith due to things unseen, crying... crocodile tears,
trying desperately to hold on to a fucked-up standard...
of living that is stubbornly still... held dear.
where was all this "love for life" when all of the "others" were dying?
Now... ALL of you sheeple can...
get the fuck outta here!!!

THE NUMBERS

"So teach us to number our days, That we may cultivate and bring to You a heart of wisdom."

Psalms 90:12

"Verily, all things have We created in proportion and measure."

Qamar 54:49

As I have repeatedly emphasized, our Ancestors regarded mathematics as the divine science because by its means we may recognize and establish order throughout the nature of BEing. It is through mathematics, that we can construct a chain of events that will show the definite relationship between a cause and its effect, an action and its reaction, a beginning and its end. Creation evolves in a perfect order, an order that is emulated in our lives and the cards we have been given to play.

The principles governing numbers were determined to be the principles of all real existences; and as numbers are the primary constituents of mathematical quantities, and at the same time present many analogies to various realities, it was further inferred that the elements of numbers were the elements of realities.

"Numbers are a key to the ancient views of cosmogony—in its broad sense, spiritually as well as physically considered and to the evolution of the present human race; all systems of religious mysticism are based upon numerals. The sacredness of numbers begins with the Great First Cause, the One, and ends only with the naught or zero--- symbol of the infinite and boundless Universe."

--Isis Unveiled," vol. ii. 407

The Art of BEing HUman

Mathematics instruction is a crucial aspect of a child's development. It equips them with problem-solving skills, logical thinking abilities, and critical reasoning capabilities that are essential for their academic and personal growth. However, it is equally important to recognize the significance of teaching children the spiritual principles inherent in mathematics.

My journey with the spiritual aspects of mathematics began at the age of seventeen [knowledge god] when I was introduced to the Supreme Mathematics of the 5% Nation of Islam. It was the first time I was invited to look at numbers as spiritual principles, and orders of operation, not just numerals. For instance, One, as the first step in a process (for the sake of this conversation, a creative process) necessarily exemplifies Knowledge because in order to begin something one must have knowledge. Knowledge of oneself, knowledge of what one is doing, and knowledge of how it is done. Knowledge thus becomes the foundation of everything. Correspondingly, in the Supreme Alphabet it symbolizes A or Allah. One represents the Oneness and Unity of the Creator, as the foundation/beginning of all things. Allah, in the Supreme Alphabet represents the same principles as the number 1. Seshat and Tehuti (numbers and letters) represent not only the principle of the Creator, but also that which has been created... it's representative... the Human BEing, in the name/composition of... Arm-Leg-Leg-Arm-Head[11]. This is how the Gods learned to decipher and decode the symbols known as numbers and letters, come to understand the natural laws and order of our Universe represented in mathematics, the motion of the planets, and the music of the spheres. Indeed, as human beings we can articulate

---

[11] 1. Weak and ignorant as thou art, O man, humble as thou oughtest to be, O child of the dust, wouldst thou raise thy thoughts to infinite wisdom? Wouldst thou see omnipotence displayed before thee? Contemplate thine frame.

The Holy Koran, of the Moorish Science Temple, Chapter 36c1

the name of our Creator with our physical appendages! I cannot say it enough, "As above, So below."

In the cosmology of the Ancients, numbers did not simply identify quantities, they were considered to be concrete definitions of formative, energetic principles of nature. The Kamau called these energetic principles Neteru (misnomered gods, goddesses), in the Yoruba tradition they are called Orisha. The Neteru (plural of Neter/Netert) are the divine principles and functions of the One Supreme Absolute BEing. They are also the archetypes that come together to form the 'nature' of our Universe, as well as our being. Etymologically all of these words (Nature, Neter, National, Natal) are all related, all speak to our... BEing.

Numerology, the study and interpretation of numbers as symbols with spiritual significance, has long been an integral part of religious studies. Numbers hold a deep symbolic meaning in various religious traditions, representing unity, duality, creativity, stability, change, harmony, perfection, abundance, completion and more. In this chapter, we will explore the importance of numerology in spiritual cultivation by examining the symbolic meanings associated with numbers 1-13 (the code of mathematics sales from 0-9, the number 10 symbolizes, among other things, the successful realization of our Human potential, 11-13 represent our self-initiation into the higher dimensions of, the surrender to, and mastery of (Queen and King) our Inner Divinity.

There are many books written about the nature of numbers and their meanings. One can spend a lifetime studying them, but for the purpose of this book I will only provide keywords for the numbers, so that the reader can begin to introduce themselves to these living principles and begin developing their interpretive skills. As time goes by and you develop your relationship with living mathematics you will gain a deeper understanding of these divine ordering principles.

Also, keeping the principle of polarity in mind we need to contemplate both aspects (modes of operation) of each number so that we can recognize them as they present themselves to us through our life experiences.

1. **One** - On the human level the aces represent the individual, self-relating levels of awareness, also the beginnings of new processes. On the cosmic level they relate to the new level attained in our transformation processes and set the design for our next level of growth.
   (+) Unity, Knowledge, Initiate, Create, Beginnings, Something New, Individuality, Leadership, Original, Desire, Focus on Self
   (-) Selfish, Overbearing, Lackadaisical, Narrow-Minded, Materialistic

2. **Two** - The twos/deuces represent union and harmony on the human level, as well as our need for purpose and direction. On the cosmic level they represent polarity and motion in relation to the new design processes that have been initiated
   (+) Wisdom, Duality, Cooperation, Agreements, Diplomacy, Union, Sharing, Security, Partnerships
   (-) Fearful, Co-Dependent, Complainer, Insecure, Fatalistic

3. **Three** - The threes represent out choices in life and group interaction on the human level. In cosmic terms they relate to the energy processes involved and their modes of bonding activity.
   (+) Understanding, Happiness, Active, Playful, Right Choices, Expansive, Restless*[22]
   (-) Worrisome, Impractical, Indecisive, Disorganized, Insecure

4. **Four** - On the human level the fours represent work,

---

[22] All of the odd numbers signify a certain degree of imbalance and strive to achieve balance through the expression of something new. They all have an innate creative drive that constantly seeks expression.

building and creating stability. In cosmic terms they represent the momentum of the energy being expended on the expansion of the base, form or foundation under construction.

>(+) Culture, Freedom, Stability, Form, Foundation, Structure, Organization, Service, Loyal, Conservative
>(-) Stubborn, Chaotic, Inflexible, Controlling, Critical, Close-Minded

5.   **Five** - Fives represent expression, movement and change on the human level. Cosmically they represent the contraction of the developmental process, the "structure" formed and its power/ability to function.

>(+) Power, Refinement, Dynamic, Amplify, Transition, Adaptability, Change, Versatile, Travel, Restless
>(-) Scattered, Detached, Irresponsible, Unstable, Disrespectful, Capricious

6.   **Six** - On a human level the sixes represent growth and learning, adjustment to circumstances. In cosmic terms they represent evolutionary processes.

>(+) Equality, Responsibility, Fate, Karma, Balance, Harmony, Flow, Stabilize, Growth, Justice, Domesticated
>(-) Stubborn, Argumentative, Combative, Naive, Righteous, Procrastinating

7.   **Seven** - The sevens on the human level represent worldly challenges, spiritual development and faith. On the cosmic level they represent the animation of the processes involved, the progress of the evolutionary design.
(+) God, Flow of the Divine, Purpose, Mystical, Reflective, Spirituality, the Inspired Self, Restless, Scholarly, Enlightened
(-) Obstacles, Mental Worry, Deception, Sacrificial, Perfectionist, Manipulative

8.   **Eight** - On the human level the eights represent the use or

abuse of our powers and how we channel those energies on all levels and dimensions. In cosmic terms they represent the transformation from one state to another, either through internal processes or external forces.

> (+) Build or Destroy, Success, Strength, Justice, Work, Patterns, Power, Material Freedom, Powerful, Practical
> (-) Overbearing, Manipulative, Ruthless, Fixed, Inflexible, Condescending

9. **Nine** - represent the concept of completion, fulfillment and acceptance. On the cosmic level they represent the regeneration, transcendence that follows from the changes we have gone through.

> (+) Born, Completion, Interconnectedness, Transcendence, Link to Higher Law/Frequencies, Restless, Universal, Mystical, Benevolent
> (-) Miserly, Abusive, Moody, Cold-Hearted, Dominating, Intolerant

10. **Ten** - On a human level the tens represent success, accomplishment and the new beginning of a higher level in development. Cosmically they represent the level of individualization attained and its operational abilities.

> (+) Manifestation, Potential Realized, Materialism, Substance, Universal Ideals, Divinity of Man, the Public Domain,
> (-) Controlling, Being Controlled, Excessive, Obsessive, Introverted, Devious, Dishonest

The Crown Cards

All of the court cards represent individuals who have entered/undergone some form of initiation into higher knowledge, wisdom, and understanding. Although, as is often the case, the individual may not be conscious of their elevated standing. Jacks represent the Entered Apprentice and Fellow Craftsman as they have just begun to do the work of self-cultivation, and still maintain a degree of immaturity. The Queens and Kings represent men and women who have obtained a level of mastery, have begun to embody their own Divinity. They are the Master Builders. Queens rule through self-mastery, inspiration and nurturing, they are the passive rulers who represent the Divine principles of creation and receptivity. The Kings, on the other hand, rule through strength, command and the enforcement of laws. They represent the male/generative principle in nature. When interpreting your cards the court cards may also represent individuals of their particular suit whom you may encounter. For that matter, because all of the cards interact with each other, any card that shows up in your spreads can represent individuals in your life.

11. Jacks/Eleven - In human terms the Jacks represent sacrifice of worldy pleasures for inspirational development or seeking personal success and losing oneself. In cosmic terms they are the neutrality of cyclic processes - the Child/Initiate.

> (+) Initiation, Creative, Inspiration, Resolution, Imaginative, Innovative, Artistic
>
> (-) Cunning, Immature, Irresponsible, Dishonest

12. Twelve/Queens - The Queens represent receptive processes, judgement of information, nurturing and creativity. On the cosmic level they represent the internalized acceptance of consciousness - the Mother.

> (+) The Divine Feminine, Nurturing Leadership, Understanding, Teaching, Continuity of Wisdom, Receptive, Service-Oriented, Sensual
>
> (-) Overreach, Exaggerate, Unpredictable, Co-Dependent, Emotional

13. Thirteen/Kings - In human terms the Kings represent the directive processes, principles in action, protecting and procreation. On the cosmic level they are externalized transformation from consciousness - the father.

(+) The Divine Masculine, Commanding Leadership, Ascension, Source Connection, Remembering, Honorable, Responsible
(-) Tyrannical, Argumentative, Arrogant, Condescending, Impatient

If you take the time to study and reflect upon the nature of numbers you will discover what many refer to as the miraculous nature of numbers/mathematics. The author agrees with this sentiment as long as we are defining miraculous as the results or works of a "Divine BEing".

Question: Do you think the mathematical example given below is a result of a coincidence or fluke of numbers? The number one represents creation, 9 represents completion... below we see the mathematical sum of nine 1's multiplied by nine 1's. Go figure! Think about it, meditate on the miracle and meanings of the numbers and let them reveal their essence and energy to you, so that you can begin to measure your movements accordingly.
111111111 X 111111111 = 12345678987654321

Coincidence is God's way of remaining anonymous.

~Albert Einstein

(Poetic Interlude)

U Betta... Recognize!

someone said, "U BETTA RECOGNIZE!"...
so i did...
i... recognized... i... re-cognized...
i thought about... he... and her... again.
continuously seeking answers that...
remained stubbornly hidden...
what foolish games...
Neteru playing people...
Neteru playing people...
playing... hide and seek...
i closed my eyes and counted to... infinity...
giving her just enough time to...
veil herself from... me?
she... covered herself with five coats of maya...
i closed my third eye and opened...
two blind eyes to a world full of smoke and...
mirrors...
funhouse mirrors...
distorting our images of self...
so we... no longer... recognize...
ourselves... in each other.
so i looked for her...
in vain...
not realizing she was closer to me then...
the blood in my... veins...
cuz... knowing me better than... i know myself...
she hid the one place my intellect...
Tends to never look...
she hid... inside of me...
while i continued to look for answers...
outside...

OlusanyaBey

The Art of BEing HUman

while all the time... intern-ally...
my heart was an... open book...
authored by her love...
someone said, "U BETTA RECOGNIZE!"...
so i did...
i... recognized... i... re-cognized...
i thought about this game called life... again...
she hid... so that i could seek...
and we... could find...
the joy of recognition... as we re-member!
we were/are... ONE!... ALL... of the time.
how many times will we do this?
close your eyes... and count to... infinity...
i'll hide this time.

THE PLANETS

HUman BEings are magnetic, the key to our existence is learning how to control our magnet in relationship to the electromagnetic nature of our Universe. The planets are points of energy transmission and what energies they transmit depends as much upon their factors of association as their given nature. While the planets do have their specific natures, they do not exist in isolation and can serve to reflect the other planets and their functions. This is simply the relativity of all life.

The essence of astro-logics and the Tzulkin is in understanding the meaning of the planets. The meaning of the polarities, is determined by the planets which rule and significate them. In the Tzulkin system the planets represent the players in the game of life. They are the mythical Gods and the Goddesses controlling the lives of human beings. As you learn to read your spreads you will be able to see what cards the planets are playing on your behalf.

☼ **Sun**: In traditional astro-logics the Sun and the Moon are not actually considered as planets, but as the luminaries or "lights" — the Light of the Day and the Light of the Night."[31] They symbolize the two (binary) fundamental aspects of that Universal Power which ancient philosopher-mystics saw as the dynamic warp and woof of the material world. The Sun represents the power which sustains all the activities of the body and their psychic counterparts and overtones. It is, to use an analogy, the fuel on which the engine of personality runs — and apparently the nature

---

[31] Genesis: 14 Then God said, "Let lights in the expanse of the sky be for separating the day from the night. They will be for signs and for seasons and for days and years. 15 They will be for lights in the expanse of the sky to shine upon the land." And it happened so. 16 Then God made the two great lights— the greater light for dominion over the day, and the lesser light as well as the stars for dominion over the night.

of such a fuel (whether it is wood, steam, gasoline, electricity, or atomic power) dictates the characteristics, the type of materials used and the structure of the engine. A person powered by an Aries or 1st polarity Sun is different from an individual whose vital energies stem from a Virgo or 6th polarity solar energy. Every person tends to use the type of energy which is most readily available and most natural to him. From this we can infer many basic traits of character, and also the nature of the experiences which the individual will attract and seek, because their experiences will demand just that type of power to meet them successfully; indeed she "resonates" to that kind of opportunity and they attract each other, because everything in our lives is basically a matter of attunement of force/energy. The Sun/Birth card in a person's life spread refers to the essential purpose of her life and to their inner "divinity" seeking its fulfillment the "higher-self," in contrast to the ego/"lower-self" or ambition of the person. The Sun governs the 5th polarity aka Leo.

☽ **Moon**: The Moon is the most ancient symbol of the basic rhythm of life everywhere on earth. The Moon is fundamentally the capacity of adaptation to the environment — the inner and psychic, as well as the outer, physical and social environment. It also refers to the mind, because mind is at first the capacity of adjustment to the challenges of daily living so that the child might make the best of them. Most important of all is the Moon's relationship to the Sun - that is, the phases of the ever-changing soli-lunar relationship, all the aspects of which constitute the lunation cycle of approximately thirty days duration — for life without light would be impossible. That the disc of the Sun and that of the Full Moon are practically the same visual size — the nearness of the Moon compensating for its really much smaller size — is one of the most remarkable correspondences. For man the attraction of light and life have the same power; yet she must choose which one will dominate her consciousness, and the degree to which she does so is an important factor in her ultimate character. The Moon is the ruler of the 4th polarity aka Cancer.

☿ **Mercury**: Mercury represents mental ability, the desire to understand, and the need to communicate. Being clever with fast responses, Mercury quickly can get a good grasp of a subject or logically solve problems. Besides being inquisitive and eager to learn, Mercury is articulate and skilled in the expression of ideas, whether through talking or writing. With critical abilities as well as mental agility, this planet can signify discriminative powers and a capacity for being adaptable and versatile. Although there can be a tendency to be nervous or diffused, Mercury is a master of communication. Through the sharing of information, Mercury is also connected to teaching or business and trading. Mercury governs the 3rd and 6th polarities aka Gemini and Virgo. Anyone relating to you from this planetary position may be a source of ideas and information. Due to its association with mental activities, Mercury relationships can be intellectually stimulating. It is an excellent influence for conversational rapport.

♀ **Venus**: Venus relates to values of love and pleasure and therefore harmonizes, bringing warmth, sociability, and a cooperative attitude. Venus would prefer to be easygoing and keep the peace rather than face confrontation and a discordant environment. Venus's function is to bring union, and is therefore connected to intimacy. Being a magnetic planet that draws from the feminine, Venus governs the ability to attract others. Since this attraction can extend to needed resources, Venus can also therefore govern money and possessions. This planet delights in the senses and has a fine appreciation for beauty and sensual indulgence. It is therefore connected to artistic, musical, and creative gifts as well as to sexuality. Bringing good taste, grace, and natural refinement, Venus dislikes coarseness but may be prone to vanity and procrastination. In men, Venus represents their feminine side and all the values associated with this, especially relationships, cooperation, and enjoyment in life. Venus is ruler of the 2nd and 7th polarities aka Taurus and Libra.

♂ **Mars**: Action-oriented, Mars is the planet that has most to do with simple activity. Mars is the planet that is closest to the earth outside of the earth. It represents the place in life where you throw off energy, fly off the handle and move the hardest to get things done. It is a planet that represents vitality, drive, and motivation. Courageous and direct, Mars represents the Warrior archetype. In the male/female polarity Mars governs male energy and sexuality. For a woman, Mars depicts the drive behind her personality and her assertive side. Mars can also represent the type of man she naturally attracts to act out her own male energy. For a man, Mars represents his physical drive and sensuality. Passionate and immediate, Mars stimulates the need to directly gratify desires or use strength and force to defend and protect. Quickly combative or confrontational, Mars can represent anger. If uncontrolled this energy can bring impatience, aggression and destruction. If controlled it can be used constructively to get much accomplished. It also exemplifies the sense of personal power that comes from inner strength and standing up for your needs. Mars governs the 1st and 8th polarities aka Aries and Scorpio.

♃ **Jupiter**: Jupiter, the largest planet in our solar system, encourages growth and expansion. Jupiter is the guru of the planets, the spiritual message of Jupiter is to seek development through higher wisdom, philosophy, and truth. The positive aspect of this enlargement is the ability to reach beyond existing limitations and experience the optimism and confidence that come from visualizing something better or greater. Jupiter also enables us to think comprehensively and see the bigger picture. This aptitude can help us perceive large concepts, philosophical ideas, or spiritual and religious values. Although Jupiter usually represents good fortune, some of this planet's less attractive qualities are excess, false optimism, exaggeration, and over-exuberance. By nature Jupiter is generous, benevolent, and full of good intentions. On occasions, however, it can inflate the ego, causing individuals to appear opinionated, arrogant, or condescending. Traveling to distant places fits particularly well with Jupiter's desire to expand and gather wisdom through new experiences. The quest for a higher truth suggested by this planet can inspire a pursuit for knowledge, higher learning, and spirituality. Jupiter as the mythological god Zeus is also associated with judgment; therefore, Jupiter represents the judicial system or law and order. Jupiter governs the 9th and 12th polarities aka Sagittarius and Pisces.

♄ **Saturn**: Saturn, ruler of the 10th and 11th polarities aka Capricorn and Aquarius, is often known as Father Time and the taskmaster. Symbolic of "that which we sow we shall also reap," Saturn represents the law of restriction or of learning through suffering. Saturn relates to discipline, organization, and responsibility. Saturn, being older and wiser, advises that everything can work if we apply methodology to our efforts. It also suggests that the knowledge gained from the restrictive influences associated with obstacles is ultimately worthwhile. In order to balance the expansiveness of Jupiter we have the reducing influence of Saturn, which can positively restrain over-inflation and maintain balance. The positive qualities of Saturn enable us to create order or work within space and form. It defines boundaries, producing rules and regulations for working systems. This planet requires us to face up to our obligation and duties. Saturn accounts for everything, for the work that has been put in, and for what was not accomplished; everything is repaid exactly. Nevertheless, Saturn's lessons are often uncomfortable, as they can point to what is wrong or missing in our lives. The negative qualities of Saturn can cause pessimism, fear, denial, and even depression. Saturn also represents anything "hard," such as bones and teeth or when we need to be "hard" on ourselves. The attractive attributes of Saturn are the ability to concentrate and to demonstrate our willpower and self-reliance. This planet will reward individuals for their dedication if they work on their determination and perseverance. With the assistance of Saturn we develop patience, order and

authority. Saturn can force us to be realistic and efficient.
Saturn also represents the last of the 'personal' and 'social' planets. Uranus, Neptune and Pluto due to the length of their orbits will be in the same polarity/sign for individuals born during multi-periods of time, making them transpersonal/generational. Another way we may express this is - The personal planets are the Sun, Moon, Mercury, Venus, and Mars aka... your ego, your emotions, your thinking, your tastes/aesthetic and how you get what you want. The social planets are Jupiter and Saturn; your perspective and your boundary, respectively. We may also say that Saturn represents the skin or the barrier between you and what is OUT THERE.

"OUT THERE" we have Uranus, Neptune and Pluto. These planets are referred to as the transpersonal, or generational because they effect entire generations of individuals. They are called transpersonal because they govern things that transcend the personal or the individual such as death, transformation, atomic energy (Pluto), fantasy, spirituality, mystery (Neptune) revolution, sudden changes, or freedom (Uranus).

♅ **Uranus:** Uranus co-rules the 11th polarity aka Aquarius. This planet governs all types of electric energy: television and radio waves, magnetic fields, lasers, computers, and new technology. Uranus enables us to develop our intuitive skills and ingenuity by being able to think in an objective or abstract way. Uranus brings enlightenment and freedom of spirit by breaking away from old habits or the restrictions of Saturn. This kind of freedom also involves leaving a space for the unexpected. These qualities can encourage individualistic expression and love of independence. Despite the pressures of conformity, Uranus dares us to express our own views or unique style. Uranus's unpredictable element is also associated with sudden happenings, erratic behavior, or eccentricity. Although Uranus highlights liberty, humanitarian ideology, and a free society, this planet's influence can produce social rebelliousness, anarchy, and revolution. At an individual level it can lead to defiance or obstinate behavior, just for the sake of being different. Nevertheless, Uranus encourages an open-minded attitude and acceptance of new ideas, change, and the latest inventions. Uranus also can widen our points of view to universal concepts such as humanity as a family of brothers and sisters.

♆ **Neptune:** Neptune co-rules the 12th polarity aka Pisces, and as lord of the sea is perceived as enigmatic and mysterious. Unlike Saturn, Neptune knows no boundaries and can merge with everything. Although this ability to blend can signify integration and unity, it can also slowly and subtly dissolve what we consider permanent or solid, diluting matter and creating ambiguity and confusion. Neptune's influence is more evident on the subconscious level, in dreams, spiritual visions, or supernatural experiences, but some aspects or areas of our lives are not as clear-cut as others due to Neptune's effects. Nevertheless, Neptune can transcend limitations by refining and purifying old or outdated perceptions. The positive qualities of Neptune can lift the spirit with inspiration and let the imagination envisage what is possible. Neptune also can break down the boundaries created by the ego. Since Neptune's receptivity can help us identify with the suffering of others, it can inspire compassion, generosity, and sympathy. Neptune's ambiguity, however, can also mislead and make us gullible. This planet's extreme sensitivity to everything can increase intuition and produce spiritual experiences or metaphysical phenomena. The unattractive qualities of Neptune suggest escapism, deception, or drug and alcohol abuse. Nevertheless, the ability to "lose oneself" in inspired creative endeavors, such as art, music, or drama, indicates that working positively with Neptune's influence can help us to aspire and to dream.

♇ **Pluto:** Pluto is the great revealer, but often there's a darkness before the rebirth. Pluto brings to mind purging, cleansing, and releasing buried power or core truths. It's the planet of creative destruction. Pluto shows the area of life where we personally face the intense powers of creation and destruction. It is a doorway through which elusive, stiff pockets of self, spirit and primal energy lie hidden, which are released either by our own efforts or by provocation from the outside world. The Challenge Card in the Tzulkin system works exactly like Pluto. This influence is intense and can bring out the best or worst in a person or situation, challenging them to transform. Pluto co-rules the 8th polarity aka Scorpio.

PHILOSOPHY OF POLARITY/SIGN RULERSHIPS

When the traditional rulerships were created, the assignments were based upon a symbolic structure that is complete within itself. Breaking any part of that symbolic structure destroys the fundamental strength and reasoning of the whole system.
Apart from the luminaries (Sun and Moon), each planet's rulership over its attributed polarity derives from its relationship to the Sun and recognizes dominion over two signs - one diurnal (of the day/Sun) the other nocturnal (of the night/Moon). Diurnal energies relate to masculinity, being active, direct and expressive, while nocturnal energies relate to femininity, being responsive, indirect, and impressive. As we can see the binary nature and function of our Universe is consistent throughout its design and operation.

As in most ancient symbolism, the pivotal point in the underlying philosophy is the relationship of the Sun to the Earth. Hence the distribution of planets to signs begins at the cusp between Cancer and Leo where the power of the Sun is greatest (at least in the northern hemisphere where, according to the author's research, Astrology evolved). We can also relate this beginning to the heliacal rise of Sirius during the "dog days of summer", which signaled the inundation of the Nile and the beginning of the Kamitic new year.

The five visible planets are then distributed between the ten remaining signs/polarities in an order based on their relative speed and distance from the Sun, in such a way that each has a 'day house' in a masculine sign and a 'nocturnal house' in a feminine sign. (It is apt that the luminaries rule only one sign each since the Sun loses its power in a feminine polarity, just as the Moon loses its potency in masculine polarities).

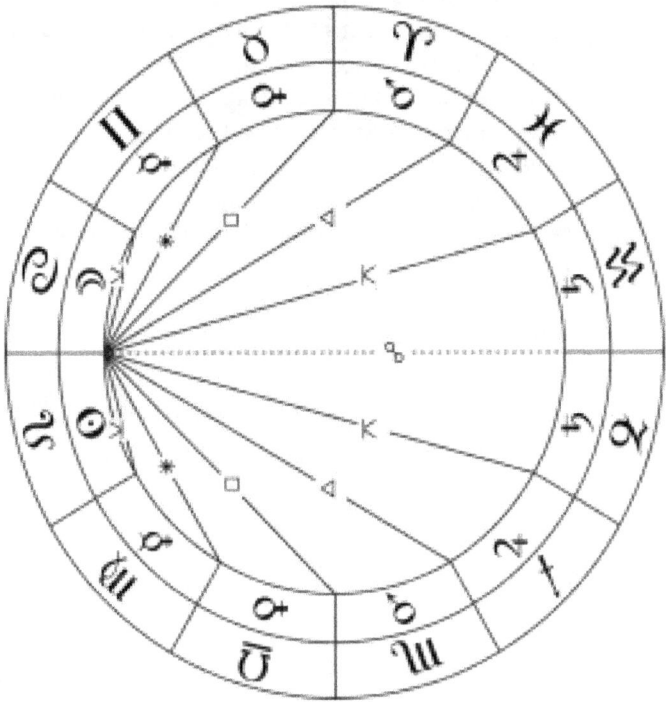

The distinction of the diurnal and nocturnal influences and the way they temper the inherent nature of the planets is extremely important and often largely overlooked by many modern astrologics texts, which don't consider the originating philosophy or explain its reasoning. Diurnal and nocturnal definitions can completely redefine planetary energies - consider for yourself how Mars in the first polarity/Aries, a diurnal[masculine] polarity, expresses itself in a very active, direct and expressive manner, while Mars in the eight polarity/Scorpio, a nocturnal[feminine] polarity is more indirect - an energy that is released slowly, deliberately and with cold control, as opposed to the natural, hot and dry energy we associate with Mars, but just as threatening nonetheless. The same applies to the polarity rulership's of Mercury, Venus, Jupiter and Saturn; each relating to a diurnal sign where its masculine energy is strengthened and its mannerisms are more overt, and also to a nocturnal sign, where its feminine traits are emphasized and its characteristics are more implicit. At this point I want to emphasize that in the Tzulkin system we are not using Signs/Constellations, therefore we do not ignore the diurnal movement of the Sun in relationship to the Earth to establish the order of polarities. We will explore this further in the next chapter.

The Planets & Personal Points

☉ SUN
Spirit, Purpose, Life Force & Identity. Masculine principle

☽ MOON
Soul, Feeling, Emotions and Instincts. Domesticity. Feminine principle

☿ MERCURY
Mentality, Intellect and Power of Communication. The Reasoning Mind

♀ VENUS
Love, Acquisitiveness, Beauty, Art and Attraction

♂ MARS

Initiative, Energy, Action, Aggression and Conflict

♃ JUPITER
Wisdom, Enthusiasm, Expansion, Optimism & Success

♄ SATURN
Restriction, Sensitiveness, Limitation, Restraint & Sorrow, Discipline

♅ URANUS
Change, Originality, Revolution & Eccentricity

♆ NEPTUNE
Imagination, Obligation, Spirituality, Inspiration, Illusion & Deception

♇ PLUTO
Power, Obsession, Forces beyond Personal Control Transformation

PRC[34]
The face you show the World. Primary motivation in Life.

---

[34] Planetary Ruling Card - I equate the PRC with the Rising Sign/Ascendant in contemporary Astrology.

(Poetic Interlude)

I'm Melting

fingertips to temples we...
worship.
bodies in motion...
like planets we...
come...
together, UnI...
verses are... born.
stargates with... blue arches...
transport me to inner dimensions where...
I seek the measure of... time, and...
eternal moments.
we made luv in a pyramid and...
gave birth to... matriarchal dynasties,
where mooning women weave black wholes.
my light... collapses into your gravity...
well...
your water... never running... dry.
my evolution is a...
revolution.
returning to the center of my BEing...
I long to be ONE...
once moor.
no longer becoming...
i choose to BE...
COME...
let's give each other the... gift of... fire!
spontaneously... Come... Bust...
combust!
nothing quite like the... transformative power of...
passion's flames.
U feelin me?

The Art of BEing HUman

Olusanya Bey

I wanna melt with U!

THE POLARITIES

"As above so below" is the only way to achieve order and harmony. As a result, our Ascended Elders adopted a matrilineal/matriarchal system, as the social manifestation of planetary laws. It was the Queen who established consanguinity, transmitted the solar blood. The Queen was the true sovereign, keeper of the royalty, and guardian of the purity of the lineage. Moorish/Kamitic Kings claimed a right to the throne through marriage to the eldest Kamitic princess. By marriage she transmitted the crown to her husband, who exercised the power of the throne on her behalf, acting as her chief executive officer and Sergeant-at-Arms.

Astro-logics, in general, is the study of the correlations that can be established between the positions of celestial bodies around the Earth and physical events or psychological and social changes of consciousness in HUman BEings. In other words, it is the study of the relationship between biological and celestial mechanics and their effect on human beings. Even if the individual in question has to focus his attention analytically on one single factor, there are nevertheless certain basic facts she should always hold in mind. The most important of these are that everything in a spread has its polar opposite, and that any factor can have a negative as well as a positive significance, regardless of whether it is usually classified as good or bad, fortunate or unfortunate. This principle of polarity is one of the seven Tehutian/Hermetic principles we introduced earlier, and is the cornerstone of any sound Tzulkin interpretation.

An astro-logical cipher or wheel of the Zodiac is divided into 12 arcs, equal either in terms of space or time. If in terms of space these arcs are all of an equal length i.e. 30° each, one twelfth of a 360° circle. This is an important point to keep in mind. All of the planets in our solar system move in the ecliptic and within a belt, which is around 16° - 18° wide. Within this ecliptic/great circle of

360° there are groups of fixed stars, there are two terms that are commonly used to describe these groups of stars namely Constellations and the Zodiac. However, that which is known as the Zodiac is not based upon the constellations. A constellation is- "a cluster, a group of stars that is physical and can be observed in the celestial sphere. These vary in shapes and forms and take up different widths*". The International Astronomical Union is the international body that is responsible for the definition of constellations and currently has defined 88 constellations in the celestial sphere, of those, 13 constellations (from Aries to Pisces) surround the ecliptic. Ophiuchus is usually referred to as the thirteenth by the IAU, sits between Scorpio and Sagittarius. The Zodiac signs (which we have clarified are actually polarities), although also 12 in number, unlike the physical constellations are equally 30° in length. These twelve equal polarities/signs are derived from a Sun based model where the Sun spends approximately 30 days in each polarity. Below is a chart provided by the IAU showing both the IAU physical constellations used in astronomy and the twelve polarities/signs used in astro-logics and the Tzulkin.

---

* According to the International Astronomical Union

The Art of BEing HUman

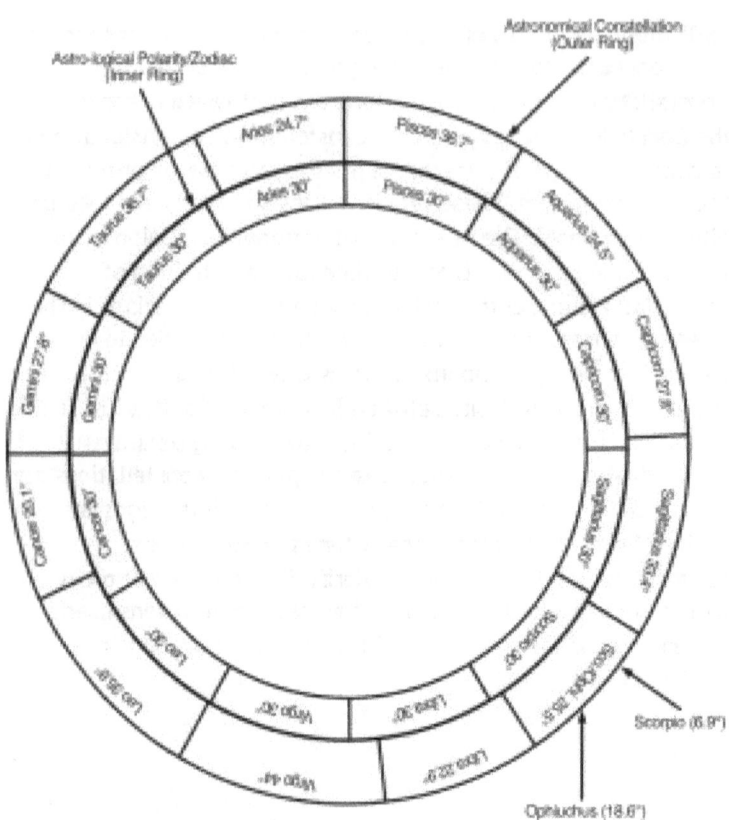

As we can see by looking at the diagram not one of the constellations is actually 30°, or fits into the twelve 30° divisions we call the Zodiac. These divisions bear no physical relation to the constellations after which they were traditionally named, but are measured from the Spring equinoctial point.

The signs of the Tropical Zodiac are 'polarities', though they follow the analogy/symbolic representation of the twelve constellations or star groups. They measure the heavens according to the Sun-Earth relationship, not that between the solar system and the fixed stars. Within the twelve-fold division of the Zodiac there is a harmonic division of the light which characterize six basic types or polarizations of the one central power represented by the Sun, source of all energies operating on the planets. Each polarization produces a male/female (diurnal/nocturnal) couple; and the Zodiac is thus divided into alternatively "masculine" and "feminine" polarities representing two sides of a particular archetype or theme: $1^{st}|8^{th}$, $2^{nd}|7^{th}$, $3^{rd}|9^{th}$, $4^{th}|10^{th}$, $5^{th}|11^{th}$, and $6^{th}|12^{th}$.

In a celestial coordinate system commonly used by astronomers and astrologers the beginning of the Tropical Zodiac, the first degree of Aries is always identical with the point of the Vernal/Spring equinox (0° of longitude on the ecliptic), not with any specific group of stars, irrespective of the fact that the sun shines in front of the constellation Pisces on the March equinox in our day and age. Studying the polarities gives us insight into these Universal themes and allows us to reconcile the "opposites.

Olney in his Mystic Test Book states, *"the manner in which this solar effect is received by the earth is very important and is fully considered in the calculations of polarity relative to the earth. These polar changes are all calculated on a time basis, for 'time' is nothing but a measure of motion of the heavenly bodies. Particularly the earth".* ⁂ He goes on to say, *"If the Earth stood perpendicular to the plain of its revolution about the Sun, the polar changes would be slight, at the same time, if the orbit of the Earth was perfectly circular and the inclination of the Sun zero, there would be no change to calculate through polarity and it would make no possible difference when a person was born. The student will understand by this explanation that the signs of the Zodiac are nothing but points of measurements dividing the heavens into 12 portions and these signs are only emblems and tokens of the 12 grand polarities of the earth as that body moves around Old Sol in his yearly journey."* This is a very important point to keep in mind! At this point I will ask the reader to refer back to my breakdown of the planetary rulers to see the

---

⁂ Olney Richmond, The Mystic Test Book, pg.196

relationship between the planets and polarities. I have observed many so-called cardologists ignore this principle of polarity and astronomical calculations, interpret the cards more from a modern Astrology basis than from the foundational rules/principles of the Tzulkin/cards. They will interpret the cards according to signs and houses, as if they are reading a natal chart, instead of the columns and lines of the 90 Quadrates/Spreads (especially the Spiritual and Mundane) with the principle of polarity in mind.

When interpreting our cards, especially our Life spread, it may be helpful to have a natal chart on hand so that we may take into consideration the placement of each planet in the heavens at the time of our birth, but it is not necessary as long as we may refer to an ephemeris for the same information.

The Tzulkin shares some of the same principles of "contemporary Astrology", but it is its own system, should not be used or interpreted in the same manner one would when practicing Astrology. The astro-logics are applicable, but there are distinct differences between the two systems.

The Tropical Zodiac is not based upon the stars but on planetary motion, mathematics, geometry, and the orientation of the Earth to the Sun. The Tropics of Cancer and Capricorn mark the positions of the Sun at the summer and winter solstices. Once again, the Tropical Zodiac begins with the Sun at the vernal equinox. This designates the beginning of the first polarity/aka Aries. It is this mathematical/harmonic division that is most important, not the individual stars within that division. The polarities are divisions of an annual cycle beginning with the Spring Equinox.
Each of the polarities has its own unique characteristics and corresponding elements that are integral to their understanding. Apart from their affect in the forming of our unique astro-logical makeup at the moment we are born, when we are in the season of a polarity, we will generally tend to feel its energies and deal with things of its nature, which will be influenced by the cards we have

in play at that particular time, in whichever spread we may be reading at the time.

When reading the brief descriptions of each polarity that follow keep in mind that I have only given ideas of the potential of these periods. It is up to you to determine the negatives or positives as you relate what you are seeing in your spreads, along with the circumstances occurring in your life at the time.

The Planetary Polarities

Each of the polarities is assigned an element (fire, earth, air, water) and a mode (Cardinal, Fixed, Mutable) which denotes whether it falls at the beginning, middle, or end of a season, respectively. All of this adds to the flavor of their energies and gives them their subtle differences. For example, a fixed fire polarity (the fifth) is different to a mutable fire polarity (the 9th). Here's a summary of their Elements and Modes:

ELEMENTS

Fire Polarities = 1st, 5th, 9th - These polarities hold fiery passion, energy, enthusiasm, and boldness.

Earth Polarities = 2nd, 6th, 10th - These are the grounded, earthy polarities of the Zodiac. They are hard-working, practical, and pragmatic.

Air Polarities = 3rd, 7th, 11th - These are the intellectual thinkers and talkers of the Zodiac. They are logical, lead with their heads, and are relationship-oriented.

Water Polarities = 4th, 8th, 12th - These are the most intuitive, emotive polarities. They are in touch with their emotions and subconscious, empathetic and fluid.

MODES

Cardinal Polarities = 1st, 4th, 7th, 10th - The leaders of the pack and self-starters. They like initiating things but may struggle with completion.

Fixed Polarities = 2nd, 5th, 8th, 11th - These polarities are hard-working, reliable, and determined. They are able to see things through but may be stubborn.

Mutable Polarities = 3rd, 6th, 9th, 12th - These polarities are flexible and adaptable. They are able to embrace the new winds of change but are prone to be fickle.

Each polarity can also be classified as either Yang/Active or Yin/Receptive. Yang polarities are more outwardly focused, Yin polarities are more inwardly-focused.

YANG: Aries, Gemini, Leo, Libra, Sagittarius, Aquarius
YIN: Taurus, Cancer, Virgo, Scorpio, Capricorn, Pisces

First Polarity aka ♈ (Aries) Mar 21 - Apr 19: The polarity of self and action.
Keywords: body, self-image, appearance, persona, vitality, how you dawn on others.
Planetary Ruler: Mars

Second Polarity aka ♉ (Taurus) Apr 20 - May 20: The polarity of possessions and wealth.
Keywords: self-esteem, self-worth, how you value yourself, possessions, money.
Planetary Ruler: Venus

Third Polarity aka ♊ (Gemini) May 21 - Jun 21: The polarity of communications.

Keywords: siblings, correspondence, communication, neighbors, local network.
Planetary Ruler: Mercury

Fourth Polarity aka ♋ (Cancer) Jun 22 - July 22: The polarity of family and home.
Keywords: home, mother, family, emotional defenses, roots, foundations, Ancestors.
Planetary Ruler: Sun

Fifth Polarity aka ♌ (Leo) Jul 23 - Aug 22: The polarity of creativity, leadership, and children.
Keywords: children, creativity, speculation, gambling, play, self-expression.
Planetary Ruler: Moon

Sixth Polarity aka ♍ (Virgo) Aug 23 - Sep 22: The polarity of health and service.
Keywords: work environment, work, service, job, co-workers, health.
Planetary Ruler: Mercury

Seventh Polarity aka ♎ (Libra) Sep 23 - Oct 23: The polarity of law, marriage and partnerships.
Keywords: marriage, spouse, business partner, clients, adversaries-open enemies.
Planetary Ruler: Venus

Eight Polarity aka ♏ (Scorpio) Oct 24 - Nov 21: The polarity of death, regeneration, resurrection.
Keywords: death, psychotherapy, transforming, occult, sex, other people's money, inheritance.
Planetary Ruler: Mars

Ninth Polarity aka ♐ (Sagittarius) Nov 22 - Dec 21: The polarity of mental exploration and freedom.
Lphilosophy.
Planetary Ruler: Jupiter

Tenth Polarity aka ♑ (Capricorn) Dec 22 14 - Jan 19: The polarity of career, organizing, and work.
Keywords: career, father, success, achievement, status, professional expression.
Planetary Ruler: Saturn

Eleventh Polarity aka ♒ (Aquarius) Jan 20 - Feb 19: The polarity of rebellion, hopes, and friends.
Keywords: friends, groups, hopes, mass media, social rapport.
Planetary Ruler: Saturn

Twelfth Polarity aka ♓ (Pisces) Feb 18 - Mar 20: The polarity of spirituality or self-undoing
Keywords: hidden strengths and weaknesses, suffering, withdrawal, inner worlds, the Divine.
Planetary Ruler: Jupiter

(Poetic Interlude)

one/time/sunrise

give thanks and praise for the times...
when she invites me to...
begin my... days as witness to the dawn of...
her gaze is a journey into the state of...
a...maze where love provides the clue in...
so many ways... it is best to be alert as...
emotions blur and... thoughts haze
poetic moons in a waxing phase will wane...
in strains and words that... string together...
things like... quarterly cycles and... seven chakras...
into twenty-eight-word quatrains!
these luna-tick... moon-tock moments when...
my entire movement is measured by...
her rhythms...
both bodies... clocks...
that get wound... a...round each other?
conscious of each... other...
time...
spent...
love...
to spend...
giving value to life's many variables...
where she begins... is...
where i end.
only to begin... so i say... again.
give thanks and praise!
a new day... dawns on the horizon, so i...
gaze into her eyes and... like a candle before the sun i...
disappear!

THE LINES

A common mistake I see many Cardologists make as they interpret the cards is a heavy reliance on contemporary Astrology. Both systems share astro-logical principles, but they differ in their mechanics and interpretation methods.

Astrologers read our Natal chart, along with other astrological charts (i.e. transit, solar return, progression, harmonic) whereas a Cardologist reads our Life Spread, along with the spreads of other Planetary progression (i.e. 7-Year, Yearly, Seasonal, Weekly). When I hear a Cardologist speak about the planets in houses or signs I immediately know that they are referring to Astrology, not Cardology, because there are no houses on a spread. In Astrology the Houses illustrate the areas of our lives being affected by the planets, in Cardology these areas are represented by the lines and columns of the various quadrations/spreads, along with the polarities. Of course, if a Cardologists wants to, they may refer to an astrological chart when advising a client, however, when doing so they are practicing Astrology, not Cardology. There are no natal charts in Cardology. All a Cardologists needs to interpret their clients' cards are the Master spreads and an ephemeris, so that they may place the planets in their respective polarities, identify their corresponding cards, and interpret them accordingly.

The lines and columns in the quadrations derive their meanings from the planets, both follow the order of the planets in speed of rotation and distance from the Sun. When one is reading the lines and columns it is customary to see the column's influence as in-flowing energy, and the rows as out-flowing energy. However I suggest that the person reading take into considerations their current life circumstances and interpret the respective cards, directions of the energies accordingly. In my experience the vertical cards (columns) usually represent in-flowing energy, but that is not always the case, as these energies can flow in both directions. I want to also invite you to see the rows and columns as construction modules in the building of your 'temple-on-two-legs'. In the same way a church or temple is built with rows and columns, your Church/Sanctum Sanctorum/Holy of Holies in built in the same manner.

Line I.

☿ Mercury - The mind, early education, youth, exchange of ideas, communication, sudden impulses, swiftly moving/changing experiences and events, stimulations.

Line II.

♀ Venus - Love, marriage, emotions, idealism, art, harmony, beauty, social contacts, domestic relations, emotional attitudes towards our family and other loved ones. The feminine principle. Women in general, as well as their interests.

Line III.

♂ Mars - Physical energy and vitality, human will and action, disputes, lawsuits, strife, where you are expending your energy/working hard. The masculine principle.

Line IV.

♃ Jupiter – money in general, returns from business, professional prestige, consideration of values, sources of wealth, benefits from any source, religion and philosophy, parental or cosmic love, relationships with people of influence or importance.

Line V.

♄ Saturn – Wisdom, experience, limitation, the tester and taskmaster, earned responsibilities and burdens, karma, your connection with sicknesses, hospitals, etc. Your state of health in general. Those who educate you the hard way or are connected with your hardships. The rewarder (of good or ill). A blessing in hindsight. Frequently matters connected to real estate.

Line VI.

♅ Uranus – Your work and work relations, group activities and relationships, progress, innovations, inventions, intuition, occultism.

Line VII.

♆ Neptune – Inspiration, idealism, utopianism, mysticism, mediumship, clairvoyance and clairaudience, travel and distant interests, commerce, ships, the sea, drugs, medicines, cosmetics, oils and gases, anesthetics, confusion, irrationality, impracticality, delusion, deception from or towards others, disappointment, alcoholism, escapism.

We look at the lines/columns to determine which planets are influencing our cards, and to identify the areas of life that our cards are influencing at any given time.

The Art of BEing HUman

Olusanya Bey

(Poetic Interlude)

patiently i... wait

as she lay sleeping i...
watch the... dream of this world through the...
five windows of my mind but...
my senses have been overwhelmed by the...
sense of... you.
now...
what's a poet to do?
how do i... write a poem that... makes sense?
see... i remember those... long midnight walks along...
the banks of the nile, that i though were... past...
how meeting you has... once again made...
ancient memories... present... but... tense.
why didn't you wait for me... this lifetime?

the moment we met i... looked into your eyes...
saw reflections and... recollections! ...of love and...
surprise... as you realized... you...
were reading my mind!
we may not understand it, but... its crystal clear...
we recognized the... tie that... binds...
our... bodies and... souls... across... lifetimes.
its at... times like these i... find words ineffectual...
to explain this experience, perhaps...
i should start practicing... pantomimes...
you know... gestures and... facial expressions,
body language! revealing the mysteries of a...
forever love...
hmmmm... virtual... road signs...
pointing the way... past... the illusion of time...
back? ... to our future.
your present relationship may very well suit you, but...
will it stand the test... will it transcend any and...

OlusanyaBey

The Art of BEing HUman

all obstacles, including... time?
these words that i write... the reason for my rhyme...
it's all about... YOU!
you... are the muse... who has always been home...
in the mansions of... my mind.

still... my commitment to... commitments...
keeps me from the... full expression of our...
eternal relationship... except... in between the... lines...
of my poetry. why? simply because...
you didn't wait for me.
so i wait.
after all... what's a... lifetime or... two...
when your love has been created to... last for eternity.
this is not the first time i... returned...
to the... dream of this world... looking for... you!
if by chance it is not... the last...
as delicious and... nutritious as... our love is...
i don't mind an occasional... fast.
it was the... "absence" of you...
that makes the... "presence" of you...
such a... "stone... cold... blast"... like...
don cornelius on soul train with... sister erykah singing,
"i guess i'll see you next lifetime..."
this is not a harlequin romance or a... zane novel...
this! ... is a... "Love Divine!"
do you remember me now?
any feelings of... deja vu?
no? that's alright... forever love...
blesses one with... infinite patience...
so i... wait...
until you do.

PURPOSE

When I began writing this book, I was quite clear about my purpose and goal. I wanted to introduce individuals to the Tzulkin calendar system, and I wanted to share my personal philosophy on the "art" of BEing... Human. My reason for doing so was simple... I attribute my knowledge and understanding of myself to my use of the Tzulkin, combined with the application of the insights I derive from my "readings", towards the cultivation of my spirit. Although I share a lot of "technical" information I have tried not to make this a "technical" book. It is a "sharing", an offering of personal insights gained from practice.

When I am invited into schools to talk to our youth, I do two things upon entering the classroom. I write the following quotation from Octavia E. Butler's book "Parable of the Sower" on the whiteboard, "*All that you touch. You change. All that you change. Changes you.*" I then turn around and greet them with the words, "Who art thou? Why art thou? and How art thou?" I explain to them that my reason for doing so is to introduce them to the idea that art is not just 'something you do', that it, is in fact, who and what you are. Yes, there are different mediums of art that one can engage in, but art is first and foremost our "state of being". As manifestations of our Creator, HUman beings are created (qualitatively & quantitatively) in the image of their Creator, and are "artful" manifestations of its nature. Think about the first Tehutian principle; All is Mind. We are the Creator's finest ideas made, complete! Therefore... we are living breathing works of art, "Divine by Design", imagined and created within a Divine Mind! I use the word complete to signify that everything we need to be everything we are supposed to be was instilled in us at birth. I consistently do this because I want our youth to remember that they have the ability to manifest the world that they want to live in, that they are the masters of their destiny. No one outside of themselves can give them better answers to their BEing than they can provide for themselves if they develop their own intuition. That is why the axiom of the ancients is "Know Thyself". I want the youth to understand that they were born with a unique purpose, and not to allow this unhealthy culture we currently live in to beat that ability out of them as they grow and develop.

I tell them of a time when all of nature was considered sacred. Knowledge, wisdom, and understanding were found in the planetary cycles, the life cycle of the plants, and the interconnectedness of our Universe. The Divine was seen as present in everything from the fire we use to cook our meals to the stars in the heavens. Our entire planet is marked by pathways of supernatural or spiritual energy that are called "ley lines" in the West and "dragon lines" in the East. Where these powerful lines intersected, monuments such as pyramids, temples and geometric circles of standing stones were built. These were all places of power where spiritual energy was most potent and could be accessed by human beings. The power at these locations not only helped humans in their relationship to the Divine, they also aided the flow of spiritual energy into all of life's expressions. Through these places of power our Ancestors were not only able to nourish their own nature, they were able to nourish the nature of our world. Our first nation-states were developed upon an understanding of our inherent, Divine origin, and a shared sense of spirituality that bound us together as a society/culture.
The rise of organized religious institutions, with their images and dogma of an otherworldly God exiled the Divine to some other-worldly 'heaven', and human beings were left on our planet to fend for themselves. We were taught to 'believe' and have faith in things unseen, the lines of power were left untapped, and although many churches and temples were built on these sacred sites, the esoteric knowledge of infusing their spiritual energy into the daily activities of our lives was lost. An all-embracing relationship with the divine, where physical embodiment of the divine was the goal was replaced by the knowledge of the physical sciences and an unhealthy fascination with materialism. The

The Art of BEing HUman

Olusanya Bey

knowledge of what spiritual power is or how it can work as a system with the entirety of our lives has largely been either misplaced, hidden, or lost, except in some of the spiritual traditions of ancient Amexem/Africa or some of the western esoteric/occult traditions.

Why do I do this? Where am I going and why am I telling them these things? As a youth I began studying the teachings of the Honorable Elijah Muhammad, sans the religious aspects, through the eyes of Allah (Clarence 13X), the lens of the Nation of Gods and Earths. One of his teachings that always stood out in my mind is, "If you notice that the ones you love are drinking out of a dirty glass it doesn't make sense to argue with them about it, just place a clean glass next to it and let them make a choice". The reality is that for many of them they do not know of, or have never been given an alternative or an opportunity to choose, especially when it comes to how they view/see the Universe.

Even when given an alternative there are those of us who will continue to drink from the dirty glass, and quite often those who seek alternatives are branded as rebellious or outlaws because we live in a society that emphasizes conformity over individuality. Due to our innate desire to connect/belong we often choose "fitting-in", favoring the comfort it offers over our unique, individual destiny/incarnation objective. Despite this fact, this book is my version of a clean glass. I have two things to offer my fellow humans... 1) my love of Universal L.A.W. [17] and order, and 2) the time that I spend sharing my understanding of these laws with

---

[17] In ancient times our manmade laws were based upon natural law, the laws of the Universe that have been encoded in symbols of mathematics and letters (Seshat and Tehuti), distilled throughout the forms and functions of our Universe. I have written it as an acronym that alludes to a simple explanation of human existence. We are here to Live in Allah's World through our Love of Allah's Wisdom. Law is order, if we can understand and align ourselves with the law and order (Allah' wisdom) that governs our Universe, then we may coordinate our movements with those of our Creator, thereby obtain a "Divine Governance" of our... BEing!

my other selves reflected in the eyes of every Human BEing on this beautiful planet. This book is an offering in the spirit of sacred economics... all the love and time I have to spend... to the Temple of your BEing! I pray that your Rabb accepts these gifts and removes any and all veils that are preventing you from seeing your inner-Divinity. Timing is everything. It's the only reason this book is coming to fruition. When it is, why it is. It is the fulfillment of a lifetime that has no beginning nor end, written in a moment of time that contains all of time.

On the day that I came to the point in the writing of this book where I wanted to share the "why" and purpose of my writing I did what I usually do to align my being with my destiny. I performed a deep dive into my cards to interpret my current energy pattern, knowing that every time I do so my cards draw me a clear picture of exactly what I need to know and exactly why I need to know it. As mathematics would have it, the card governing the "theme" of my week at that time was the 6 of Spades, also called the card of fate. When I first started reading cards this would have amazed me a bit. The first card I look at is speaking about fate, and the reason I am looking is so that I can identify the purpose of a book I consider to be a part of my fate. This was just another one of the many "synchronicities" I am constantly experiencing and have learned to recognize in my practice, so instead of being awed by this incident... I dove deeper.

Next, I looked at my cards for the day. It was a Saturday, which this year represents my Jupiter day, and Jupiter was playing a 3 of Diamonds (direct), supported by a Jack of Clubs (vertical). We'll talk more about direct and vertical cards when we look at our "card spreads". Jupiter represents wisdom, expansion, optimism and success. Jupiter playing the 3 of Diamonds denotes successful expansion in the diversity of values, or a successful expansion of alternative values. Three is Mercury's number, in this instance it also conveys the communication/exchange of ideas. The Jack of Clubs symbolizes a creative expression of knowledge, or an

Olusanya Bey

initiation into higher knowledge. So, we can see by this analysis that my cards were implying that the purpose of this book is... the creative expression of higher knowledge for the purpose of communicating alternative or diverse values. It should be clear to the reader, by everything I have expressed thus far that the cards hit the nail right on its head, this is precisely why I had chosen to share this information. I know that this information, when practically applied to our lives may expand our sense of what is truly valuable and make us better Human Beings, thereby transforming ourselves into a better society.

This in and of itself is a great explanation for the purpose of my book, but I couldn't just leave it there. I went further into my divinatory exploration and I related the same cards to their I Ching[*] correspondences, as each card has a corresponding I Ching gua or trigram. I have included these trigram correspondences in an appendix for your further exploration. When I want a deeper look at what my cards are alluding to, I will usually look at their corresponding trigrams and the resulting hexagrams. In this case I derived the trigrams K'un (Earth) from the 3 of Diamonds, and Ch'ien (Heaven) from the Jack of Clubs.

The trigram K'un symbolizes the spirit of Human Beings, which acts subconsciously to carry out our "will". Ch'ien represents "heaven" and by extension our "will", it also signifies the 11 Divine laws illustrated by our "living mathematics". This is how I perform what I have come to know as Tarot/Card analytics. I am not looking to predict futures or coming events, I am seeking to identify the energy matrix at play and to align myself accordingly. Analyzing my cards along with their I Ching correspondences I saw a pattern emerging between my personal experience writing this book, and the current state of affairs we find our society engaged in.

---

[*] The I Ching or Book of Changes is another divination system that developed in China, which unknown to many is another one of the "pyramid cultures".

The Art of BEing HUman

We experience many different crossroads over the course of our lifetime. I found myself standing at one of these crossroads. I was looking towards my cards for inspiration because I felt that I was stuck in my writing process, without a clear path forward. It has been my habit to only write when I felt inspired, when the words would flow intuitively. I didn't need to put forth much intellectual effort because the words were flowing through me, not coming from me. This book however was a different matter. I had accepted a grant to write my book within a time frame. It was a generous time frame, but it still represented a constraint, a condition placed upon a creative process that, until then, was unconstrained, free of any self-imposed or external limitations. My writing was never an intellectual process, it was an outpouring of spirit, from a man who had been broken open by time, circumstance, and love. All I had to do was stay out of the way.

This time it was different. Having accepted financial compensation, I was obligated to write this book. I set myself up by voluntarily placing myself in a position where I had to write, whether I felt inspired to or not. If this book was going to come to fruition I would have to, somehow, align my intellect and spirit, so that they could cooperate and collaborate in ways that I had previously never encouraged. This meant the application of some self-imposed discipline that, honestly, I strive to apply as little of as necessary.

My intuitions were picking up these insights from my spirit, but as is often the case when I would find my spirit in opposition to how I was choosing to live my life... I would ignore my spirit, instead cater to my flesh, my pre-disposed conditions/habit-energies. And so, I found myself stuck at the point in my book where I needed to clarify its purpose, but... I was still getting in my own way.

Now here were the cards and the I Ching making it plain, not allowing me to ignore what I already knew and kept refusing to put into application. One of my mother's oft-repeated phrases to me, as a child and adult, was "hard heads make soft behinds". She was reminding me that my stubbornness and refusal to obey rules, good advice or any admonition that I chose not to follow would result in me facing consequences that would, more likely than not, cause me to suffer during their administration.

The 3♦ and J♣ were pointing to the rewards I might receive if I stop ignoring the efforts of my spirit to align me with my destiny, but the I Ching was delving below the surface and revealing my lack of will and inability or reluctance to follow the laws of spirit. I could look at these messages and act like I was being given insights into our culture in general, or I could be honest with myself and understand that I was being given a clear sign that the lack of spiritual discipline I was recognizing as an issue in our nation was just a reflection of my own internal struggle and inability to follow the dictates of 'my' essential self.

K'un and Ch'ien come together to form the 12• hexagram P'I (K'un/Earth below, Ch'ien/Heaven above) which translates as Stagnation/Standstill. The hexagram P'I implies the disharmony that is caused by a lack of spirituality, a government devoid of "spiritual wisdom". Where the 3♦ was alluding to me needing to make a choice in what I truly valued and the J♣ was implying a need for my self-initiation into higher knowledge, the I Ching was illustrating my current situation on another level/dimension; how my own choices were getting in the way of my spiritual development, as well as the writing of this book.

How could I expect others to recognize the importance of Divination and its practical application when I, too often, choose to ignore the information I am being blessed to receive. Especially when I had been so clearly admonished on previous occasions and should have learned my lesson, but like Mama used to say, "hard heads make soft behinds". Here was the man who refers to himself as a "Son of Saturn" once again ignoring the lessons and discipline that Saturn represents.

The Art of BEing HUman

On occasion, when I point out to others our culture's general lack of accountability, I often am told, "Olusanya, you think you're better than everyone else", I am accused of being "Holier than Thou". At these times my response is usually, "Actually... it's the complete opposite!" I speak the way I do because I have come "up from Devil". I recognize my "fall from Grace", and my struggles to "rise". I have not learned to recognize the things that I do because I am free from temptation or the desire to indulge in harmful or life-negating behaviors. I know what I am speaking of because too often I ignore my spirit and indulge in behaviors I know I should avoid. I then suffer the consequences of said behaviors and learn the lessons that result therefrom. Too often it is my stubbornness, 'refusal' to obey spiritual law that teaches me to honor it, not my devotion to said laws. My name literally translates to "God compensates for suffering/sacrifice", I experience this every moment of everyday.

So, when I looked at these cards and trigrams it was impossible for me to ignore what they were once again pointing out to me. I was stuck because I was still refusing to behave correctly, to 'act right'. I was still refusing to let go of values, a lifestyle that was no longer serving my best interests, and to initiate myself into a higher knowledge, a more 'creative' way of expression and BEing. If I was going to write a book about the art of Human BEing[*] then I needed to, in fact, practice what I was preaching. I needed to not only finish my book as promised, I needed to get out of my own way and embrace my destiny. Basically, the I Ching's comment was, "you're not stuck... you're standing still and stagnating, there's a difference."

The great boxer Joe Louis said, "You can run, but you can't hide!" The unforgettable Teddy Pendergrass said, "You can't hide from yourself... everywhere you go, there you are." I found myself wanting to write a book about the dysfunctional society I live in,

---

[*] Although the title of this book is "The Art of BEing... Human, the reader may notice that I sometimes flip it around and write Human... BEing.

and what I think is a solution to our malfunction only to realize that these malfunctions were so evident to me because they were exterior reflections of my own internal contradictions and conflicts. The Most High, via the oracles, was admonishing me, "Physician... heal thyself!" Evidently, it is impossible for one to evaluate a quality that he himself lacks.

Now is the time, In the words of my father, "to shit or get off of the pot!" This was his colorful way of saying, "take care of business or get out of the way of those who will". Here I was thinking I was writing a book for the masses, when in reality I was writing an instruction manual for my own personal development.

So, no... the purpose of this book is not to give the reader answers to any questions they may have. It is simply me sharing how I 'ask' my questions and arrive at my answers. With this book I am striving to present general principles of divination, along with concrete examples of how I have used these principles, to transform my life into one filled with enlightened moments and joy. I am inviting you to investigate a system of divination, a way of living that will allow you to do the same. I am sharing the revelations of my self-fulfilling prophecy in the form of an invitation. An invitation to... Know Thyself.

As a result of my contemplations I have reached a personal conclusion... the key to 'my' success in life is not money or the accumulation of material things. It is developing my self-awareness (knowledge of self) so that I may make my life choices free of any external or internal forces that are contrary to my BEing, to my pre-determined measure. The planets and stars may compel me, but they do not control me, neither do the many external forces that I fall, or allow myself to, come under, the influence of. Although you may not think this applies to you and your life it absolutely does.

So, let's start 'reading', learn how to make better, well-informed life choices, exercise our freedom instead of complaining about its absence.

Olusanya Bey

(Poetic Interlude)
the sun is... shining

the... sun is shining...
the... sun is... shining...
the sun is... shining...
the sun is shining it... always is... that is its nature...
although... at the time of this writing...
it is through the haze of... Canadian wildfires
the wind... still whispers in my ear...
the birds in the trees tell 'A'... story only they can tell...
their... musical language in praise of the... Most High...
the only... "spin"... being put on it... is the gentle revolution of her...
Earth... as she revolves... around the sun...
his light... fingers... softly tracing the... surface of her skin...
i see an... underlying beauty... throughout this... creation...
my secret... to love, peace, and... happiness... is found therein...
while... man tells tall tales of his... own glory...
nature speaks with... every facet of her BEing... a witness...
to the beauty of the... ONE. you wonder why?
i meditate on the... ocean... the sun and... moon... attracting
powers...
put her... watery garments in... motion... the churning of her...
primordial element... gives birth to the... cycles of...
life and... time as... thoughts of her BEcome the... fertile soil...
wherein ONE may cultivate a... BEautiful mind...
a mind that... measures time by... moving in... tune...
harmony with she... is a... celestial alignment like...
the Earth and Sun at... high noon... ONENESS!
casts no shadows... there is no illusion of... creator and... creation...
the essence of... U and I is... ONE...
the singular shades of our... individuality... cannot...
stand up to the light of... love's unity...
if this is not BEing... clearly received by your... spirit... then...
adjust your mental station... fine tune your mind to a... higher
frequency...

OlusanyaBey

The Art of BEing HUman

manmade TV tells... lies to your vision... you cannot trust what you see...
or what your... ears may hear... over a... radio...
learn the language of your mother Earth... before you make what...
may become a... life and death decision...
nature broadcasts in... organic surround sound... you see...
everywhere you go... there... YOU are!
there is nothing to worship... i am the god... you are the goddess...
it is the... light of our love... made manifest in the...
sun... the moon... and the stars... shiva and... shakti...
the interaction of... yin and... yang... is the story of... our love...
told time and... time again throughout this... unfolding creation...
yeah! every time we... allow ourselves to... melt... this...
coming together... this! is the... original BIG BANG!
Hmmph! this is the story that... nature told me this morning...
as i watched... the sun through... Canadian wildfires... the wind...
whispered in my ear and... the birds in the trees sang...
how do you do it?
allow yourself to be... continually distracted...
by... televisions... radios and... all of those... manmade shows...
while the... ONE who is... ALL... is producing the...
"Greatest show on Earth"... before your very eyes...
the roles of... leading man and... leading lady...
although Universally cast remain... Universally un-acted...
the Most High's play... which is real... has been adapted...
into a... movie reel... when will we stop... acting according to...
man's script... learn our... divinely inspired... role... stop
acting... out... of character... according to... how you feel...
help to make the Earth... whole... again...
when will we listen... to our creator's story... as told by... Mother Nature...
and... pardon my language but... F@#% the story of men
the sun is... shining... it always is... that... is my nature.

THE MASTER SPREADS

In the previous chapters I introduced you to the symbols and language of the cards. Now, it's time to take a look at the Master spreads. There are 91 spreads in total, two of these spreads serve as keys to the entire system. These are the Spiritual or Natural spread, and the Mundane or Life spread.

The Spiritual, Pure, or Natural spread represents the Divine Order or plan behind our Universe. The Life, Mundane or Material spread represents the distillation of spirit into flesh. Whereas the Pure spread symbolizes the Divine order, the Mundane spread symbolizes manmade order. In order to understand our cards, we need to understand the layout of the Master spreads. Let's begin by determining what our Birth/Natal/Sun card is and start learning how to read the spreads.

Our Birth card/Sun card represents our most important life measure, it identifies our life's purpose, what we have come here to do. It is our solar signature, the card of our destiny. I refer to it as our "HU Art Thou" card. Our birth card represents our "essential/divine" nature. It is calculated using the day and month we were born. We have a very simple 4-step method to determine our birth card;

1. Take the number of the month you were born and multiply it by two.
2. Add to this number the number of the day of month you were born.
3. Subtract the total from 55, this will give you the solar value of your birth card.
4. Look up the solar value of your birth card on the chart below. For example, using April 15th as our birthday we multiply 4 x 2 = 8, we then add 15 + 8 = 23, subtract 23 from 55 (55 - 23 = 32) leaving us with 32 as our solar value. We can see by the solar

value reference chart below that the playing card with a solar value of 32 is the 6 of Diamonds.

SOLAR VALUES OF THE CARDS

#	♥	#	♣	#	♦	#	♠
1	A♥	14	A♣	27	A♦	40	A♠
2	2♥	15	2♣	28	2♦	41	2♠
3	3♥	16	3♣	29	3♦	42	3♠
4	4♥	17	4♣	30	4♦	43	4♠
5	5♥	18	5♣	31	5♦	44	5♠
6	6♥	19	6♣	32	6♦	45	6♠
7	7♥	20	7♣	33	7♦	46	7♠
8	8♥	21	8♣	34	8♦	47	8♠
9	9♥	22	9♣	35	9♦	48	9♠
10	10♥	23	10♣	36	10♦	49	10♠
11	J♥	24	J♣	37	J♦	50	J♠
12	Q♥	25	Q♣	38	Q♦	51	Q♠
13	K♥	26	K♣	39	K♦	52	K♠

THE JOKER = 0

You can practice this formula by calculating the birth cards of your family and friends. At some point you will want to do this, so that as you learn to read your different charts you will be able to see where your loved ones are in your spreads, giving you valuable insights into your relationships with them.

Now, check your math to make sure you understand the formula. Calculate the birth cards for the following dates; April 20th, June 14th, and January 29th.

If you did the math correctly you should have, correspondingly, come up with the A♦, 3♦, and J♣. Of course, you can always take the easy route and look at a birth card chart, but then you won't promote the development and performance of your prefrontal lobe and higher functioning cognitive abilities which mathematical calculations and other forms of abstract thinking stimulate.

In his "Mystic Test Book" Olney Richmond demonstrates how to determine our birth card using the Astral powers of the days and months of the year. Since that method is the basis for how the birth card chart came into being I have included this method in the appendices for those who want to familiarize themselves with Olney's method. The formula above is very easy and convenient, but I think it's important that individuals interested in using this system understand how the birth card chart came into being. Each of the 52 cards corresponds to a day of the year (including the Joker which represents Dec. 31st). At this point we need to look at two days in our calendar and how they are currently being used within the system. The days in question are December 31st and February 29th.

We learned in a previous chapter that the deck of cards corresponds to a solar year. The total value of the pips in each suit is equal to 91, represents the 91 days in each season of the year. When we multiply 91 by 4, we get a sum of 364, this correlates to our solar year, with the Joker expressing the last 1.25 days. It is a common practice among the Cardology community to treat individuals born on 12/31, symbolized by the Joker, as wild cards. Therefore, they treat these individuals as exceptions to the rule, who can choose to be any card in the deck. This is an error, the result of misunderstanding the ancient's concept of a "day out of time", and trying to adapt a mathematically precise natural cycle to an imperfect calendar. An obvious question for those who want to use this metasymbolic system is; If we can read these individuals using numerology or Astrology, which operate upon principles shared by the Tzulkin, then why can't we read these individuals using the cards? Have the planets stopped radiating their energy? Did the Earth's magnetic field suddenly shut off? The same planetary movement and measure that took place for 364 days of the year, that produce the energy patterns that we read, are still in operation. How is it that we cannot read them on the 31st of December. It is important for us to remember that all calendars are manmade instruments used to keep track of planetary movements, the primary reason is to aid Human BEings in their efforts to align themselves with the pulse and rhythm of the cosmos, so that they may be in time with Universal movement. The Tzulkin divination system is mathematically precise in its measurement of Universal movement. When there is a discrepancy between the system and our imperfect calendar it is the calendar that needs to be adjusted, not the Tzulkin. Our solar year is 365.25 days, but our calendar is only 365 days, so every year there is a quarter of a day that is unaccounted for. To compensate for the missing quarter of a day we add an "intercalary" day every four years. This day is February 29th, we call it "leap year". Thus our calendar is adjusted to align it to the actual length of a solar year and this accounts for the so-called "day out of time".[*]

This relationship between February 29th and December 31st provides us with the key to understanding the "day out of time", the proper way to read the cards of a person born on either of these days. Considering the relationship between these two days out of time, keeping Olney's birth card calculation chart (which I refer to as the Universal spread) in mind, I have resolved the issue in a manner that makes sense for me, I present it to you for your consideration.

The entire Tzulkin system is based on the fact that the deck of cards represents a solar year, each day of the year has a unique energy signature represented by the symbols on the cards. Now how to we determine the cards for each day?

In all of my readings about the Tzulkin I have only found 3 ways to determine an individual birth card, or card of a specific day. We can look at a birth card chart, but that still doesn't let us know how the cards came to represent the days. We can use the well-known formula shared earlier in this book, or... we can use the astral powers of the days and months to calculate the cards for

---

[*] The reader should keep in mind that what we refer to as "time" is a result of the mathematical measure of planetary movement. The original calendars of the ancients, as expressions of the cosmobiological laws of nature, ruled all measurements. The concept of a "day out of time" is in reference to the inaccuracy of our calendar. Thus we have 3 consecutive years of 365 days followed by a year of 366 days to make up for the "day out of time".

each day. I surmise that the formula commonly used is a simplified version of Olney's calculations of the astral powers of months and days. I've reached that conclusion by using Olney's method to determine the cards for each day, as well as the simplified formula, arriving at the same cards each time. Until I find another source for the determination of the cards for each day that makes as much sense, I recognize Olney's birth card calculation chart as the source of all of the birth card charts. Once that determination was made, I was comfortable using the simplified formula to calculate February 29th, arriving at the 9♣. Thus every four years our calendar will have 366 days.

The Tzulkin and the laws of its operation are maintained throughout this creation, are perpetual, constantly in operation. When we use either the formula or Olney's birth card calculation chart for people born on December 31st we are left with the sum of zero. This is why individuals born on this day are considered wild cards/Jokers. Individuals born on December 31st may still be read in the same manner as the rest of the days of the year. However, because they are born during the transition between the beginning and end of our "count of days", we may read them as either an A♥ or a K♠ depending on their time of birth (if they were born before noon, we read them as an A♥, after noon we read them as a K♠).

In order for us to fully understand our birth card and determine our card charts/spreads we need to reference the layout of the Master spreads; The Spiritual/Natural and the Mundane/Earthly. These two spreads are the Master keys to the Tzulkin system.

When looking at the spreads we see that there are planetary lines running horizontally and vertically across the card layout. The lines and columns in our spreads represent the various areas of our life being affected by the planets, obtain their meanings from these planets. For example, looking at the Spiritual spread we see that the Queen of Clubs is positioned horizontally along the

Jupiter row and vertically in the Jupiter column. This tells us that on a spiritual level Jupiter plays an important role and will have a particularly powerful influence over the Queen of Clubs destiny.

Jupiter is the "guru" of the planets, represents wisdom, expansion, its message is to seek development though higher wisdom and spiritual truth. The Q♣ represents self-mastery through the development of higher truth and wisdom, ruling by the virtue of one's knowledge of Divine Laws and Principles. The Q♣ occupation of this position on the spread makes it clear that the central point of our spiritual education and development, the source of our blessings and good fortune in life is the attainment of self-mastery through the cultivation of our spirits.

Now if we look at the same position on the Life/Mundane spread we see that the key to our good fortune on the physical plane is represented by the 10♦, symbol of the embodiment of divine principles, as well as material success. Looking at these two central cards we can surmise that a human being who develops self-mastery will almost surely also obtain material success. It is important when reading our cards that we keep in mind the principle of polarity and look at both the positive and negative aspects of our cards. One may become obsessive in their pursuit of material gain, lose sight of the need to continuously develop knowledge and wisdom, so that we make good, ethical decisions while pursuing our material desires. In the 120 lessons of the Nation of Gods and Earths this behavior is identified as "being a savage in the pursuit of happiness".

As we can see, interpreting our cards is simply a matter of gathering our different factors (suits/elements, planets, polarities) and blending them together in the same manner a chef blends their spices until we arrive at the 'recipe' for our life.

The Art of BEing HUman

Olusanya Bey

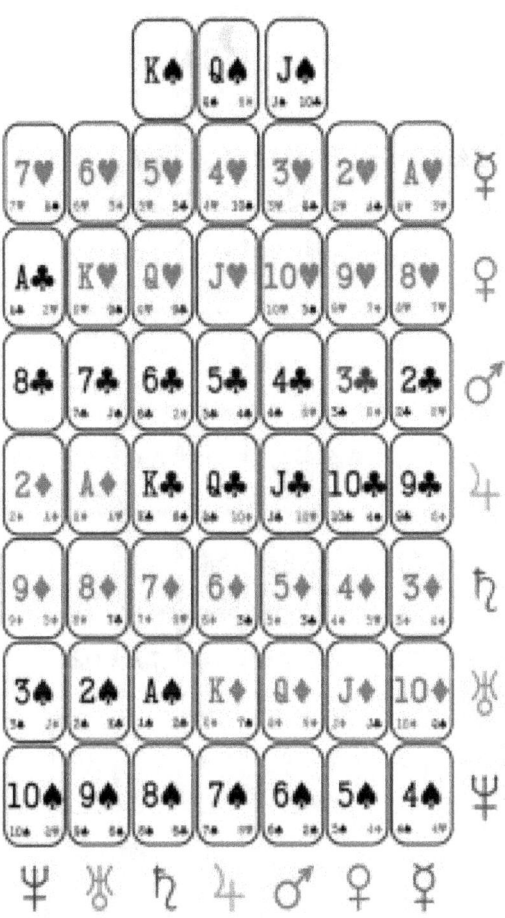

MUNDANE/EARTHLY SPREAD

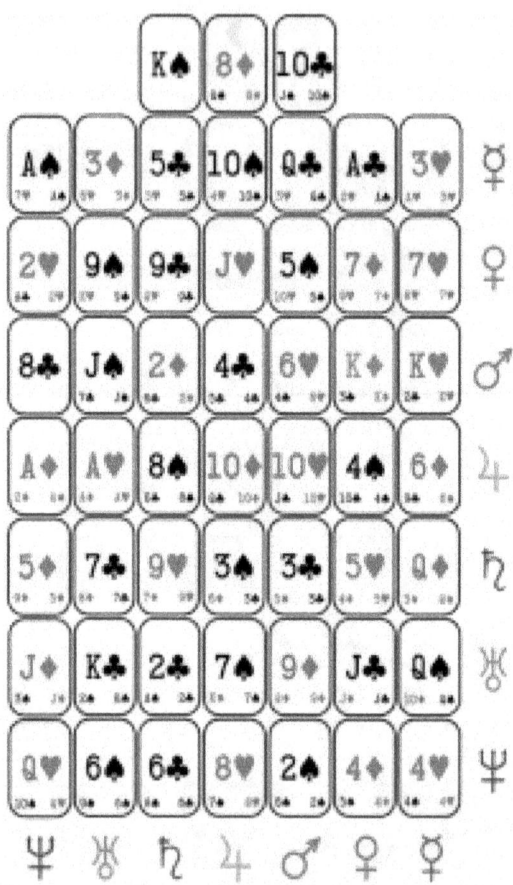

Olusanya Bey

Although we may use several different intervals of time (cycles/progressions) to calculate our charts/spreads we will focus on our Life chart and Yearly chart as we learn to cast and interpret. We will use the same birthdate we used previously (04/15/1989) as an example, we'll call the individual Harmony. Using the formula provided earlier, or by referencing the Birth Card chart in the appendices, we have determined that Harmony's Birth card is the 6♦. To arrive at a full understanding of our personality, the Tzulkin system incorporates two more cards to determine our personality, they are our Planetary Ruler card, and the Planetary Number card. Remember, our Birth card/Sun card represents our most important life measure, it identifies our life's purpose, what we have come here to do. I mentioned previously that I refer to it as our "HU art thou" card. The next personal significator, our Planetary Ruling card, represents the personality trait that will lead to our personal success. It represents how we show up, face the world. I call this card our "How art thou" card. Our birth card represents our divine purpose, our planetary ruler card identifies our key to unfolding our purpose, how we may use the energy and untainted/refined spirit of our birth card during our current incarnation.

We determine our planetary ruling card by our birth polarity, also known as our Zodiac sign. I have listed the polarities below, along with their traditional planetary rulers. The reader may refer back to our chapter on the polarities for further understanding. Once again using Harmony as our example we know from her date of birth that she was born while the sun was in the 1st polarity/Aries, that would make her planetary ruler Mars. We would then look to see which card occupies the Mars position in her life/yearly spread. In this case Harmony's planetary ruler card is the 10♦. We will go over how to read our spreads after I introduce our last personality significator card.

Sun - 5th polarity/Leo
Moon - 4th polarity/Cancer

Mercury - 3rd & 6th polarities/Gemini & Virgo
Venus - 2nd & 7th polarities/Taurus & Libra
Mars - 1st & 8th polarities/Aries & Scorpio
Jupiter - 9th & 12th polarities/Sagittarius & Pisces
Saturn - 10th & 11th polarity/Capricorn & Aquarius

Our last personal significator is our Planetary Number card, we determine this card by reducing our birthdate to a single digit through addition. I call the planetary number card the "Why Art Thou" card. In my experience this card represents what we must master to unlock our life's purpose, to express the full expression of our birth and planetary ruler cards. Let's go back to Harmony's birthday 4/15. To obtain her PRC we use addition to reduce her birthdate to a single digit... 1+5=6.

We then refer to the table below for her planetary ruler. The ruler for a single digit 6 is Venus. We then go to the Mundane spread to locate the Venus card, arriving at the 10♥. I've jumped ahead a bit. Let me back up a little and explain how we construct and read a spread. According to the Tzulkin system every individual on this planet has their own calendar that is set in motion on the day of their birth. As we pointed out earlier, this calendar can be broken down into several different intervals.

To construct Harmony's Life spread we use the Earthly/Mundane spread, or the "0" quadrate. Our Life spread is the very important because it rules over our entire life. It is the "road map" for our life's journey. There are 90 quadrates or years of influence, if we start our count from age 0, then we have 91. Over the course of these 91 years, we have 7 periods of planetary influence, starting with Mercury and ending with Neptune, giving each planet a 13-year period during which it will have a major influence over our lives. All of the planets will influence us throughout our lives, but each one will have a more significant influence during their respective 13-year period. The planetary periods follow the order of the planets in their speed of rotation and distance from the sun. Our Mercury period covers our first 13 years (0 -12), followed by

Venus (13 - 25), Mars (26 - 38), Jupiter (39 - 51), Saturn (52 - 64), Uranus (65 - 77), and Neptune (78 - 91). After 91 years we go back to the age 1 quadrate.

Following our planetary period cards are five more cards that I refer to as headliner/overall theme cards. I have given brief explanations of the meanings of all of the cards in our spread below. As you begin to work with the cards and their energies, developing a more intimate relationship with them, you will use your experience to expand upon these meanings.

When reading our spreads we always read our direct cards (the rows) from right to left, when we reach the end of the row, we move down one row and continue reading from the right to the left. When we read our vertical cards (the columns) we read upwards, when we reach the top of the column we move one column to the left, start from the bottom of the column and read upwards. This is demonstrated on the following blank quadrate.

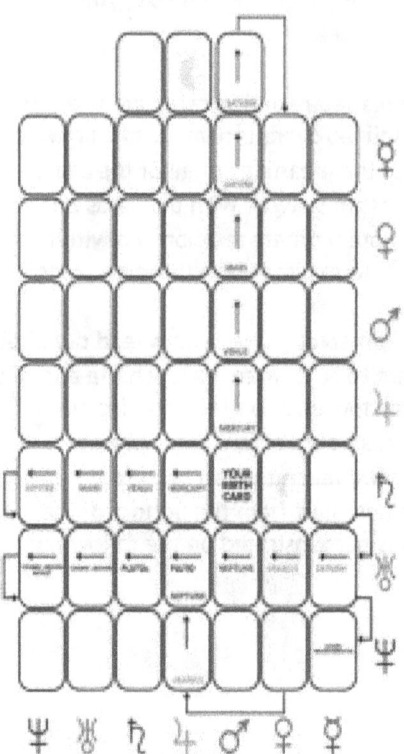

Now we may look at the Mundane spread and determine the various cards that compose our spreads These cards are;

1. Birth/Sun card
2. Planetary Ruler card - determined by the polarity occupied by the Sun at birth.
3. Planetary Number card - determined by reducing the birthdate to a single digit.
4. Moon card - the card preceding (on the right of) our birth card.
5. Mercury period - located on the immediate left of our birth

card.
6. Venus period - two spaces from the immediate left of our birth card.
7. Mars period - three spaces from the immediate left of our birth card.
8. Jupiter period - four spaces from the immediate left of our birth card.
9. Saturn period - five spaces from the immediate left of our birth card.
10. Uranus period - six spaces from the immediate left of our birth card.
11. Neptune period - seven spaces from the immediate left of our birth card.
12. Pluto card - eight spaces from the immediate left of our birth card.
13. Pluto Result - nine spaces from the immediate left of our birth card.
14. Cosmic lesson - ten spaces from the immediate left of our birth card.
15. Cosmic result - eleven spaces from the immediate left of our birth card.
16. Cosmic Transformation - 12 spaces from the immediate left of our birth card

Mercury - Your Mercury Card will provide insight into your communication style, travel plans, educational pursuits, mental state, relationships with siblings, and sudden events or changes. It will reveal the content of your thoughts and how you think, and may give insight into your identity and self-perception.

Venus - Your Venus Card provides insight into various aspects of your life, including what attracts you, relationships, home, finances, possessions, artistic pursuits, social events, and how you interact with women. It also reveals your feminine side, what you value and find beautiful in life, and may reveal both positive and negative influences on your romantic relationships.

Mars - The Mars Card in a Tzulkin reading represents the things/people that motivate you. It is your masculine, aggressive side and the goals you have in life, and it reveals information about your work, aggression or conflict, where or how you will be spending your energy, and your dealings with men in general, both positively and negatively.

Jupiter - Your Jupiter Card indicates expansion in various areas of your life, including business, legal matters, and travel. It indicates your blessings or good fortune during this period. This card brings a sense of abundance and can open up new opportunities, but it is important to be mindful of the potential for inflated ego.

Saturn - Your Saturn Card reveals the negative patterns of behavior that limit you in life and the lessons that need to be learned in order to achieve balance and stability. It also provides insight into your responsibilities, career, dealing with authority, long-term goals, and lessons to be learned.

Uranus - The Uranus card in a Tzulkin reading represents unexpected changes and disruptions in one's life, particularly in regards to work, real estate, technology, and social connections. It can also indicate a need for breaking free from old structures and patterns in order to reach one's full potential. Our cards can have both positive and negative connotations, depending on the context of the reading and the individual's current circumstances.

Neptune - Your Neptune Card reveals information about your dreams, escape, long distance travel, issues with drugs and alcohol, hidden matters, spiritual matters and any dealings with or around water, as well as the subject of your recurring daydreams and fantasies. It can indicate the potential to get lost in illusions or the opportunity to work towards building a solid foundation to accomplish your dreams.

Pluto - The Pluto Card represents a powerful transformation or goal in one's life, symbolizing the unconscious and hidden aspects of oneself. To evolve, it is important to integrate and express the positive attributes of this energy, but one may also fear and unconsciously act out its negative aspects.

Pluto Result - The Pluto result card is related to the experience or events defined by the Pluto card, and can assist in overcoming its

Olusanya Bey

influence. The Cosmic Transformation/Phoenix card represents the main outcome of the current spread, while the Pluto result card indicates a secondary outcome. This card reveals the desired reward for the current period, which can be obtained by successfully addressing the challenges presented by the Pluto card and responding to the other cards in the spread.
Cosmic Lesson - What we must strive to learn as we 'self-initiate' ourselves to higher levels of energy and dimensions of being.
Cosmic Result - Our cosmic result represents the divine energy we are learning to embody as a result of our self-initiation and adherence to natural law.
Cosmic Transformation - Our cosmic transformation reveals the means by which we may exercise mastery over our reality, remove ourselves from the wheel of karma, become God-in-Person.
Moon - Our Moon card represents our foundation and support. It grounds us in our 'being human, also signifies any emotional fears we need to recognize and overcome. I also identify the card that sits in the middle of the crown line (the top line of the spread) as our Cosmic Moon[41] card. This card shows us what the basic theme of our spread will be, it's influence can be felt throughout the duration of our spread.

It is important to keep in mind that although our planetary period cards influence us heavily during their respective periods, we will feel their influence throughout our lifetime/year. In other words, our Mercury card represents how we will think and communicate for the duration of whatever spread we are reading, just as our Venus will show who or what we are attracted to, and our Mars will represent who or what energizes us.

We can view our cards from Pluto to Cosmic Transformation as long-term cards, the effects of these cards can be felt throughout the duration of our spread, whether we are reading a yearly spread or our life's spread. They give us the big picture and through our

---

[41] Some cardiologists refer to the Cosmic Result card as the Cosmic Moon

The Art of BEing HUman

interpretation of them and our planetary period cards we can begin pinpointing finer details, allowing us to seek greater alignment with the Universal energies around us and within us.

I have included the 91 quadrates/spreads in the appendices for your consideration, however for the purposes of this book we will only focus on the Master spreads (the Spiritual & Mundane). Using the Mundane Spread we may construct Harmony's Life spread as shown below. The "D" indicates her Direct cards, the "V" indicates her Vertical cards.

6♦		Mercury 4/15/1989	Venus 4/15/2002	Mars 4/15/2015	Jupiter 4/15/2028	Saturn 4/15/2041	Uranus 4/15/2054	Neptune 4/15/2067
	D	4♠	10♥	10♦	8♠	A♥	A♦	Q♦
	V	K♥	7♥	3♥	4♦	J♣	5♥	4♠

Pluto	Pluto R	Cosmic Lesson	Cosmic Result	Cosmic Trans
5♥	3♣	3♠	9♥	7♣

Moon
8♣

10♦		Mercury 4/15/1989	Venus 4/15/2002	Mars 4/15/2015	Jupiter 4/15/2028	Saturn 4/15/2041	Uranus 4/15/2054	Neptune 4/15/2067
	D	8♠	A♥	A♦	Q♦	5♥	3♣	3♠
	V	4♣	J♥	10♠	8♦	6♣	2♣	9♥

Pluto	Pluto R	Cosmic Lesson	Cosmic Result	Cosmic Trans
9♥	7♣	5♦	Q♠	J♣

Moon
10♥

Now, using what you have learned up to this point you can now calculate your own birth card and construct your own life spread.

Olusanya Bey

BREAKING THE CODE

We have now reached the section of the book that caused most of my hesitation when I was deciding whether or not I was going to share this divination system. Unfortunately, America has become a nation of reckless followers who crave instant gratification, but possess very little self-imposed discipline. As a result, most Americans who want answers do not have the wherewithal to discover the answers for themselves, they want their answers handed/spoon-fed to them. I imagine that this is not just a tendency of Americans, but my experience of other countries is limited, I can't speak on something I have not experienced for myself. Having fallen for the ease of looking for our answers outside of our own being, many of us do not engage in the necessary self-contemplation and introspection to seek the answers that are within OUR... BEing.

The cards serve the same purpose as an astrolabe, sextant, GPS or road map. They allow us to navigate our courses of action as we move through life. They may be used to predict, but not in the sense of fortune-telling. Our cards allow us to see the various energies that are influencing us at any given time, internally as well as externally. If we understand the nature of these energies and their influences, we may be able to make accurate predictions of what may occur IF we make certain choices and behave accordingly. This is not fortune-telling. The predictions are predicated upon specific choices being made, followed by the right behavior. A so-called fortune-teller cannot predict an individual's choices or behavior, so to act like they can tell you your future is reckless and dangerous. If you consult a healer in regards to improving your physical health they will examine you to determine your current state of health (your energy matrix). They will then share their assessment with you and give you remedies based upon what they have determined to be the cause of your dis-ease. If you follow their regimen and your health improves does that make them a fortune-teller? No, it doesn't, no more than you choosing not to apply the remedies and your continued decline in health makes them a fraud. Human Beings, even when provided with information that will allow them to give shape to their future by behaving in a certain manner, will often choose to either ignore the instruction or seek to conform it to how they prefer to behave. Every sacred scripture I have read shares repeated stories of Human Beings choosing to ignore the advice/wisdom shared with them by their Creator and the results of their choice. Look around, do an objective assessment of those you know well. Do they have a "belief system", a way of living they "believe" to be true? Do they adhere to it faithfully, or do they throw it out the window in every instance where it does not conform to their preferred way of BEing? The information I am sharing will not allow you to predict your future, but it will allow you to define your essential nature, the current energies influencing you at the time of your reading, and how you may manage these energies accordingly to "shape" your future. This is why I do not do "readings" for others when I am asked, instead I teach them to "READ" for themselves.

Now, before we start reading, let me make one more important point. My Ancestors were not guided by their spirit. They cultivated their spirit under the guidance of their indwelling intelligence/essential nature, which is Divine. The cultures we established all had systems in place that insured each individual was capable of cultivating their own spirit, based upon their understanding of their essential nature. These systems were self-initiated and encouraged self-imposed discipline. Individuals were never coerced or forced into these systems. We adhered to them willingly because we had generations of evidence proving their efficacy. We passed them on from generation to generation through rites of passage, this was the "generational wealth" that enabled us to build the greatest civilizations that this planet has ever seen, which have never been equaled to this day. Every one of these cultures had an oracle, or system of divination that allowed them to consult the Divine. These oracles helped every individual in the culture to bypass their ego, develop their intuition, and tap into their indwelling intelligence.

In the chapter where I share my purpose for writing this book, I have already given you an example of how I divine and interpret the cards. Using Harmony's life spread I will now give you a few more example of how you may begin to analyze your cards and begin working with this beautiful system.

6♦	☿	♀	♂	♃	♄	♅	♆
	4♠	10♥	10♦	8♠	A♥	A♦	Q♦
	K♥	7♥	3♥	4♦	J♣	5♥	4♠

Pluto	Pluto R	C. Lesson	C. Result	C. Trans	Moon
5♥	3♣	3♠	9♥	7♣	8♣

Let's start with her birth card. The number 6, a symbol of balance and harmony, carries a deep sense of responsibility and the wisdom of "what you reap is what you sow". All sixes are cards of "fate". Born to play this card Harmony is likely to be worldly and emotionally balanced. She has a caring nature, while admirable, can sometimes turn towards interference and dominance as she seeks to help others. Her greatest challenge on the path to peace is to begin with herself. Her compassion and ideals shine bright. Strong family bonds make her a great parent or a supportive presence. Her knack for aesthetics makes beautifying her home a pleasure. Sixes must be on guard against anxiety and harsh judgements. They are trustworthy, kind souls, and a natural advisor to those in need.

Belonging to the suit of Diamonds she will naturally understand life's code of values. The 6 of Diamonds knows that effort paves the way to true rewards. Through life's lessons she will find her self-worth, understanding that settling her debts and being frugal can ease her journey, leaving her worries behind. If she embraces this wisdom daily, she will surmount inertia and material trials and tribulations. The number 6's touch brings fairness and balance; making equity her goal. She is sociable and warm, cherishes her home and kin. The influences of Mercury and Jupiter in the Earthly/Mundane spread blends optimism with practicality. Her mind is agile, full of ideas, seeking material abundance. Jupiter and Saturn's influence in the Spiritual spread teaches her patience and resolve. If she follows through with her plans success will open its doors. However, she must be careful of discontent and self-doubt may drain her vitality. Their maturity will blossom through lessons surmounted and scars transformed.

Take a minute to look at the above interpretation, then refer to the meanings of the numbers, suits/elements, planets and polarities that you were given earlier. Can you see how I have arrived at my interpretation? It is a product of blending the different components that compose the language of the cards. Next, we'll take a look at Harmony's Mercury card.

The 4♦ is known as the 4 of 4's because it contains some of the energy of all of the other fours. It also switches positions with the 4♥ in the Spiritual and Mundane spreads giving them a special relationship, making them the most four-like cards in the deck. The four is all about security, stability, the home, our foundation, hard work, our lifestyle and spirituality. The 4 of Spades in Harmony's Mercury position will give her a mind that tends to focus on all of these things, thus she will be a hard-working, marriage-minded individual, the influence of both Jupiter and Venus in her Earthly spread will give her the protection and loving influence to accomplish her goals. She will spend a lot of time thinking about settling down and establishing a base of security upon which she can build her family unit. During the early part of her growth and development she will more likely than not be in a family environment that allows her to experience these things, influence her desire to establish them within her own family. She may also experience their loss, which will increase her desire to make sure that she can provide them for her future family. She will have a straightforward mental approach to life, this is a good influence for working in the communications fields; teaching, writing, studying, or speaking. She will also have a deep concern for the health of her siblings. Having a 4♣ in the Mercury position also means that she will have to be mindful of becoming fixed or stubborn. She should have a mental affinity and good communication with people born to play the 4 of Spades, as they will trigger her Mercury card.

Harmony has the 10 of Hearts in her Venus position. Tens are associated with success because they represent one who has gained the experience of whatever suit it is found in. This is represented by the 1+0, the zero symbolizes one having completed a "full cycle" from 1 to 9, having gained experience/success as a result. With its Jupiter and Mars influence in the Earthly spread this card can give her much success and power with people in general, as well as with her personal relationships. The 10 of Hearts shares the same position as the Jack of Clubs in the Spiritual spread, giving Harmony a very creative mind, her creative interests and emotional power can inspire others. She is friendly and charismatic, can be successful in careers that are related to the public or to successfully promote beauty products, items for the home, music, art, or other Venus-related things. With the 10♥ in this position Harmony can benefit from all people-related activities. This is also an excellent influence for artists. Moving on, let's look at her Mars card.

Harmony has the 10 of Diamonds in her Mars planetary period, with a double Jupiter influence in both the Life and Spiritual spreads (the 10♦ shares the same space as the Queen of Clubs in the Spiritual spread). With the 10 of Diamonds in this position material success will be a major motivation for Harmony, as the 10 of diamonds occupying the central position is one of the most blessed cards in the Life spread. However, Harmony will have to be on guard against becoming obsessed with money, that potential can be countered if she draws upon the mental mastery and influence of the Queen of Clubs. Keep in mind that the 6♣ is the "responsibility in values card and those individuals blessed with abundance who misuse or abuse their gift will undoubtedly create problems for themselves. Her blessing of money or material abundance can easily flip into the loss of money or poverty. Remember the sixes represent the "karma" cards in the deck, karma is not fate, it is the law of cause and effect and is determined by the choices we make every moment of everyday.

I have made it clear that I think our culture has developed an "easy-way-out" mentality and desire to be spoon-fed, so I am not going to interpret any more of Harmony's cards for you. There are many Cardology "cook-books" that give easy answers and many experts on the internet who try to teach the cards by giving "cookie-cutter" interpretations. I am purposefully using the term "cookie-cutter" because in my studies I have noticed that even when Cardologists differ on which suits represent the different elements their interpretations somehow remain the same. This could never be the case unless they are sharing interpretations, despite differing on some of the principles. By now I have given more than enough examples to begin interpreting the cards for yourselves, based upon the fundamental principles of the system I have shared. I have also included a bibliography of Cardology books that you may read that will allow you to continue your own studies. Some of these books will "give" you interpretations if that is your desire. My goal was never to provide a book of card interceptions, but simply to introduce you to the inner workings of the Tzulkin system, so that you may begin using it and interpreting your own cards. View the Cards and Planetary influences as a code consisting of ten numbers (0-9), four suits, nine planets, and twelve polarities each with their own fundamental qualities. The more you familiarize yourself with these components and meditate on their relationships, meanings/potentialities the better you will be able to interpret your cards and the cards of others.

At this point I have described the banana for you in detail; what it looks like, how to peel it, what it tastes like. Now, you have to go

Olusanya Bey

get said banana, peel it and taste it for yourself, because... she who tastes... knows! Kua Ba Dati... NOW... is the Time! for you to start teaching yourself how to read your cards...your "Book of Life", the "roadmap" of your destiny.

The Art of BEing HUman

(Poetic Interlude

She... and I...

I...
wrote a poem...
about how the Sun set on her lips...
coloring them the perfect shade of love, making them... irresistably kissable,
like... kissing a candle and having your heart suddenly burst into flames...

She...
acts as if my heart did not step sideways in my chest upon meeting her...
redirecting love's journey in... Her direction,
as if any conversation held with Her... could cover any subject other than...
Her...
effect upon the UnIverse.

I...
wrote a poem...
about Her...
read it at the foot of a mountain, where witnesses swear the mountain moved closer,
to hear me speak about my love for Her, but...
SHE... remained distant

Do U love music?
Do U know me?
then U know why I... describe Her... as 'love's finest instrument'...
waiting to be loved... to be learned... to be played.
I... long to lay hands upon her and... coax her soul's music to the surface.

The Art of BEing HUman

Olusanya Bey

She...
is the 4 bars of perfect music used to compose the song of the Universe!
the song sung by every bird and whispered on every wind!
Simply put...
LOVE... is too weak to describe my experience of Her, but it will have to do... until the day we make love turns into forever... and the Creator reveals love's true name.

She...
is pulling the Sun and Moon out of my sky and replacing them with her BEing...
becoming the measure of my day and night, but never spending any time... my days and nights have no value, become endlessly lonely without...
Her!

She...
is a summer storm raining pearls from one hundred cloudless skies, filled with one hundred suns and... one hundred moons.
a ray of light in every single drop... upon every spot Her essence falls... we should build temples... to worship... every woman ever born in HER image.

I...
write poems to... celebrate Her signs, but...
these celebrations will not suffice, unless you know the... inner workings...
the path of this poem... the movement of breath and the soul's sacrifice.

I...
am the sound of a flute... the song of a guitar.
the song may come from me, but...
it is the delicate touch of her spirit as She... caresses the body of my thoughts,

The Art of BEing HUman

breathes life into my soul and... sounds my love into BEing!

heart beats, and... dawns break as She... makes me...
poetry and... music!

She...
is the embodiment of the Creator's grace and... beauty,
I...
am the song She sang into a soul to record's Love's divinity.

I...
write poems because...

She...
is, in substance, pure beauty but cannot remember what she looks like,
my response to her amnesia...

"borrow my eyes Beloved... their view is always of you"

I...
write poems because...
my words are mirrors I hold up to my love, so that She can remember...

Me!

The Art of BEing HUman

THE BOTTOMLINE

At the heart of each of us, whatever our imperfections, there exists a silent pulse of perfect rhythm, a complex of wave-forms and resonances, which is absolutely individual and unique, and yet which connects us to everything in the Universe. The act of getting in touch with this pulse can transform our personal experience and, in some way, alter the world around us.

~George Leonard*

W.A.T.C.H.

Watch your **Thoughts** for they become Words.
Watch your **Words** for they become Actions.
Watch your **Actions** for they become Habits.
Watch your **Habits** for they become Character.
Watch your **Character** for it becomes your Destiny.

The Art of BEing Human is a relentless pursuit for Knowledge of Self, Self-Inquiry, Introspection, and Self-Contemplation, however..... to know thyself is to know that which is Most High.

Now, as I bring this book to a close, I want to clarify exactly what I have identified as the "art of BEing Human". In my introduction I stated that the art of BEing Human in its most basic terms underpins two very basic truths;

1. There is no "god out there" managing our existence from some distant place called heaven. There is only the One Absolute BEing HU, for the sake of this book I have denoted by the name Allah [articulated by our limbs; Arm Leg Leg Arm Head]. It is this BEing which comprises our essential reality, whose qualities we should be striving to embody.

2. Human Beings - in terms of the Most Beautiful Names (Al Asma al Husna) and qualities of Allah comprising our essence... are immortal. Therefore, we should align our lives in accordance with our inherent endless potential within and seek to fully embody these attributes so that we may represent that which is Most High, according to our individual, unique measure.

I find it ironic that ALL of the sacred scriptures I have read refer to human beings having been created in the image of our Creator, yet many of the religious traditions spend an inordinate amount of time talking about the limitations and faults of being human, making excuses for our seeming inability to do the right thing. How are we created in the image of our creator, yet born in sin? I often questioned the seeming contradiction, striving to resolve it in a way that made sense to me. I think that Zen master Thich That Hanh explains the paradox well,

"It is said that God has created man in his own image. But it may be that humankind has created God in the image of humankind."

Therein lies the solution to our dilemma. Humankind have allowed the knowledge and experience of their humanity (an admittedly wonderful, though somewhat chaotic experience) to overshadow the reality of the Creator, and the 'nature' in which they have been created.

I invite you to think for a few moments about the law of cause and effect. Causality is influence by which one event, process, state, or object (a cause) contributes to the production of another event, process, state, or object (an effect) where the cause is partly responsible for the effect, and the effect is partly dependent on the cause. Keeping this definition in mind think about what could possibly be the cause of the effect we have labeled human. While you do this, I also want you to observe the intelligent thought that is taking place and contemplate its cause as well. Can your intelligence be the effect/result of chance. Can single cells that lack a brain evolve into forward-thinking intellectual beings? Can

The Art of BEing HUman

Olusanya Bey

a UnIverse that began in a random fashion evolve into an orderly UnIverse?

Consciousness exists in every part of our body, even in the smallest atoms. We have evolved in a way that we primarily rely on our intellectual mind to hold our consciousness. Instead of following our intuition and instincts, which stem from our heart and subtle energetic perception, we allow our thoughts to guide us. If we can adjust our inner processes to recognize consciousness in other areas of our body and let our intuition and instincts process information before our minds analyze it, our entire experience of our UnIverse will shift. We will become more in tune with our surroundings, the wisdom of nature, and our inner light. Our entire body acts like an antenna, receiving electromagnetic information from the world. We have to allow ourselves to become the "piece with the magnetic", learn to manage our 'per-son-al' electro-magnet in relationship to the electromagnetic nature of our UnIverse.

Our environment is constantly exchanging energy, stimuli, and responses, transforming one thing into another. When two objects vibrate at the same frequency, they resonate with each other. Wherever we go, we either harmonize with our environment or we don't, when we don't it is called dissonance. I find it very interesting that as a society we seem to have come to terms with the huge amount of "cognitive dissonance" that is prevalent in the culture, but seem to have no clue as to the amount of "spiritual/energetic dissonance" that exists alongside of it. By and large we have lost our ability to harmonize with our planetary and galactic environments.

I love words, I love language. I love language because I think that it allows the different species of humans to communicate across the genus/genius of humanity, even when our native tongues are not the same. I know that some may not think or agree that there is more than one species of human, but this is how I resolve the biological differences in humanity using words. I know and understand that many still use the term race to make this distinction, but I find that expression to be not only inaccurate, but also historically loaded, full of baggage and... dirty laundry. So much so that... most dictionaries have now stopped using that terminology as a biological system of classification. Besides, I'm not here to write about genus, species, or race, this particular train of thought is about my love for languages and their words because it is integral to my art of human being, and to the work of art denoted by the name Olusanya.

My fondness for words has a trail that can be traced directly to the first books I developed a delight for while reading. The "Encyclopedia Brown: Boy Detective" books not only sparked my 'positive obsession' with written words, they also activated an ability to follow a trail towards its conclusion, that graduated into a passion for research. It didn't hurt to be the youngest of seven children, in a household of individuals who all loved to read. My joy of reading was fed by my parents and my elder siblings (who were already in high school when I entered kindergarten). The result of this is that I was often reading books beyond my so-called "reading level". These newfound skills would come to serve me well once I realized I had an inborn knack for getting to the root of problems and discovering ways to solve them. Published two years after I was born, it seems like the Universe timed them perfectly to be available to me when I began my journey into words and language, research and problem-solving. As I think and write about these things I feel a sense of kismet, as if I was destined to reach this point in my life, where I am aware of myriad issues in our culture that trigger my art of human being, and my particular skill set, allowing me to trace a route to their roots and address them from their foundations. Most of them are "castles made of sand" destined to fall and be washed away when and if we decide to... change... for the better. Change is inevitable, but as a child of the sixties still living in 2023, most of the changes I have witnessed do not fall within that "better" category. This is

Olusanya Bey

because many of us have forfeited our ability to "shape" change and have simply become the victims of change.

When viewing the Universe around me I spy a beautiful and magnificent work of art, operating according to an infinitely intelligent design. The design is so intelligent that, for me... it is proof positive of a Creator. The appellation Creator is being used to signify a Divine, Operating Intelligence... operating the Department of my Interior... the Original Artist. It's not a religious or spiritual thing per se. It is what it is. I'm perceiving an intelligent Universe, where intelligence is a behavior, not necessarily a capacity to learn, think or understand. The result of this intelligent behavior is a staggeringly beautiful Universe, a masterpiece of craftsmanship that functions with the precision of a cosmic Swiss watch. Time and... time again.

Unfortunately, this watch... has an element that has been instilled with a sense of autonomy that allows it to go outside of its function, often interfering with the other components of this transcendental timepiece, causing major malfunctions. This... mischievous and quite often malignant part would be... humans. It seems we have grown up and forgotten that we are artists, gifted with imagination, the ability to co-create ourselves, our planet and the Universe. Instead we have become the authors of a society that preaches peace and prosperity while engaging in war for roughly 229 out of the 247 years we have been a nation. That's 93% of our entire history as a nation! Now, here's the challenge I have given myself... how may I use my passion for words and language to convince a culture that has mastered the art of war to lay down their manmade/artificial arms, so that their natural arms can embrace their humanity once again, allowing US... to master our art of human... being.

The "Art of BEing HUman" is not a textbook, it's a journal. It's basically just me... thinking out loud about what I know as the cause of my effect and recording my thoughts for future generations of the Springer, Russell, Stoner, Andes, Gill, Bey lineage. It is an opportunity for my grandson to read the words of his grand pére and decide for himself who I am and what I represented. It is a physical record of one of the "causes" of his "effect". It is a trail of crumbs for him to follow to a loaf of bread, eventually to the master-baker, the bread's Creator. It is also a call-to-arms.

Yes, indeed! It is a "call-to-arms". Not fire-arms... Human arms. Arms that are attached to hands, with both having the ability to articulate... to make movements and gestures that communicate clearly. See... I can embrace you or push you away, both actions clearly communicating how I am feeling or thinking about our relationship. This book is a finger pointing at the moon and a helping hand for humanity. Stop staring at my finger... the moon is full and she's beautiful!

I'm just a not-so-humble artist who dared to meditate on the moon instead of staring at the finger pointing to it. I chose to put away the many maps I had been given and instead explore the territory/this BEing for myself. What I discovered was... there is nothing to discover, just... a whole lot of truth that needs to be uncovered, so that we may come to truly know our "essential being" and its relationship to the source of ALL being.

The Art of BEing... HUman is not a book of answers to all of your life's questions. It is a personal journal and manifesto, a re-defining of what art is and who is an artist... from the perspective of a living, breathing work of art viewing itself from the eyes of its Creator. It is an owner's manual to your own personalized GPS, allowing you to always know your place in the Universe and how to navigate your life/movements accordingly (in relationship to the movements of our fellow humans being and the Universe as a whole). Here is the thing about using a GPS. If you only follow its directions, but do not pay attention to the territory you are traveling through, then even though you may arrive at your destination you will still not "know" your way. So, although you have traveled to this destination on many occasions you still don't know the actual path to it. How do you view you? How we identify ourselves, our BEing is the foundation of the life we build. That is why the Ancients stressed "knowledge of self" in the manner in which they did. That is why the God's say, "knowledge is the foundation of the UnIverse".

The journey called life has as many paths as it has beings. Each manifestation has its own path to travel. We all begin from and return to the same source, but the road in between is determined by our individual makeup and composition. As an "individuated" manifestation of the One Being denoted by the name Allah we have "fallen" into a fractured/dualized consciousness of our experience. We see Creator and creation as two different things, one having given birth to the other. The knower, the knowing, and the known appear to no longer be the same thing. The unity that is a natural result of understanding the One has been lost. We believe that "we" are having this experience, so we "identify" our "self" as the sum total of thoughts, feelings and memories stored within the database we call our brains, as well as our bodies. The Kitab Al' Qadr, the art of being human, in fact ALL art, is a reminder of who and what we are, an invitation to inspire the Divine within ourselves. Using the Tzulkin as our key we can identify our "creation program", learn to "read" our book of life.

Say, "Everyone acts according to his own creation program (natural disposition; fitrah)" This is why your Rabb knows best who is on the right path!"

~ Holy Quran Surah 17, Ayat 84

Set your face (consciousness) as a Hanif (a "pure" one without the concept of a deity-god, without making shirq to Allah, i.e. with the consciousness of non-duality) towards the path (the only system and order), the natural disposition of Allah upon which Allah has created man. There is no change in the creation of Allah. This is the infinitely valid, 'straight' system, but most people do not know.

~ Holy Quran (Surah 30, Ayat 30)

As I stated earlier, I never wanted to write a book. Although every form of divination I have ever used clearly indicate that I am a communicator and writing is one of the fields in which I can be successful. Even so, I had no intention of writing a book. I chose to write this book for a variety of reasons, all of which I vigorously questioned up until it's completion. The desire to share with others the sources of my inspiration and how I use them is just one. Not because I think that I have answers for you. I am simply sharing... the answers I found for myself.

Individuals who have enjoyed my poetry would often ask me when am I going to write a book. For a long time, my answer was, "Probably never". I've never seen myself as a poet. I began writing poetry as a form of catharsis, to sort out a whirlwind of emotions I was feeling as the result of a broken relationship. During the process I realized that I didn't know myself as well as I thought that I did, so writing poetry was my first real attempt at the kind of self-inquiry that may lead us to the knowledge of ourselves. One of the first things I discovered while writing is the transformative nature of art, of tapping into our potential for creativity. While writing poetry I realized that I was being written as well. Thoughts and ideas started coming through me that clearly did not come from me. Mind you, when I say, "me", I am referring to my ego. However, the inspirations I found myself receiving were coming directly from my Rabb. I was able to recognize this because of the level of self-inquiry that I had engaged within myself due to my writing. I stopped acting like I was the author of my poetry and began to trace its inspiration to its source. Surprise, surprise!!! I realized that the source of my poetry was the source of my being. Every ounce of my creativity is a gift from my Creator, it is my proportion and measure. It is my purpose for existing. When I say

Olusanya Bey

this, I am not simply speaking about my ability to craft a poem. I have what most would call a 'gift for gab'. When I was twelve years old our next-door neighbor Mr. Hubbard nicknamed me "Preacher Man", not only because I obviously loved talking, but also because he noticed that when I spoke my peers listened. I am a gifted communicator; poetry is me demonstrating this with the written word. However, I am not as gifted in my writing as much as I am in my speaking, which is one of the reasons why I was never interested in writing a book. I function more along the lines of a djeli or griot, sans a musical instrument (although I often like to sing along with my poetry). I finally chose to write a book because my cards make it clear that publishing is one of the vehicles I may use to share my gifts and I am determined, at the tender age of sixty-two to begin walking the straight path of my destiny more than I deviate from it. If I have gained anything from the ability to read my cards it is the understanding that I have a rebellious nature, a tendency to bend the rules and often break them. I wouldn't call myself a criminal, but I am most definitely an outlaw by nature. On a mundane level I a I have a tendency to question, often rebel against authority... even my own! I have been unconsciously/consciously striving to exercise my sovereign nature as a human being since the day I was born, sometimes to my own detriment! With great freedom comes great responsibility and a great deal of discipline. I had yet to learn or understand this. It was this same reckless disregard for manmade law that led to my incarceration at the age of 21. It was this tendency to rebel against my father's advice that led to me almost losing my life at the age of 26. Now, having gained the insights into my BEing provided by the practice of divination I can follow the recipe for this BEing denoted by the name Olusanya. Imagine how much grief I could have saved myself, my parents, and my loved ones if I had these insights provided for me and my family as a youth. However, it is truly better late... than never. Using the Tzulkin as my sextant and astrolabe I have finally established my proper orientation, so that I may navigate my "Sirat Al' Mustaqim".

The Art of BEing HUman

When the inspiration for this book was conceived, I had no idea what "rope flow" was, although I had taught myself various elements of graphic design, I had never attempted creating Islamic geometry or Islimi patterns previous to this writing. Both of these elements of creativity were presented to me by my Rabb over the course of my writing journey, as the Creator continues to use me to express it's BEing, in the same manner in which I use my art to express... IT'S BEing! Everything we see as creation is a divine self-revelation constantly being renewed in different forms at every given moment. Human Beings have the capacity to receive the complete revelation since they encompass all the levels of existence, and the potential to become a complete reflection/mirror to Reality, ideally integrating all of life's many aspects in a balanced and harmonious way. My introduction and immersion into rope flow and Islamic geometry revealed to me that life/existence... HU thou art... is a movement of love for the sake of revealing a UnIverse's beauty, music is this same mathematical movement through sound.

Practicing Islamic geometric patterns revealed to me something that had never dawned on me before, that was the need to return, reorient and restore my 'self' to my "natural state of being", so that I may begin to function and behave according to my true/essential nature, my indwelling intelligence. That is the bottom-line of this entire book. The "Art of BEing Human" was written to inspire the Human family to practice divination so that ALL of us may develop awareness of our Rabb (our indwelling intelligence/essential nature) and began to live our lives in accordance with the nature in which we have been created. It is a call to embody our Divinity, so that Thy Kingdom come, Thy Will be done on earth as it is in heaven.

I'd like to leave you with this; There is no place in the art of BEing HUman for dogmatic controversy affecting the current convictions of those who choose to practice. In its highest contemplation the Art of BEing HUman is solely concerned with and addresses itself

The Art of BEing HUman

Olusanya Bey

to the "Grand Architect of our Universe," respecting all of the Beautiful Names under which this Unique BEing is apostrophized in every place, by every so-called race, and by every school of thought. There are no religious differences attached to the adoration of Supreme Being. In reality HUmans only differ with respect to some of HU's manifestations of love and solicitude for humanity, making claims to an exclusiveness in one respect or another, are too often the outgrowth of fast-vanishing racial isolations, social-constructs, soial-engineering and the diverse trends of thought that are a natural consequence of differences of origin, climate, and environment. In arguing over these differences, so frequently the result of misunderstandings of identical premises, viewed from diverging/different angles, we are too eager to forget that the goodness and abundance of the Almighty is forever flowing in a never-ending stream 'upon', 'through', and 'within' us, manifesting itself infinitely and impartially in everything that either experiences or can be experienced.

From the selfish standpoint of the unintelligent ego, each individual is alternately blessed with good times and cursed with trials and tribulations, often to the the extremes predominating in many instances, without apparent reason. Our ascended Elders, many of the ancient philosophers, therefore, taught that HUmans could attain 'peace of mind' only by realizing his identity with the All. Sensing this, she perceived the resistless operation of the natural laws of Being, in perfect poise, harmony, and impartiality, requiring only to be acknowledged and followed for man to escape the evils and enjoy the benefits gained during his portion of infinity, the accidents and mishaps experienced not being subject to the whims or impulses of an antagonistic Mystery God, but simply the consequences of her own unguarded collisions with unchangeable law.

For those who gain this level of understanding the whole goal of human life becomes the attainment of more and more knowledge, wisdom and understanding of the natural laws of our Universe, upon which all progress and all 'true' security to life and happiness depends, and the divine gift of the reasoning faculties which rendered this possible, was appreciated as God's most precious blessing to man. Thousands of years of experiment and ceaseless vigilance on the part of eager observers has never resulted in the detection of a single principle so unrelated to the rest of the universal machine as to have no dependence upon it. Nothing in this Universe exists independently of itself, everything is related to... everything!

Year by year, day by day, hour by hour, minute by minute, the infinite details of this magnificent cosmos-pervading law keeps on unfolding to human perception, filling all space with its greatness. The capacity of mind to see and understand has limitations, and his-tory - that of which it takes cognizance through the medium of the senses - is limitless and without historical beginning or end. Every past age has attempted to place bounds upon what it is legitimate for man to know or think he knows about the origin and constitution of the Universe around him. Each era has attempted to end its book of human knowledge with an italicized *"The End"* at the conclusion of an ultimate chapter, and yet the dawn of every other day has ushered in new wonders, fresh revelations, and original truths.

"Dogma" is the name given to all the futile finalities which do not finish, to the cancel-culture entanglements and defensive obstacles set by each generation at the limit of its attainments, in the vain thought that the "End" had been achieved. In most cases dogmas will be found to revolve round the privilege of 'classes' to rule 'masses', regardless of the fact that it's a natural law, just like how the ocean always has waves, there's a constant change happening among people. Today's slow-moving depths can turn into tomorrow's big waves. Yet the minds of HUmans BEing (framed in the image of our Creator, even as the receiver of an acoustic instrument must be attuned -to the vibrations of the transmitter so that the message may be received as it is sent) have discovered constant and unchanging elements in this magnificent order of varied manifestations. We have uncovered chaos-banishing laws which must be the same in an atom as they are in a Sun, and so may be exhibited in symbols of dimensions convenient to the level of all contemplative individuals. Such, are the symbols of the Tzulkin -- evidences of the truth attributed to Tehuti, "that which is above may be discovered by examination and contemplation of that which is below".

Those who engage in the Art of BEing HUman must concern themselves with every branch of research that is capable of throwing light upon the causes that have led HUmans to crystallize their perceptions of immutable law into emblems and symbols. She may pursue each of the various paths of investigation and research indicated by the obscure phraseology of the various religions and spiritual traditions/rituals until she emerges into the full splendor of Divine light embracing its fundamental truth. She may unearth the intricacies of ancient philosophies and mythologies, in order to convince herself of their ultimate source in the fountain of their revealed wisdom. She may set her own value upon anthropomorphisms or the embodiment of attributes and principles in the flesh, so that what really are the play of natural forces, the play of the elements, the cycles of worlds, are described in terms taken from the vocabulary of human lives and direct experience. Each mind is a little UnIverse, a cell of the Great UnIverse, one as eternal as the other, and subject to the same law of gradual evolution. Some day we may all know the intricate and the complicated as well as we, at present, know that which is simple and plain; but of that infinite aggregate, the unfathomable, unseen indivisible totality of BEing that transpires behind ALL that is seen, our knowledge and use of the Tzulkin can teach us the value of THAT... NOW!

The greatest truths, the simplest and most beautiful gifts, are free. No amount of money in the world can purchase the magnificence

The Art of BEing HUman

of a full moon, or the sun's rising and setting on the horizon, or the translucent colors of a rainbow. We should learn to view our world through the lens of creation, then innumerable wonders surround us, from a sweet baby smile to a butterfly perched on the petal of a rose. This is the way to truly live! When we pause to sense, to absorb, to BEcome! that's when we embark on the journey of self-discovery, harmonizing our inner world with our outer environment and the entirety of existence. Here, is where we begin our voyage to meld with the boundless Universe of creation.

READ! In the name of your Lord who created-

Created humans from a clinging substance.

READ! And your Lord is Most Generous

Who taught by the pen-

Taught humanity what they know not.

~Surah 96, Al 'Alaq, Ayats 1-4

Olusanya Bey

(Poetic Interlude)

No Ordinary Love

A full moon appearing at night:
my view of her face amidst the pitch black of her hair.
My perception gives birth to thoughts of sadness:
tears fall upon my face;
this black narcissus shedding tears for a rose.
The quality of her aesthetic... is truly overwhelming:
even beauty becomes silent!
Her wonder; fleeting,
constantly escapes the pursuit of my thinking,
her nature... beyond the spectrum of my sight.
I seek to quiet my mind, so I do not tarnish her subtle essence
[my thoughts lack the finesse to fully perceive her].
This BEing true... how can I expect to see her correctly
with this clumsy organ called an eye?
Poetry's thief: whenever I seek to describe or explain her,
she... defeats me!
At every attempt I find myself at a loss for words;
they sprout wings and take flight.
Knowing that I am trying to define what has no definition...
they... want no part of this madness!
There are those who would lower their aspirations
[settle for an experience of... "ordinary love"]... –
sometimes, even I wish I could, but...
I can't.
THIS... IS! ...
no Ordinary Love.

APPENDICES

BIRTH CARD CHART CALCULATION

Astral Powers of the Months

Jan. 161623	Jul. 491281
Feb. 266435	Aug. 324824
Mar. 334149	Sep. 353658
Apr. 498658	Oct. 227944
May 597719	Nov. 217412
Jun. 693378	Dec. 188169

Astral Powers of the Days

1. 157741	12. 622346	23. 386139
2. 213144	13. 491125	24. 468758
3. 256883	14. 361848	25. 683569
4. 358942	15. 236459	26. 524160
5. 461973	16. 186886	27. 362807
6. 533819	17. 169589	28. 269494
7. 616519	18. 154727	29. 246165
8. 656370	19. 221875	30. 198556
9. 722465	20. 233538	31. 163543
10. 881872	21. 274361	
11. 719547	22. 376420	

Take the astral power of the month, the astral power of the day and add them together. Find the spirit sum, which will indicate on the Universal Spread the card for that particular calendar day.

Here's an example to practice.

September 28•

Month 353658
Day.   269494
       623152

The spirit root of a number is equal to the Nth root of one-ninth of the number, plus ten times the enumerator of any fraction that may arise from the division of the number by nine. To calculate the spirit number by an easy method, simply divide the number by nine, reduce the quotient to the Nth root and place the remainder if if there is one, to the left of it.

Example: What is the root of 623152? Answer: 12

Found as follows: 623152 ÷ 9 = 69,239.1
The Nth root is found by adding the figures composing a number together, continuously until one figure remains. 6+9+2+3+9 = 29
2+9 = 11 1+1 = 2
We then place the remainder (1) to the left of the 2, arrive at 12. This indicates the card on row #1, in the second column from the left on the birth card calculation chart below - the 9♥." This is called the Universal Spread, it allows us to identify the planetary energies that each card manifests. [ie. The 9♥ manifests a mind of pure love - ☿/♀]

The Universal spread allows us to see the planetary energies that come together to give each day its respective card. If we take the time to contemplate these energies and their designated card it will help us to better understand how each card has received their unique meanings. For example, when we look at the 5♣ we see the planetary energies of Mercury and Mars, which we can simply interpret as 'an energetic mind'. Now, with these two keywords for the planets Mercury and Mars we can see why the 5♣ has been given the name "the versatile mind", "the adventurer", or "mental curiosity" by different Cardology authors. I have included a table of card titles in the appendices.

The Art of BEing HUman

THE UNIVERSAL SPREAD

BIRTH CARD CHART AND TIME TABLE

Locate your date of birth, read row left to right to identify your 52-day planetary periods. [ie. Sep 1, Oct 23, Dec 14, feb 5, Mar 29, may 20, Jul 11]

THE TITLES FOR THE DAY CARDS

CARD	TITLE	CARD	TITLE
A♥	Desire for Love	A♣	Desire for Knowledge
2♥	Union in Love	2♣	The Communicator
3♥	Indecision in Love	3♣	Mental Creativity
4♥	Stability in Love	4♣	Mentally Strong
5♥	Changes of the	5♣	Versatile Mind
6♥	Making the Peace	6♣	The Messenger
7♥	Unconditional Love	7♣	Intuitional Power
8♥	Emotional Power & Charm	8♣	Mental strength
9♥	Universal Love	9♣	Universal Thinker
10♥	Public success	10♣	Mental Strength
J♥	Sacrifice for Love	J♣	Mentally Inspired
Q♥	The Loving Mother	Q♣	Intuitive Knowledge
K♥	The Loving Father	K♣	Master of the Mind

CARD	TITLE	CARD	TITLE
A♦	Desire for Money	A♠	Desire for Work
2♦	Wheeling & Dealing	2♠	Partnership in Work
3♦	Financial Creativity	3♠	Internal Energy
4♦	Financial Stability	4♠	Stability through Work
5♦	Changes in Values	5♠	Changes in Lifestyle
6♦	Financial Stability	6♠	Fate & Karma in Action
7♦	Financial Success	7♠	The Faith Card
8♦	Financial Power	8♠	Power in Work
9♦	Universal Values	9♠	Universal Life Card
10♦	Financial Success	10♠	Success in Work
J♦	Finances for Higher Good	J♠	Revelation through Labor
Q♦	Financial Nurturing	Q♠	Mastery of Self
K♦	Financial Responsibility	K♠	The Master

I CHING CORRESPONDENCES

We can use pairs of cards to form I Ching hexagrams by using each cards trigram correspondence. Our direct card forms the lower trigram and our vertical card forms the upper trigram. We can then consult the hexagram using our preferred I Ching/Book of Changes.

CREATING AFFIRMATIONS

If you have a copy of your current spread you can create affirmations from the cards you are playing in each period. This can be a powerful tool in helping you understand the energy you have 'at play', while using it in a practical application!

How to write affirmations about the cards in each Period:

1. Get the main keyword/phrase for the card
2. Look at the chart below for the phrases to use for each Planet (Use the Planet of the Period you are currently in)
3. Create a present tense, positive, personal affirmation by combining both the card's meaning and a phrase from the planet. (Start each statement with I have..., or I am... or I experience...)

Planet Words / Phrases

Mercury - Communication, Commerce, Analyze, Ideas/ I'm aware of... I'm thinking a lot about... I'm analyzing...

Venus - Pleasure, Beauty, Attraction/ I'm attracted to.... I'm attracting... I receive pleasure from... I'm seeing beauty in...

Mars - Passion, Energy, Motivation/ I am taking action on... I am driven to... I am confronting...

Jupiter - Expand, Blessings, Gifts/ I receive blessings from... I have success with... I am positive about... I am expanding...

Saturn - Lessons, Restrictions, Discipline/ I am disciplined about... The lesson of... is teaching me about... I will mature and become wiser because of...

The Art of BEing HUman

Uranus – Unexpectedly, Surprisingly, Spiritual/I am open to this new idea of... I am now aware of... I am grateful for... pushing me out of my comfort zone.

Neptune – Fears, Confusion, Inspiration, Illusions & Deceptions/I am inspired by... I am facing the illusion of... and bringing it into the Light. I will face my secret desire of...

An example of this is:
If you have the J♣ in Jupiter –
Here is the phrase for the J♣: success through mental creativity

Examples:

Using the single words –
I experience the blessings of success through mental creativity.
I experience the gift of growth from my mental creativity.

Using the phrases:
I am positive about my success through mental creativity
I have success now through my mental creativity.
I am expanding my gifts through mental creativity.

Do any of the phrases resonate with you or reflect what is currently going on in your life?
You can also turn the affirmation into a question to check in on that topic within your life.
For example, using the first affirmation created above – turn it into a question: Can I experience success through my mental creativity?

Questions are great for journaling and doing an inner check-in on how you feel and what you are telling yourself and/or believing about yourself. Is it positive or empowering?

THE SOLAR QUADRATES

DIVINE/PERFECT/SPIRITUAL SPREAD

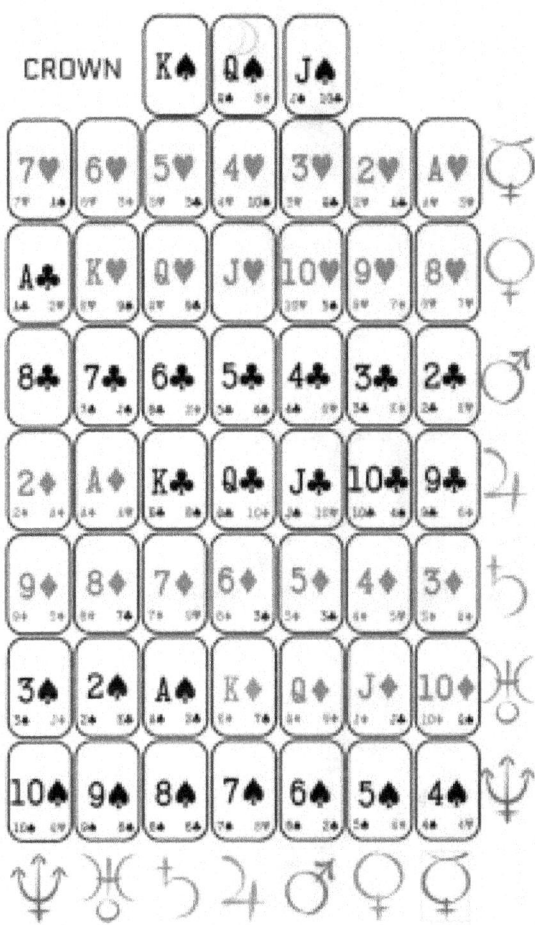

OlusanyaBey

The Art of BEing HUman

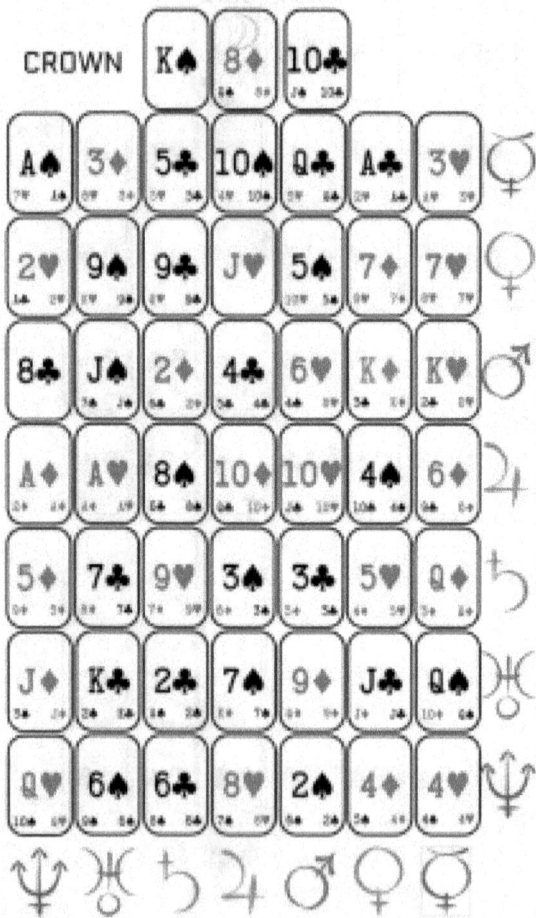

The Art of BEing HUman

Olusanya Bey

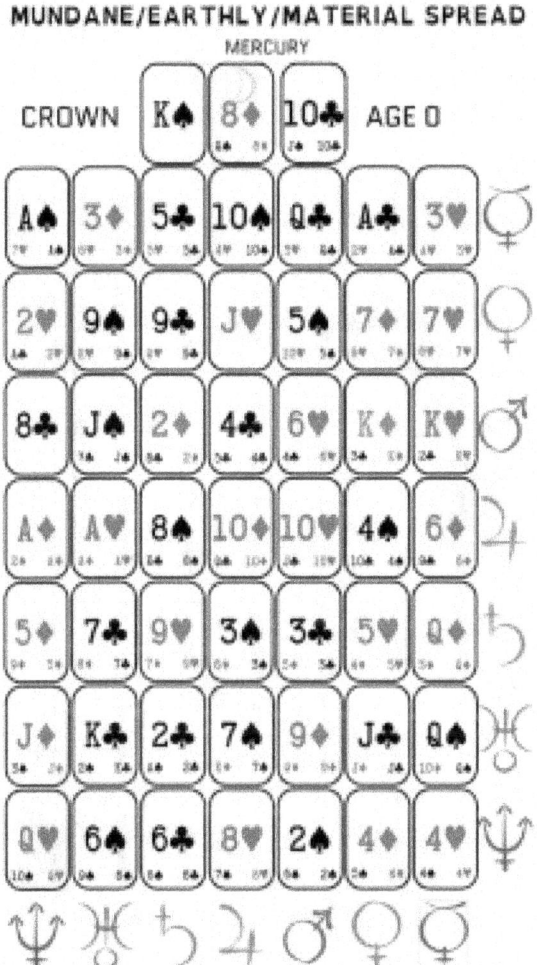

OlusanyaBey

The Art of BEing HUman

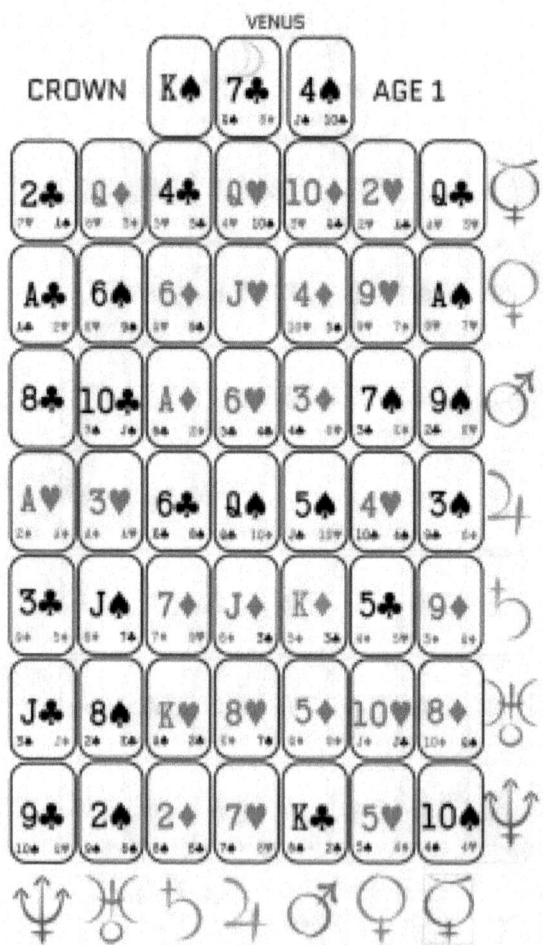

The Art of BEing HUman

Olusanya Bey

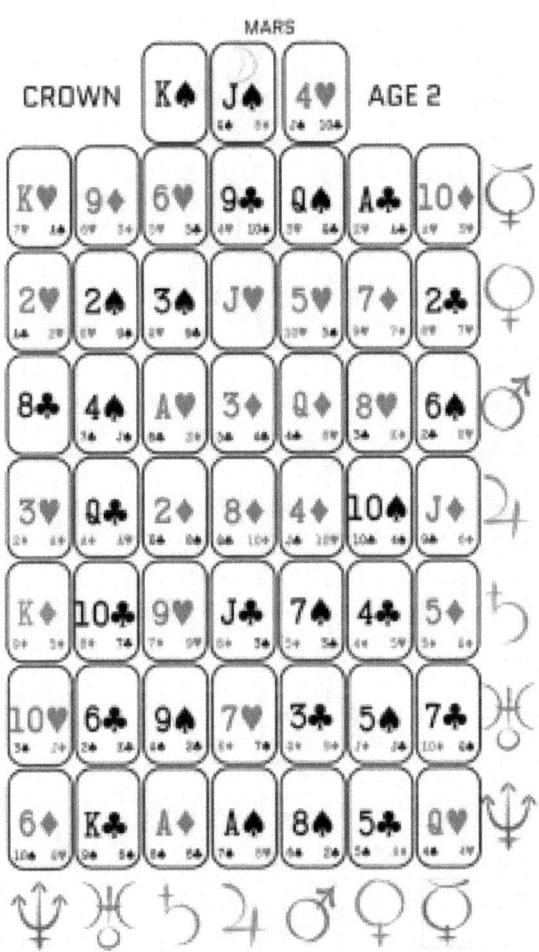

OlusanyaBey

The Art of BEing HUman

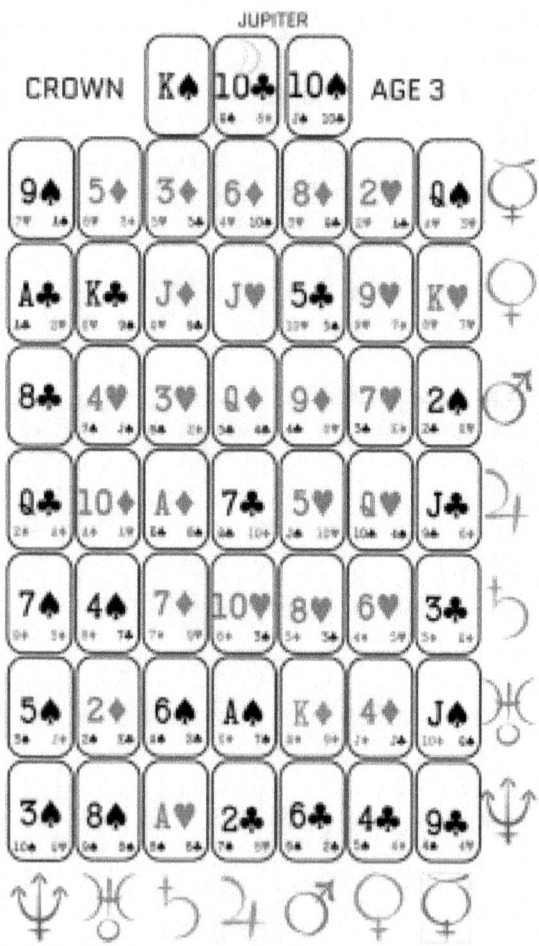

The Art of BEing HUman

Olusanya Bey

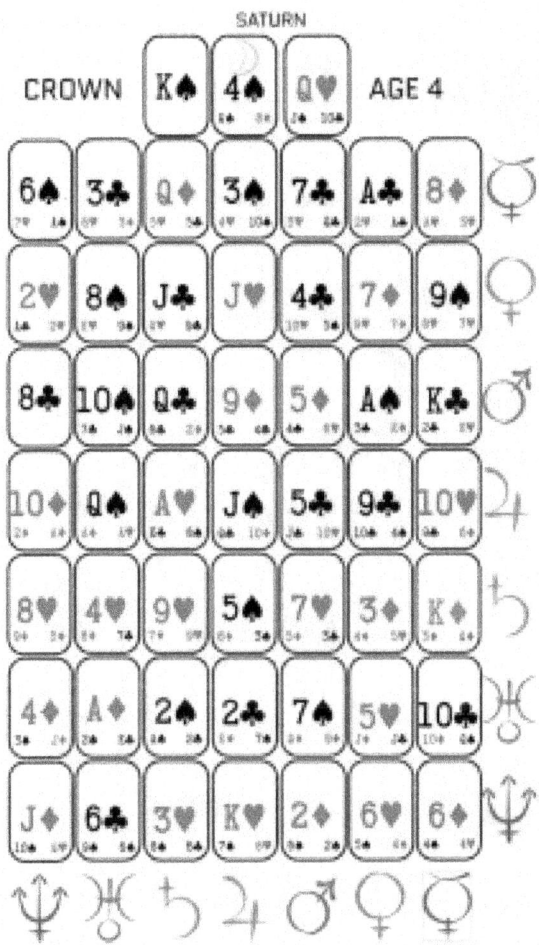

OlusanyaBey

The Art of BEing HUman

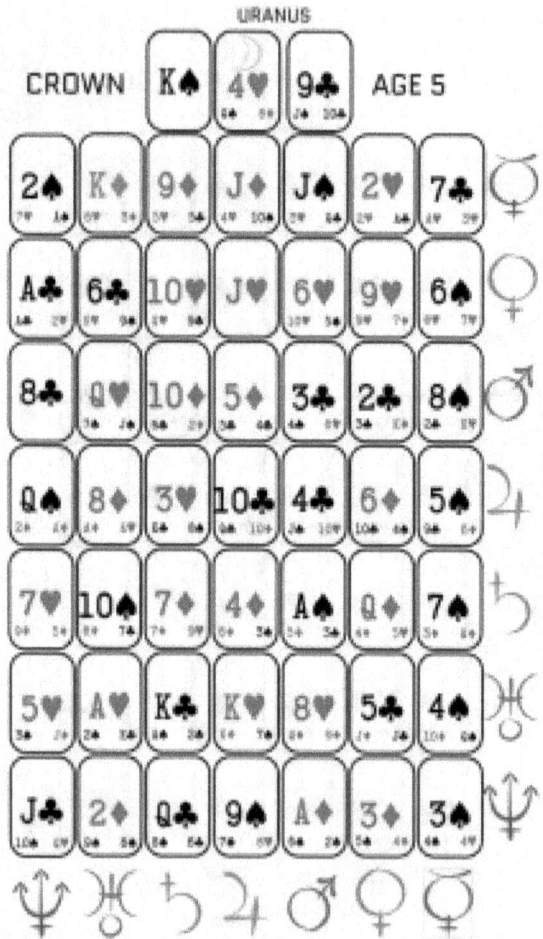

The Art of BEing HUman

Olusanya Bey

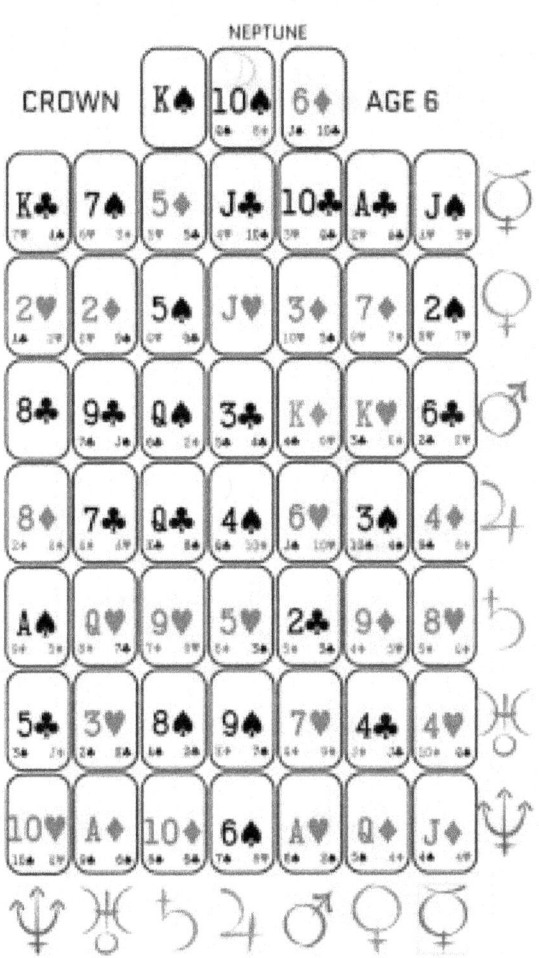

OlusanyaBey

The Art of BEing HUman

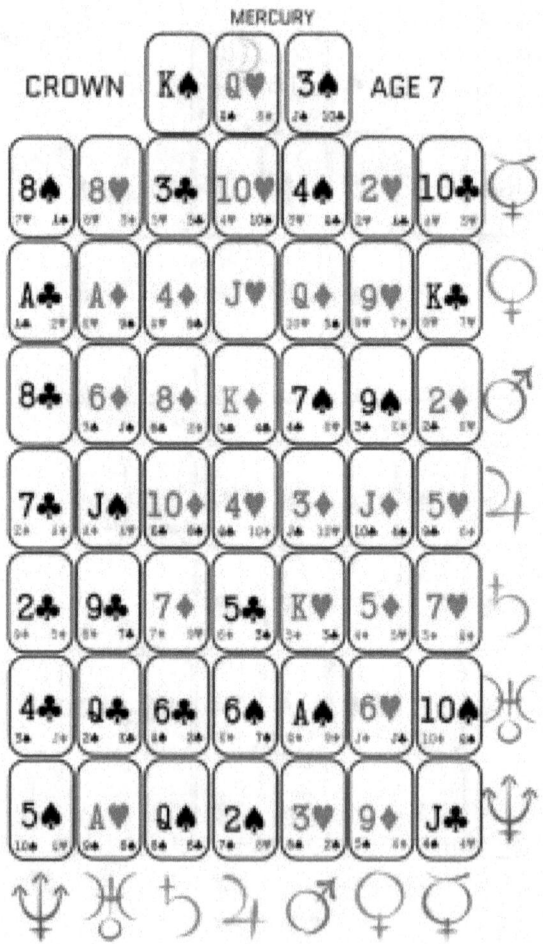

The Art of BEing HUman

Olusanya Bey

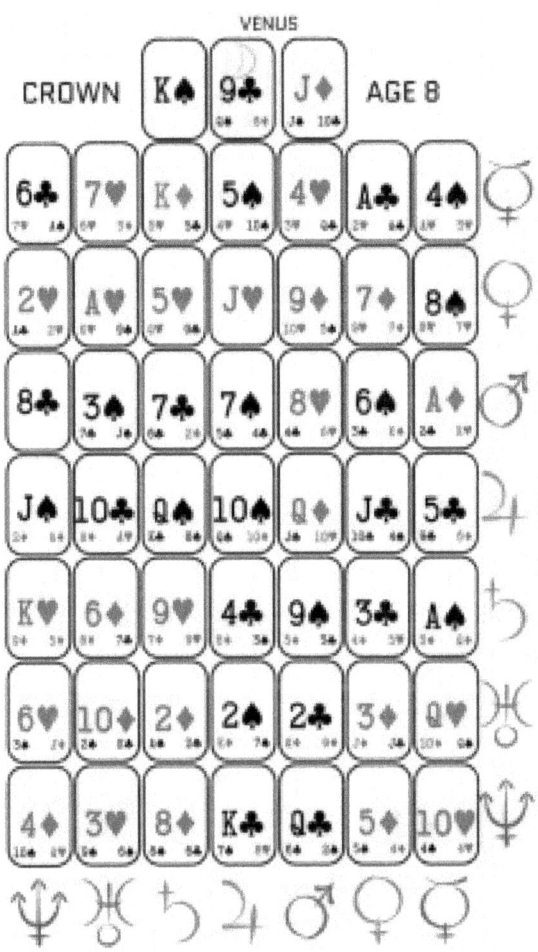

OlusanyaBey

The Art of BEing HUman

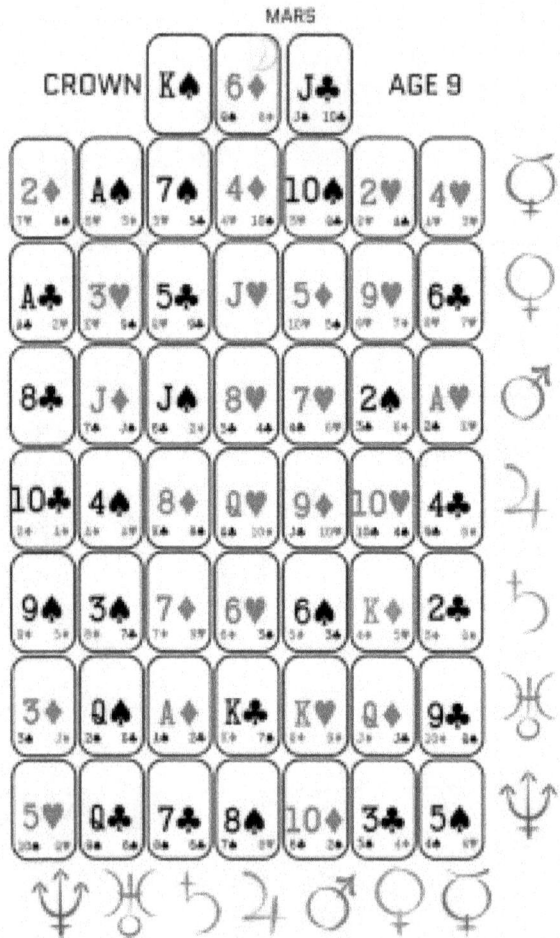

The Art of BEing HUman

Olusanya Bey

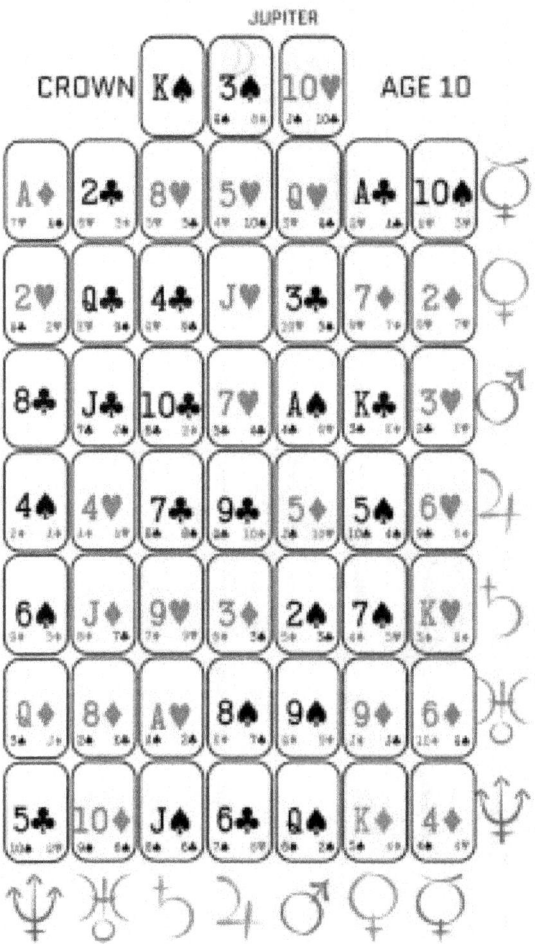

OlusanyaBey

The Art of BEing HUman

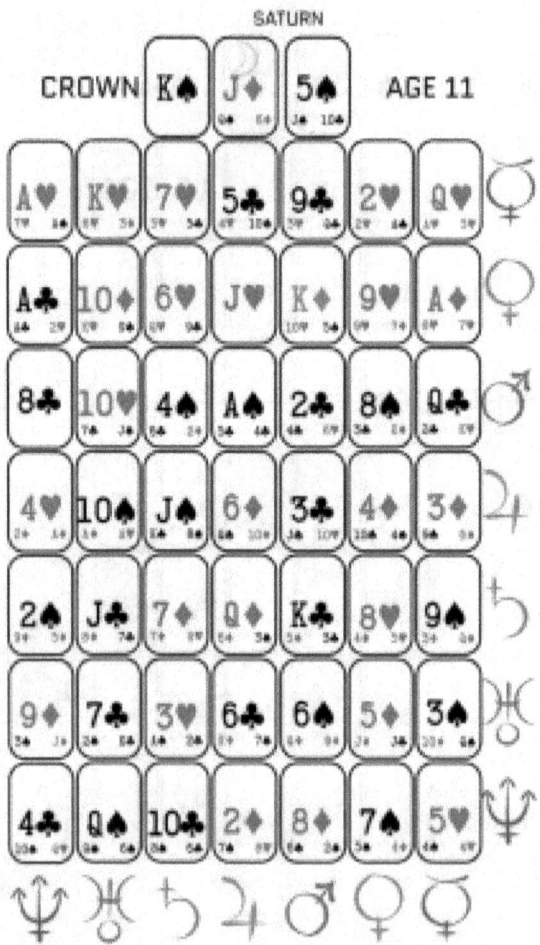

The Art of BEing HUman

Olusanya Bey

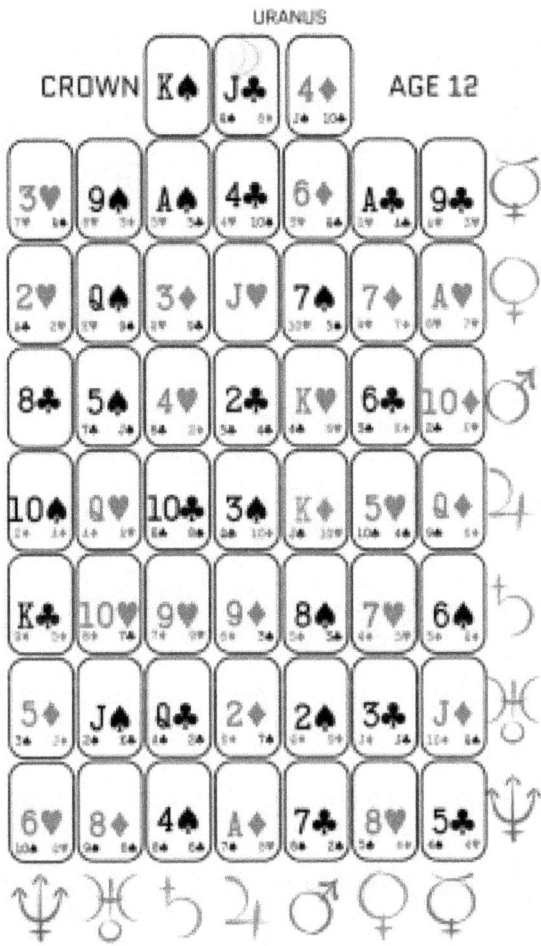

OlusanyaBey

The Art of BEing HUman

The Art of BEing HUman

Olusanya Bey

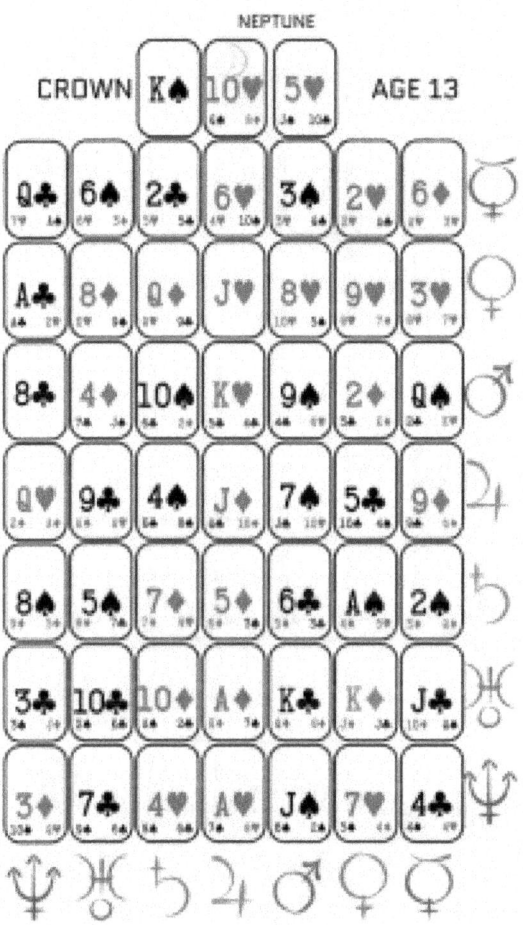

OlusanyaBey

The Art of BEing HUman

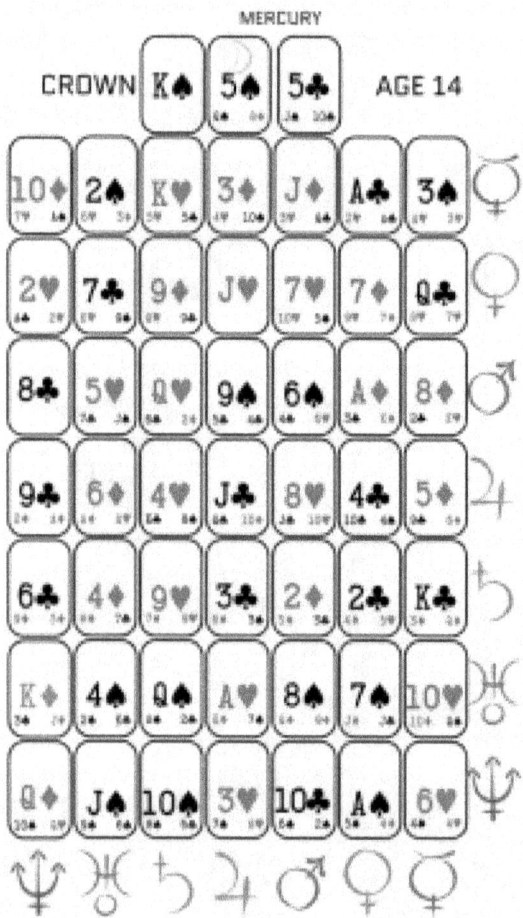

The Art of BEing HUman

Olusanya Bey

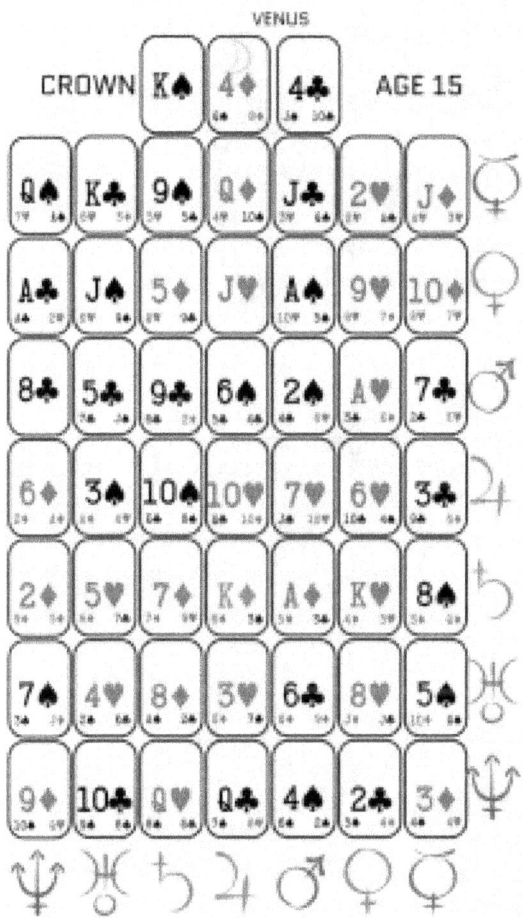

The Art of BEing HUman

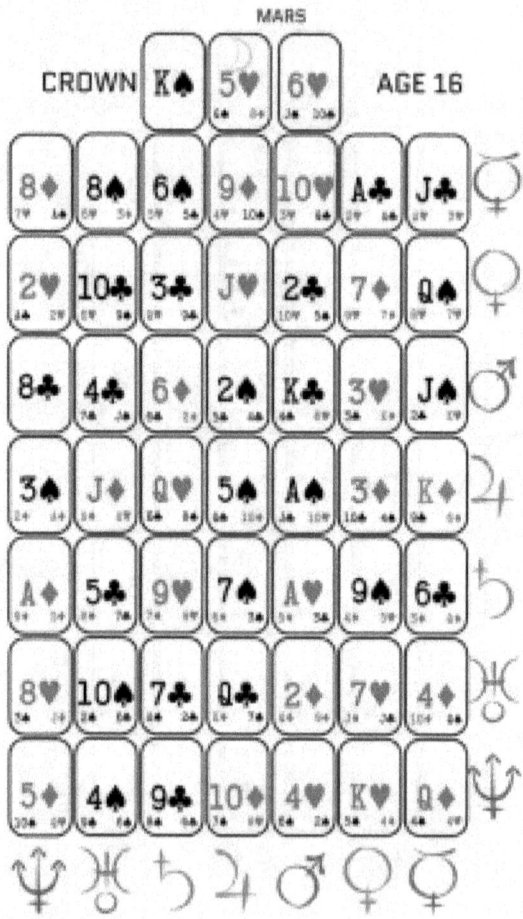

The Art of BEing HUman

Olusanya Bey

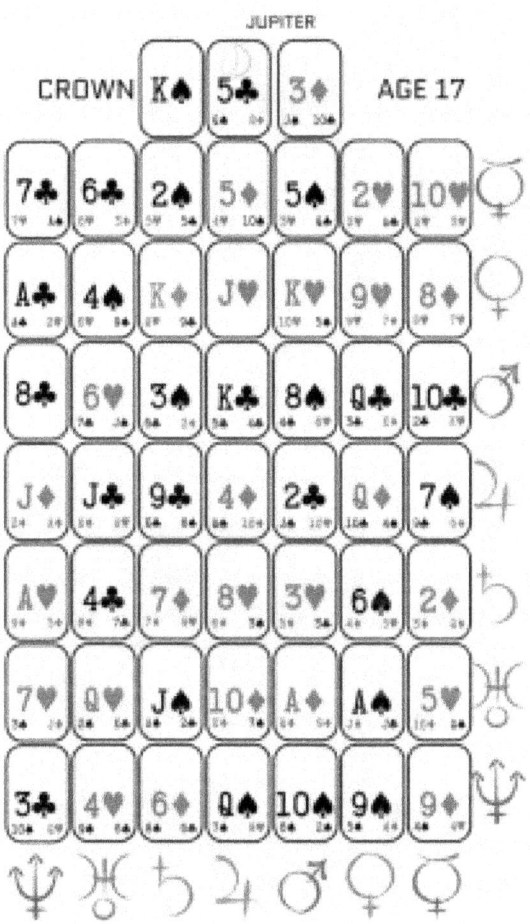

The Art of BEing HUman

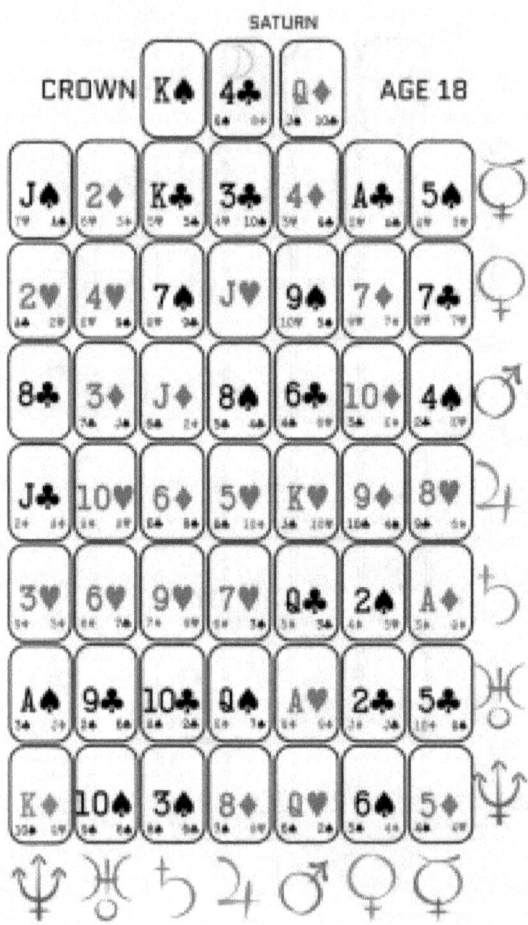

The Art of BEing HUman

Olusanya Bey

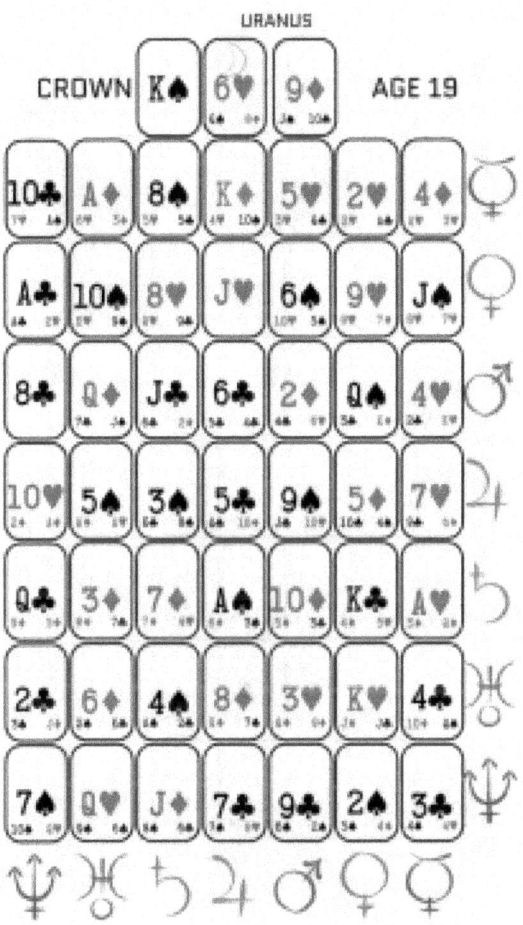

OlusanyaBey

The Art of BEing HUman

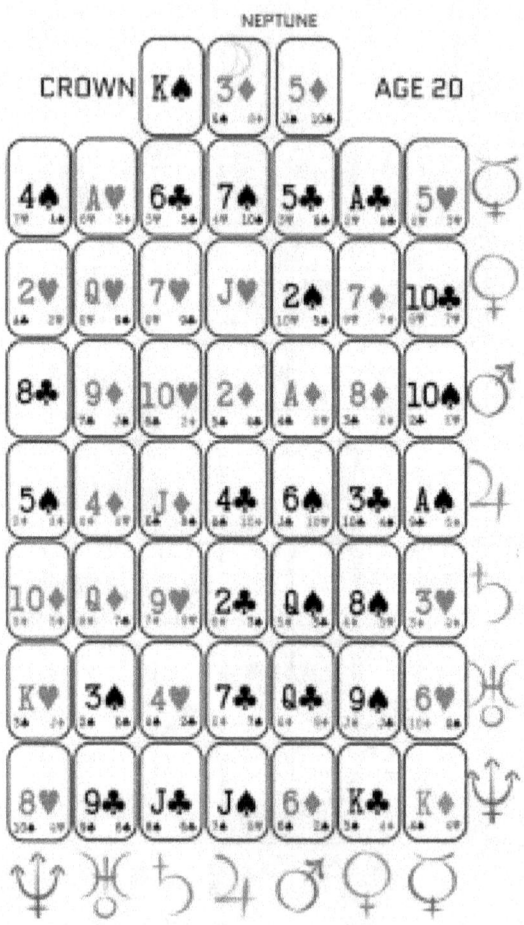

The Art of BEing HUman

Olusanya Bey

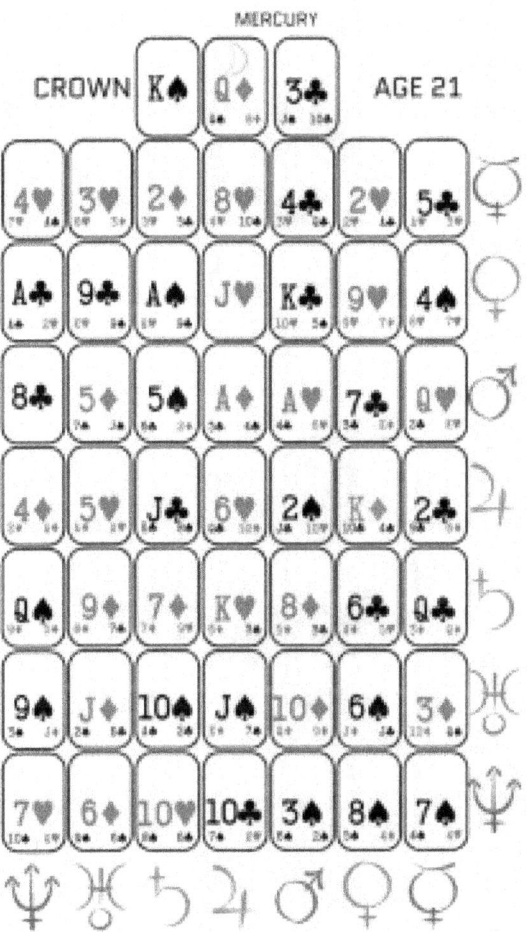

OlusanyaBey

The Art of BEing HUman

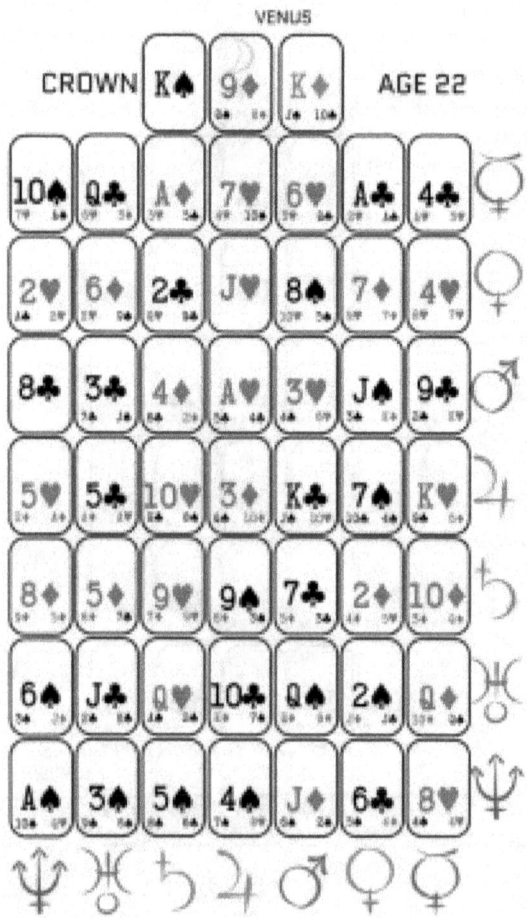

The Art of BEing HUman

Olusanya Bey

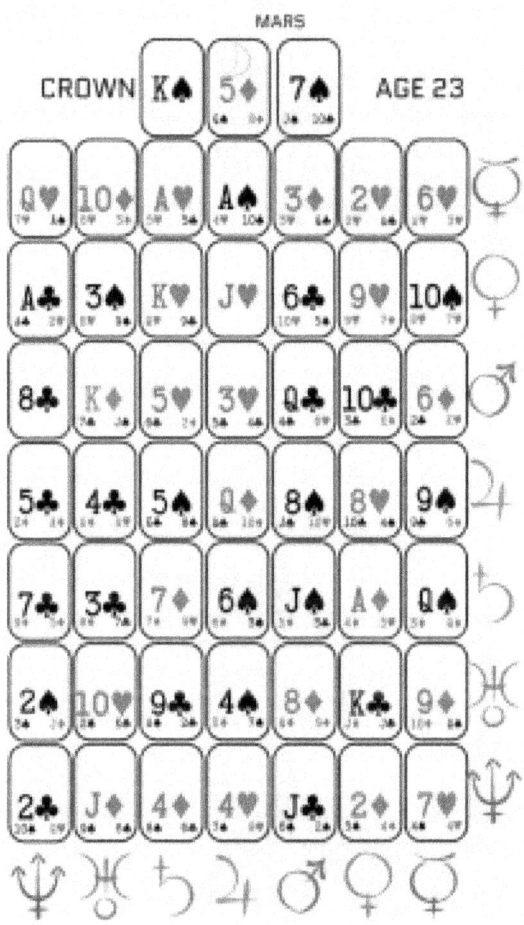

OlusanyaBey

The Art of BEing HUman

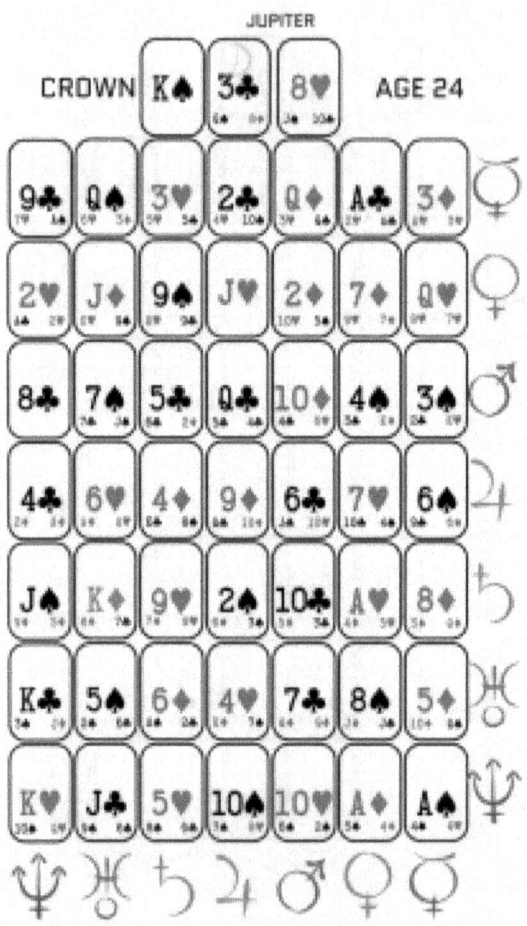

The Art of BEing HUman

Olusanya Bey

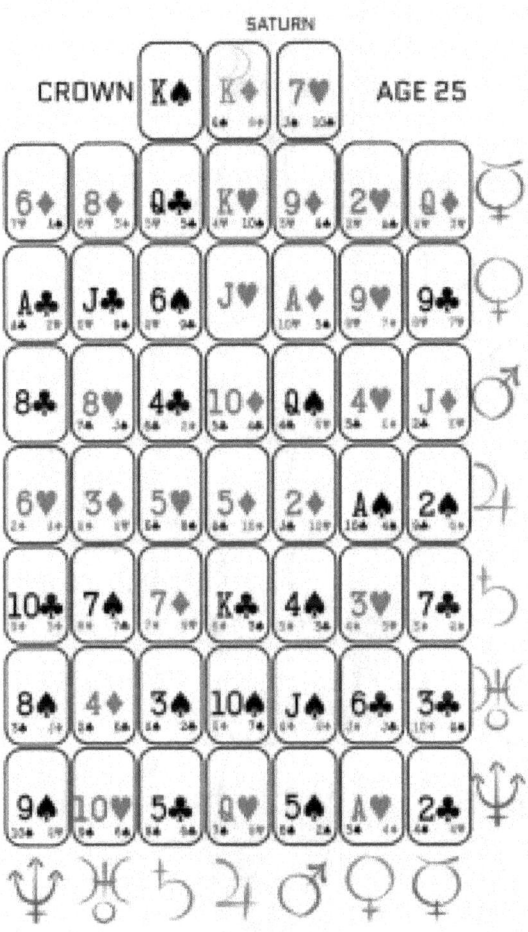

OlusanyaBey

The Art of BEing HUman

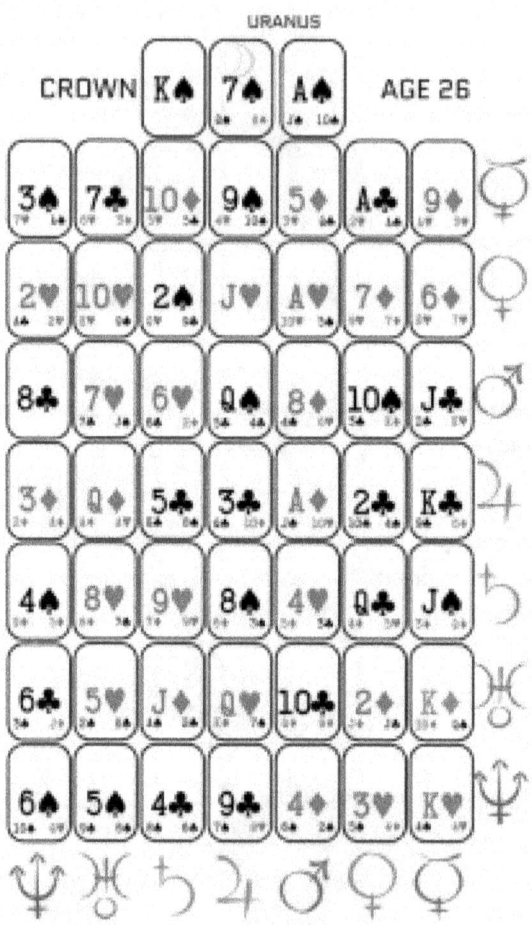

The Art of BEing HUman

Olusanya Bey

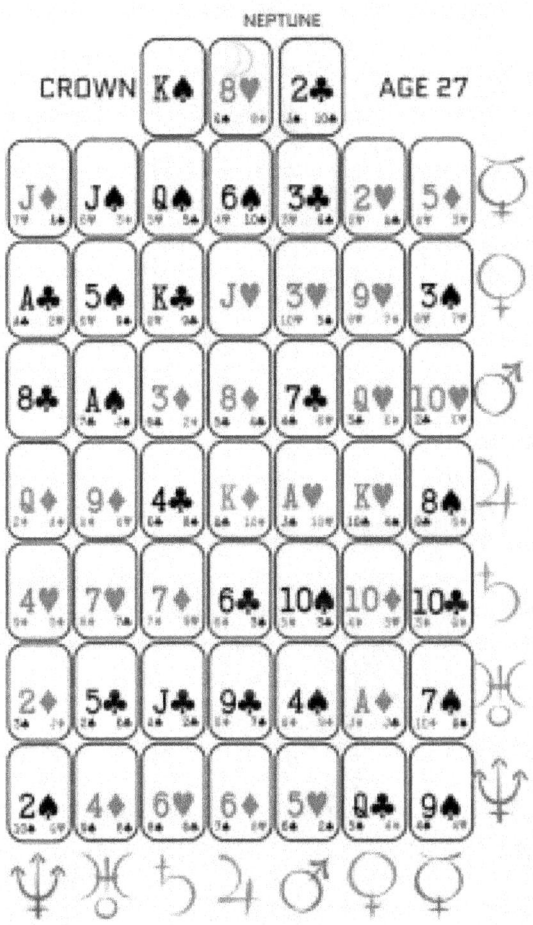

OlusanyaBey

The Art of BEing HUman

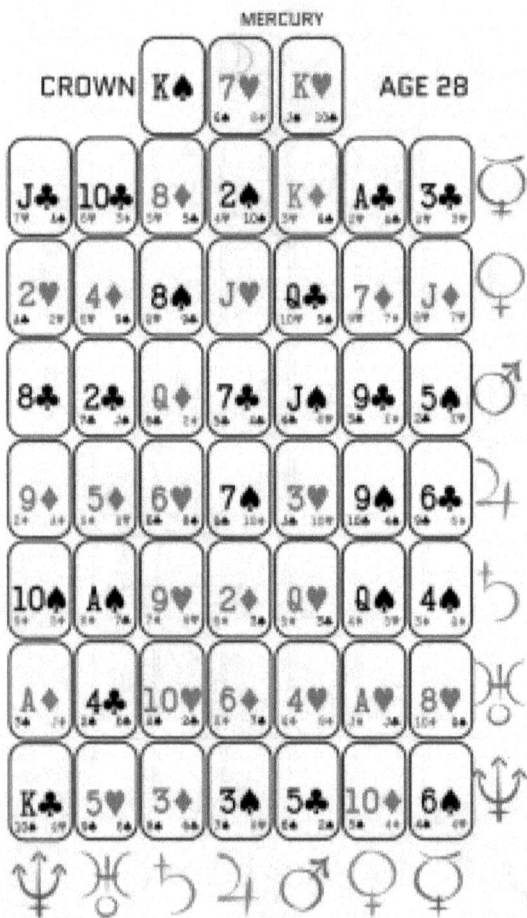

Olusanya Bey

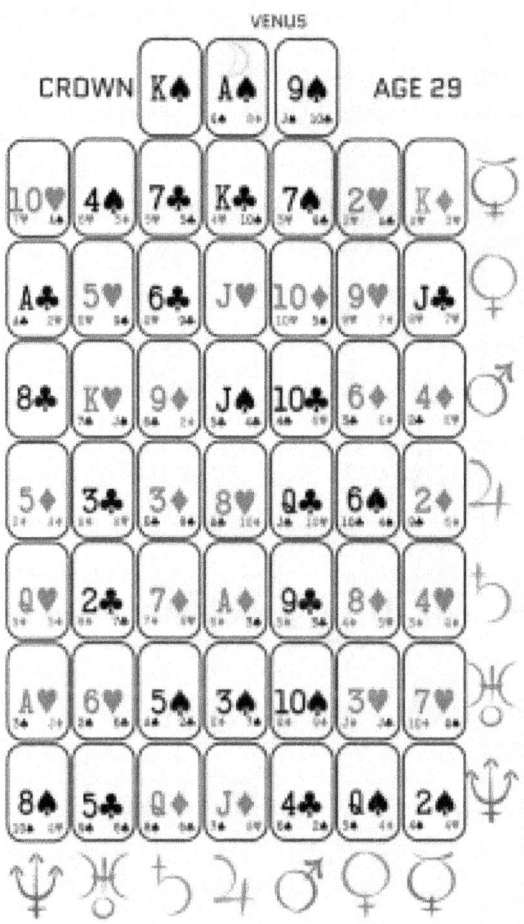

OlusanyaBey

The Art of BEing HUman

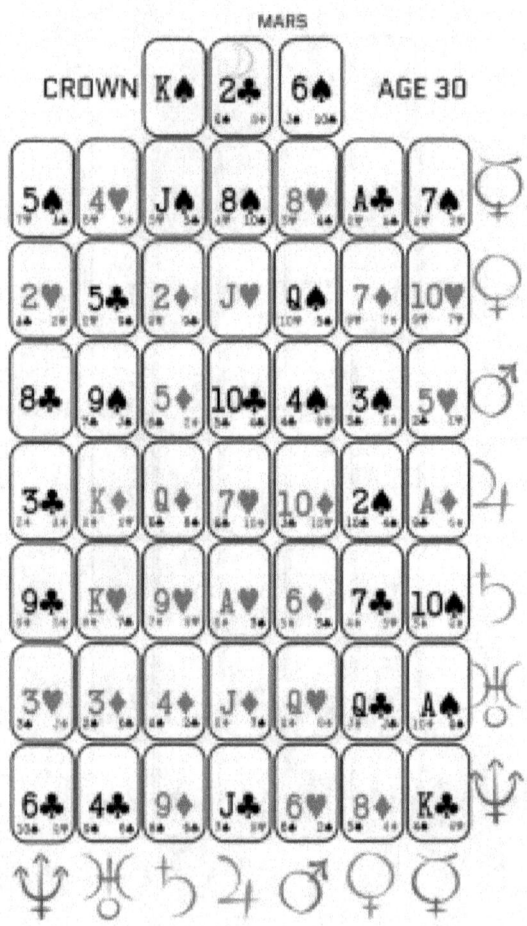

The Art of BEing HUman

Olusanya Bey

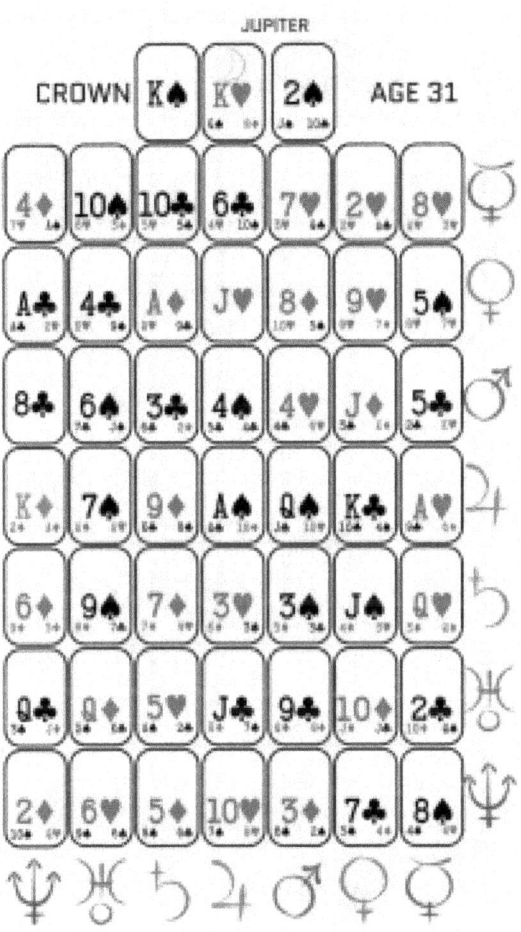

OlusanyaBey

The Art of BEing HUman

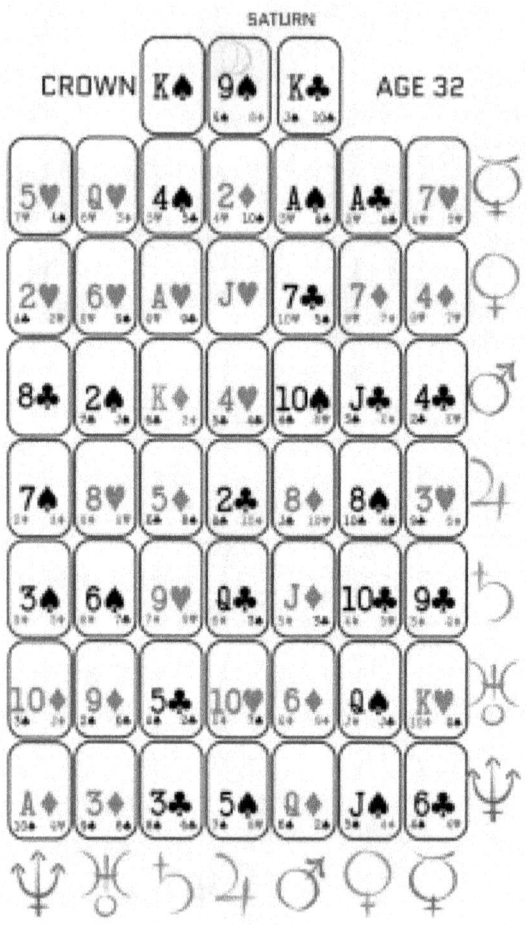

The Art of BEing HUman

Olusanya Bey

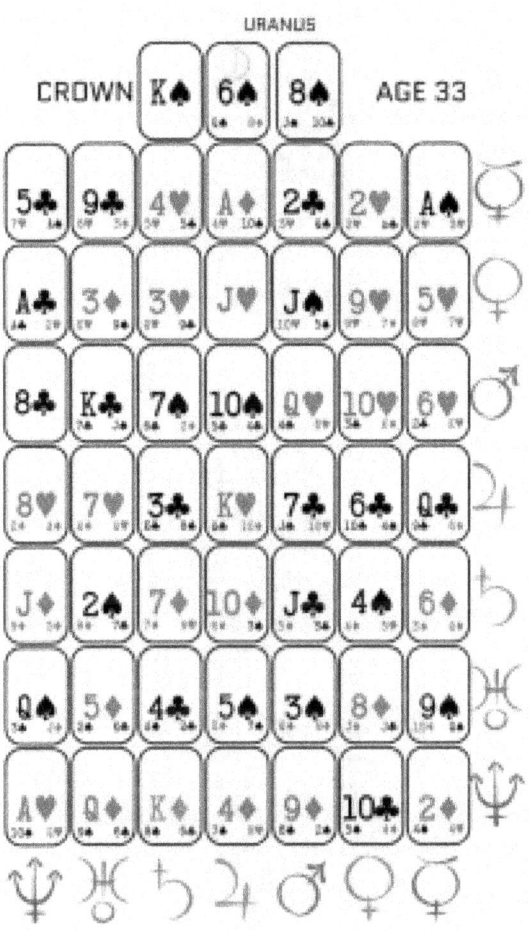

OlusanyaBey

The Art of BEing HUman

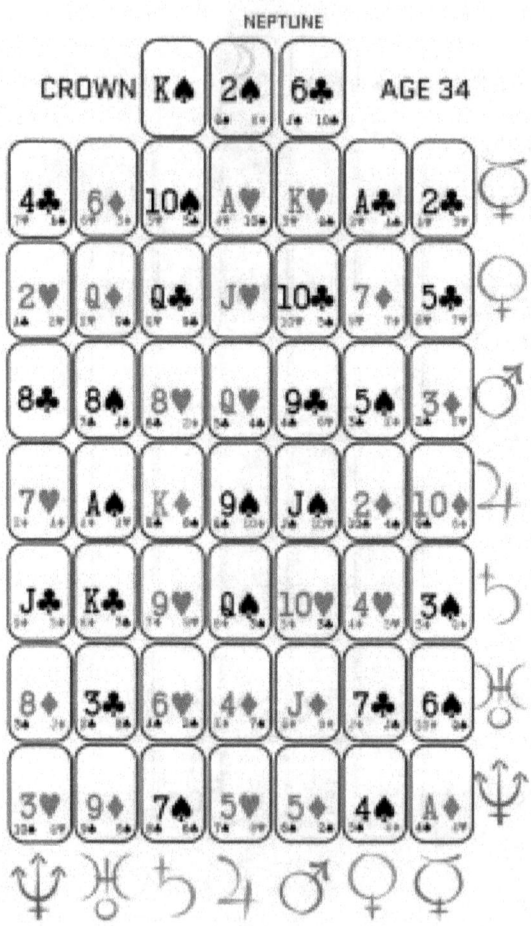

The Art of BEing HUman

Olusanya Bey

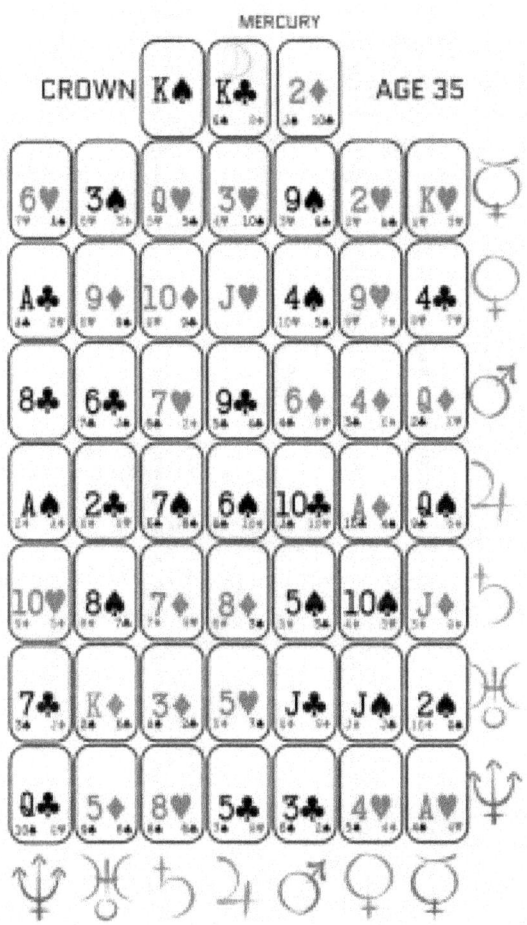

OlusanyaBey

The Art of BEing HUman

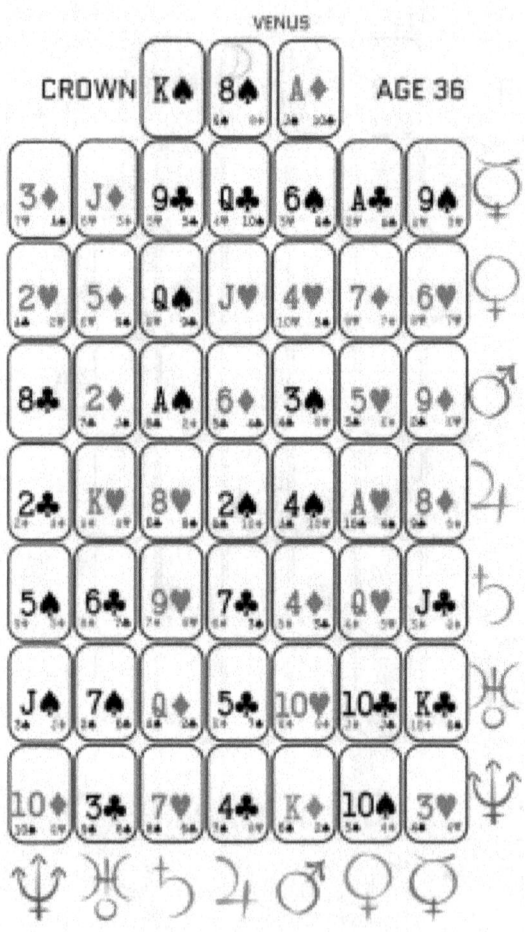

The Art of BEing HUman

Olusanya Bey

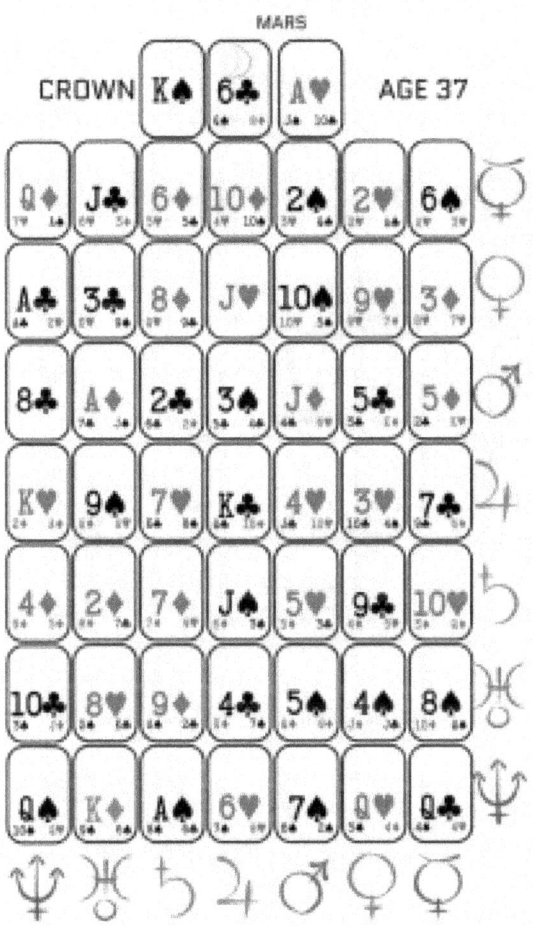

OlusanyaBey

The Art of BEing HUman

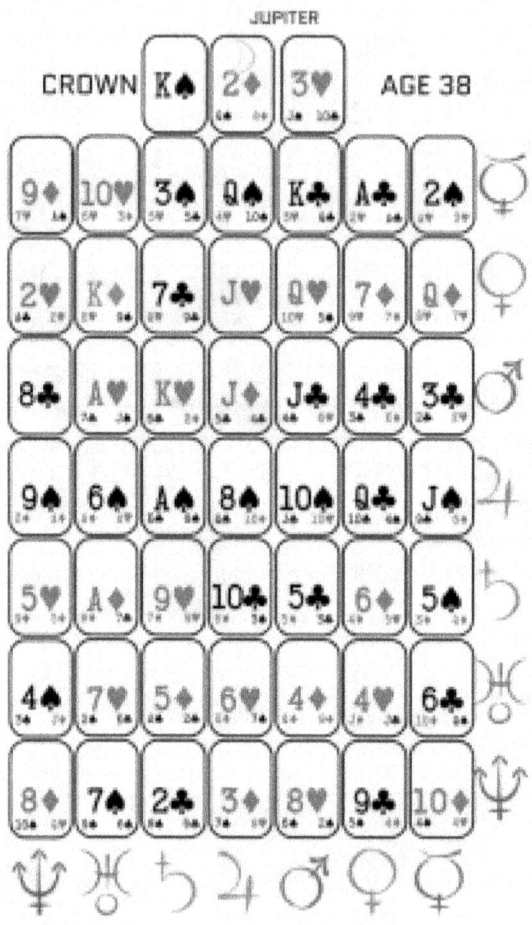

The Art of BEing HUman

Olusanya Bey

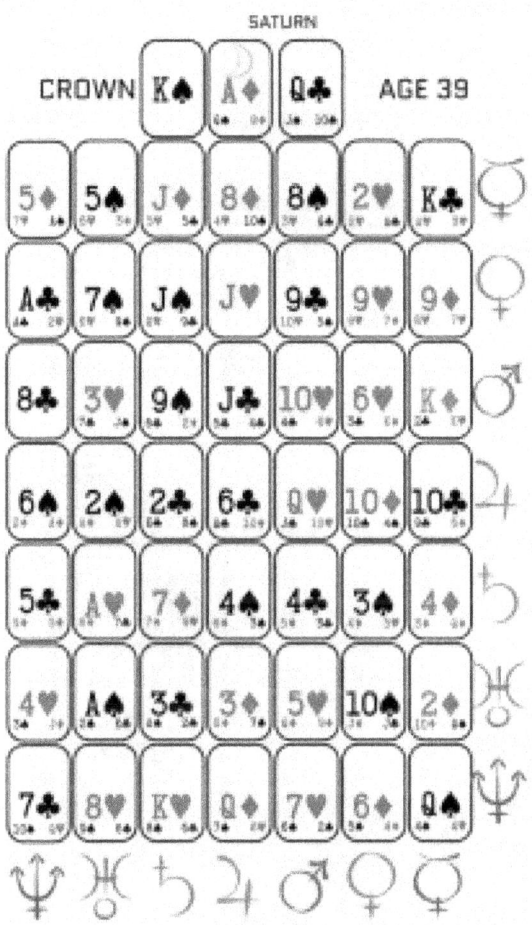

OlusanyaBey

The Art of BEing HUman

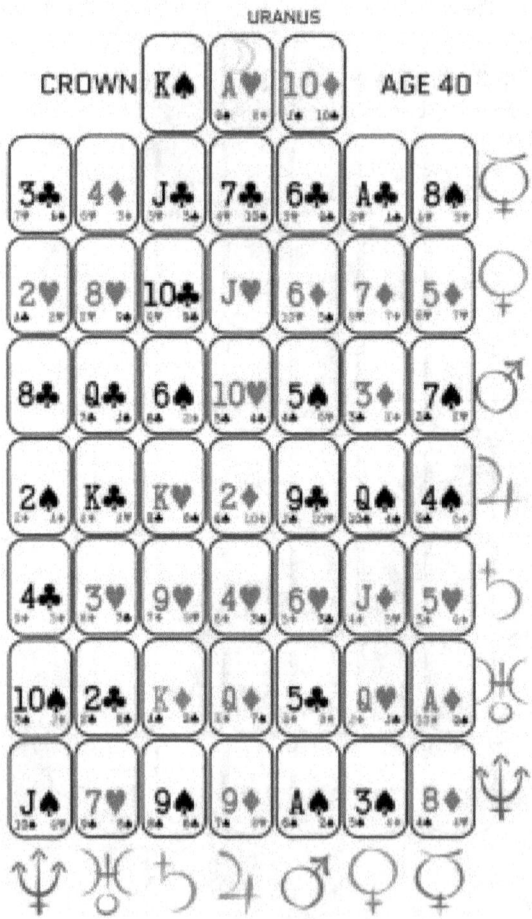

The Art of BEing HUman

Olusanya Bey

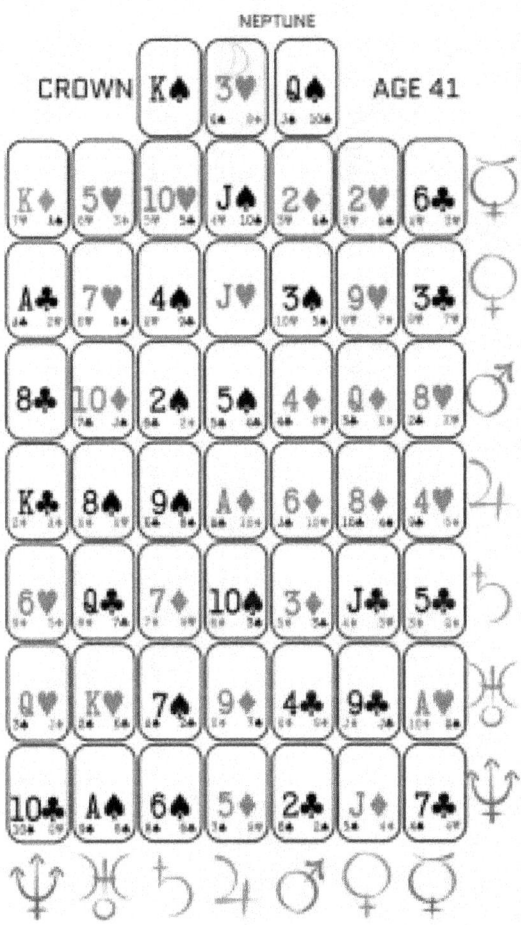

OlusanyaBey

The Art of BEing HUman

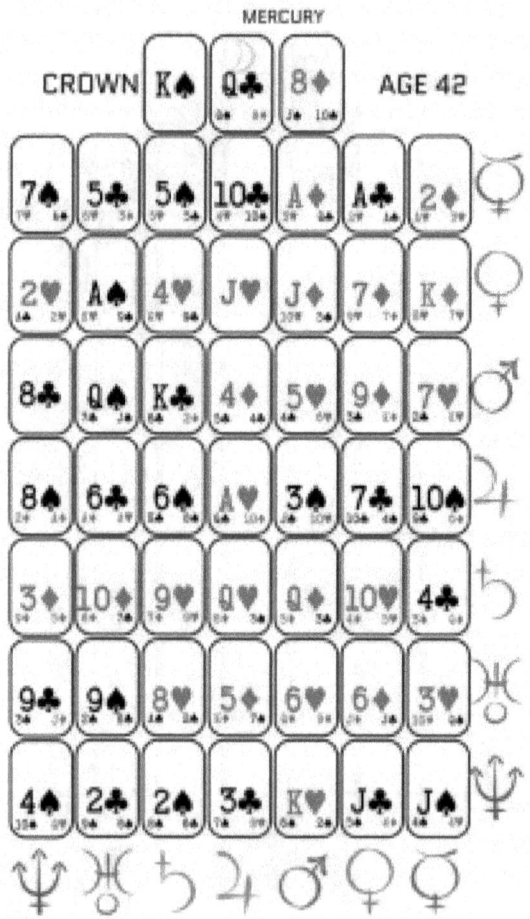

The Art of BEing HUman

Olusanya Bey

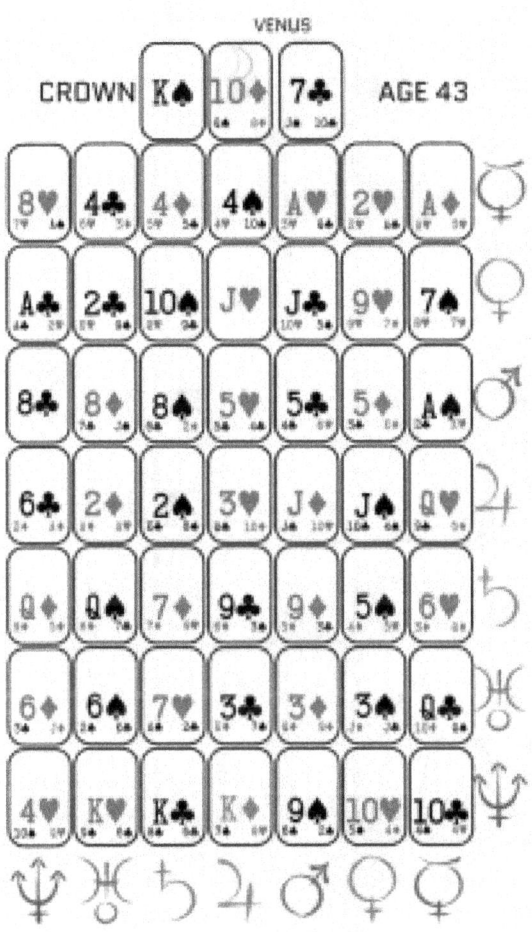

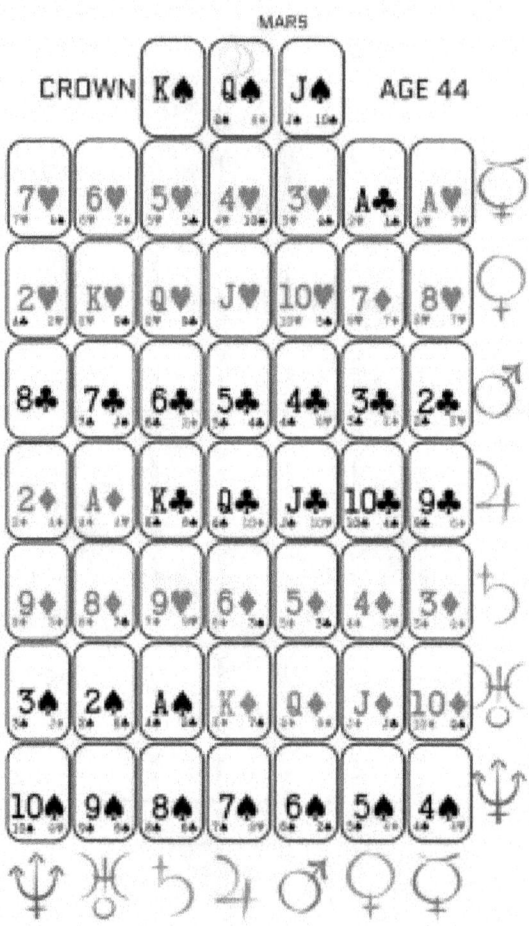

The Art of BEing HUman

Olusanya Bey

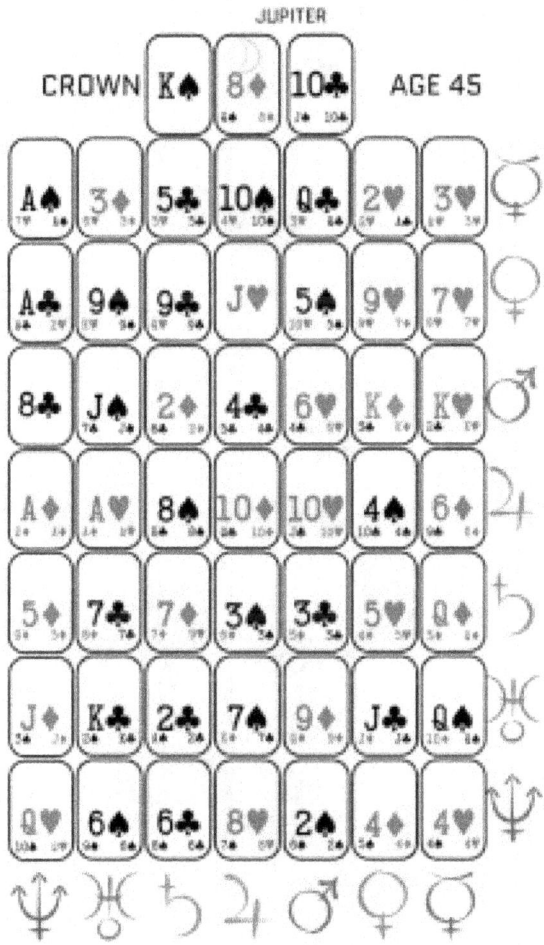

OlusanyaBey

The Art of BEing HUman

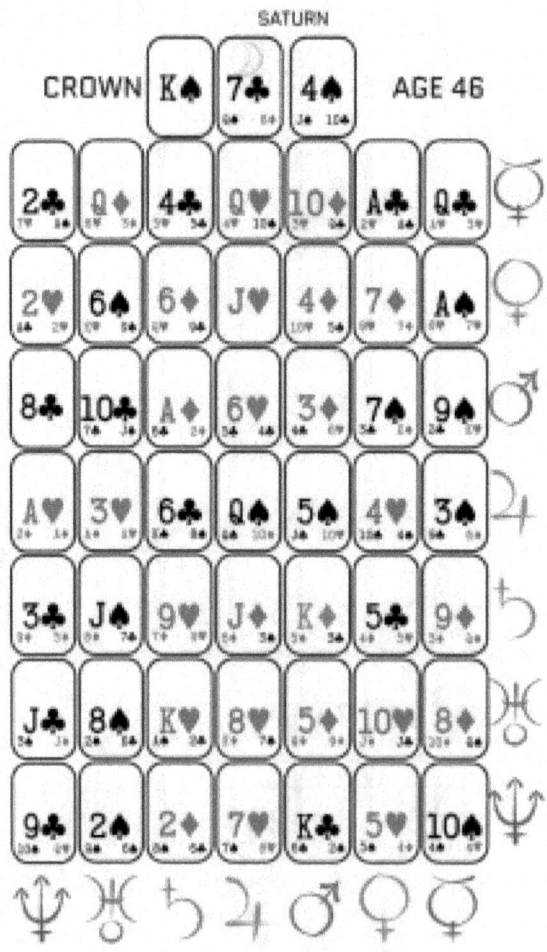

The Art of BEing HUman

Olusanya Bey

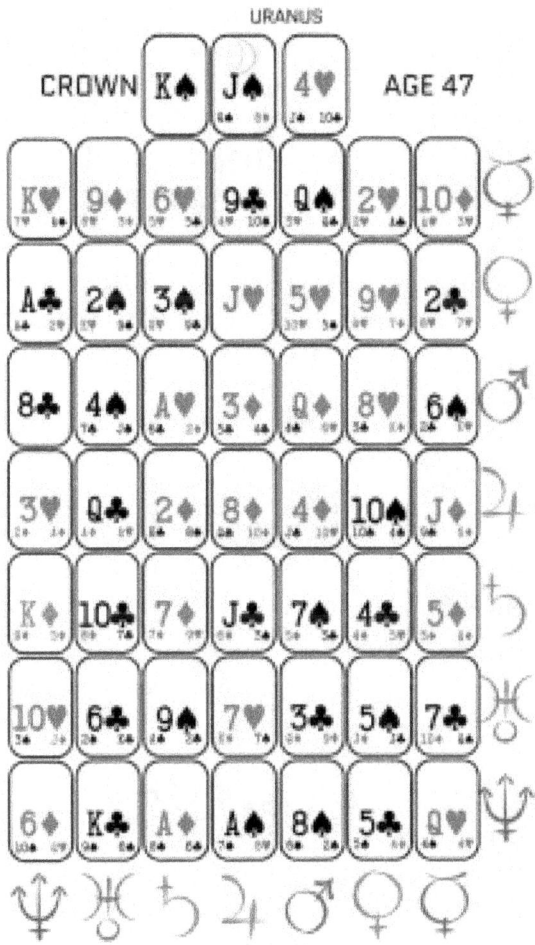

OlusanyaBey

The Art of BEing HUman

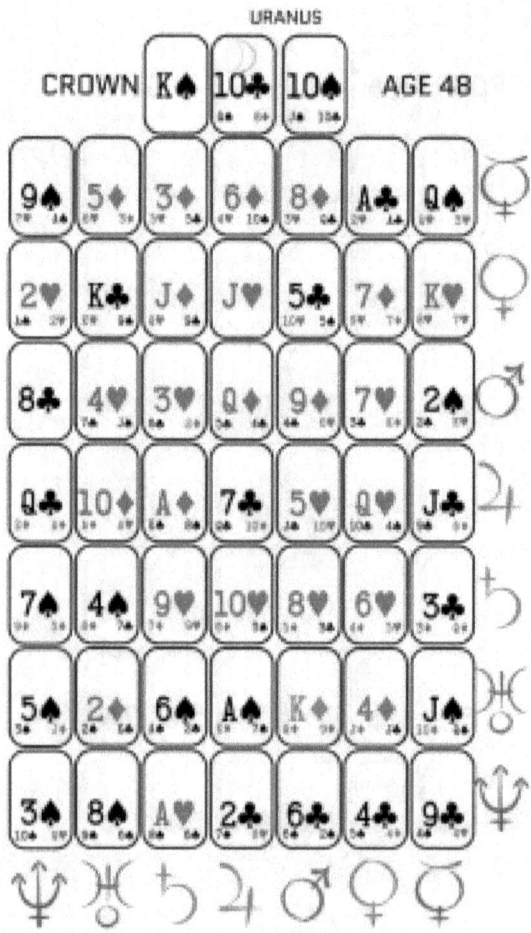

The Art of BEing HUman

Olusanya Bey

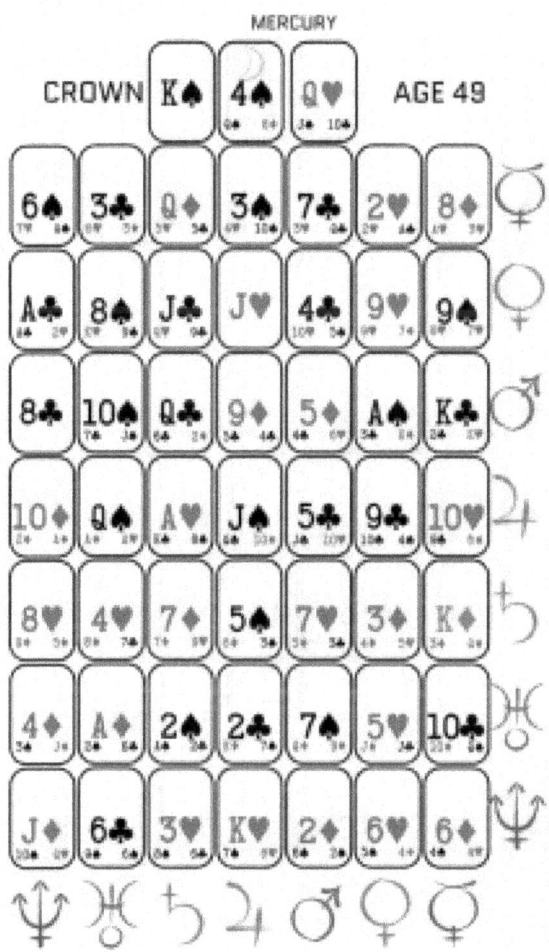

OlusanyaBey

The Art of BEing HUman

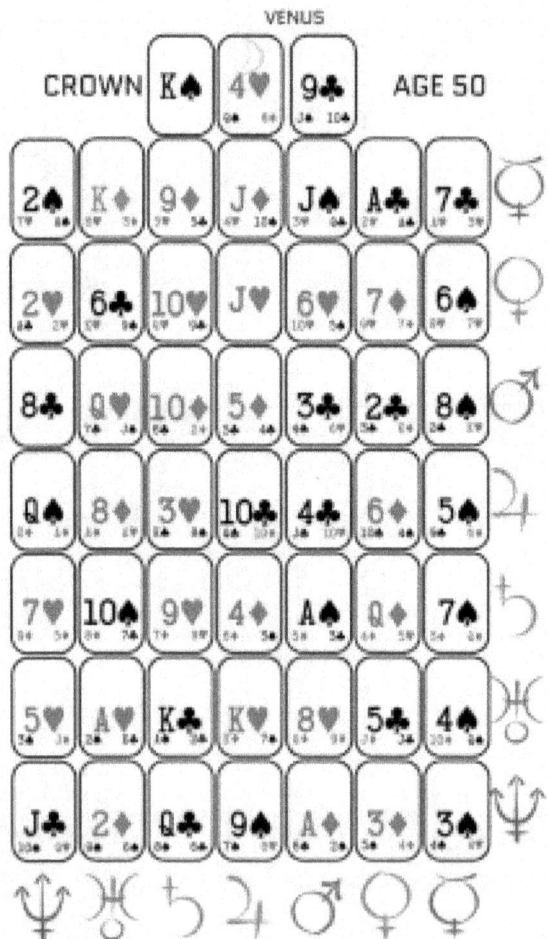

The Art of BEing HUman

Olusanya Bey

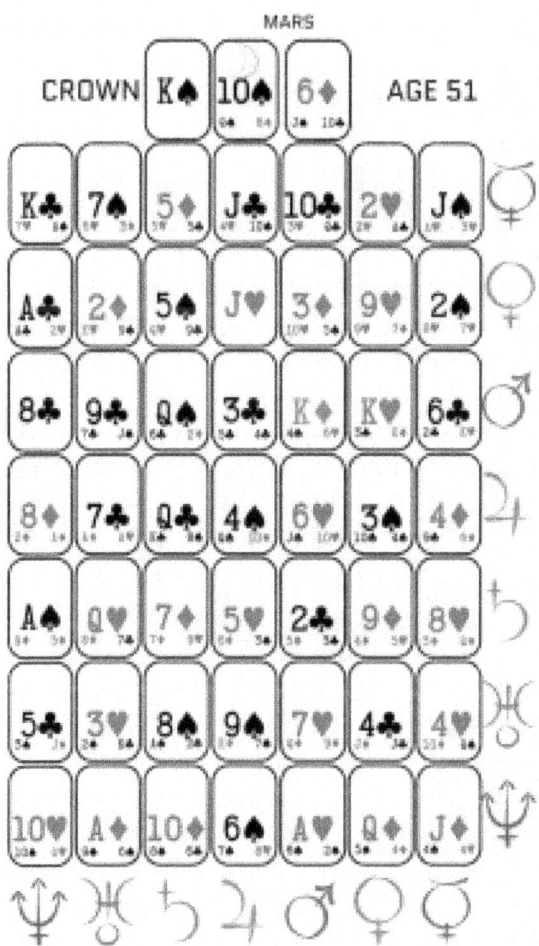

OlusanyaBey

The Art of BEing HUman

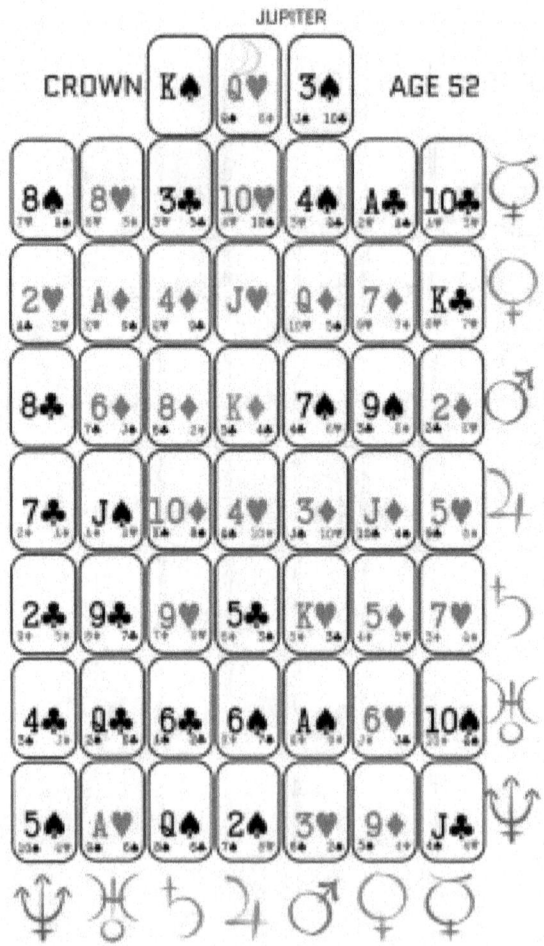

The Art of BEing HUman

Olusanya Bey

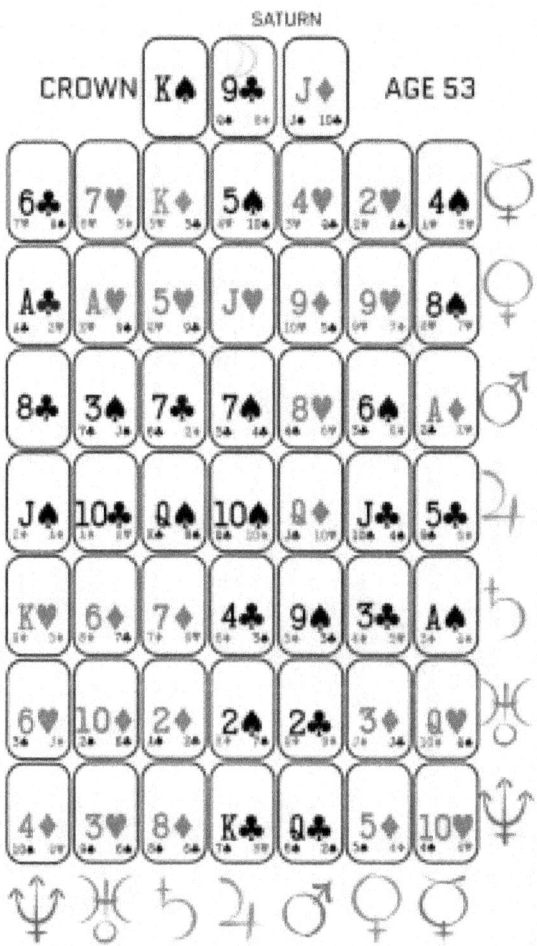

OlusanyaBey

The Art of BEing HUman

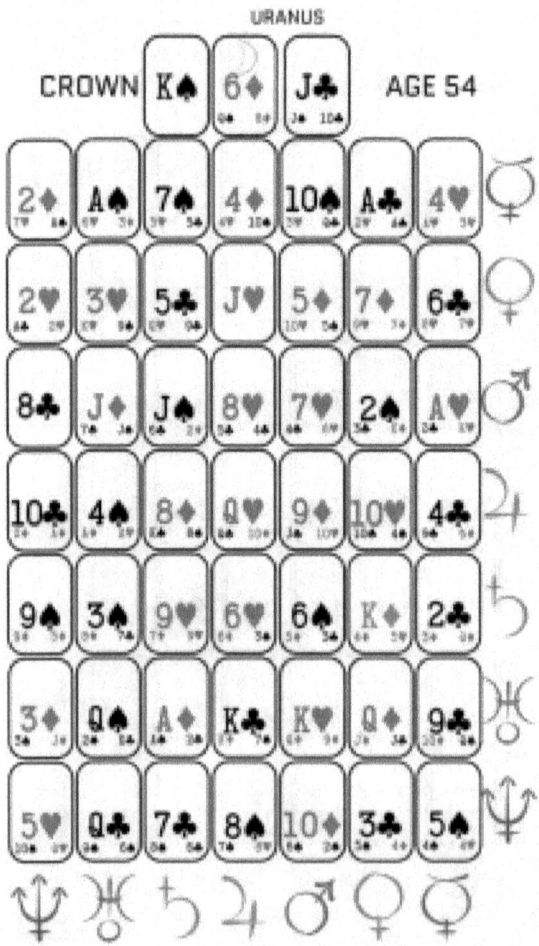

The Art of BEing HUman

Olusanya Bey

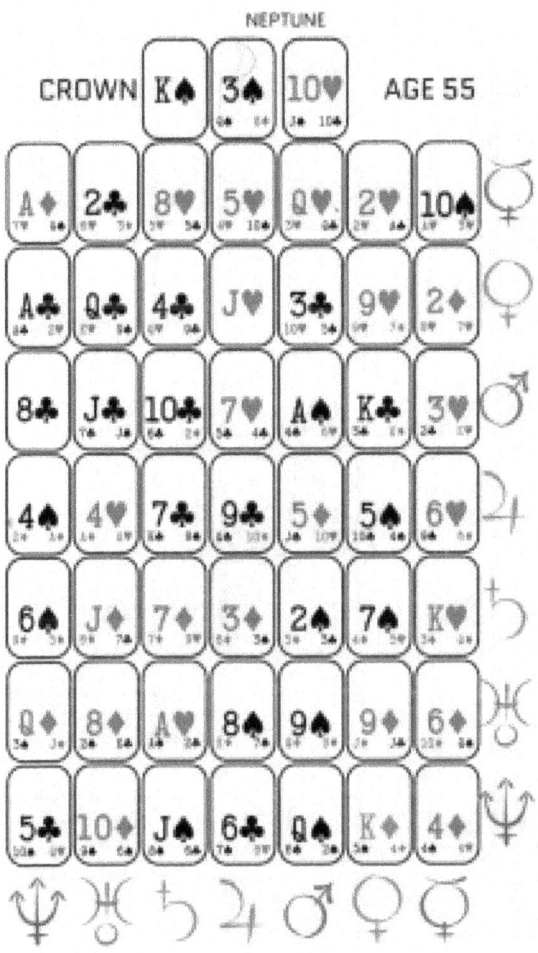

OlusanyaBey

The Art of BEing HUman

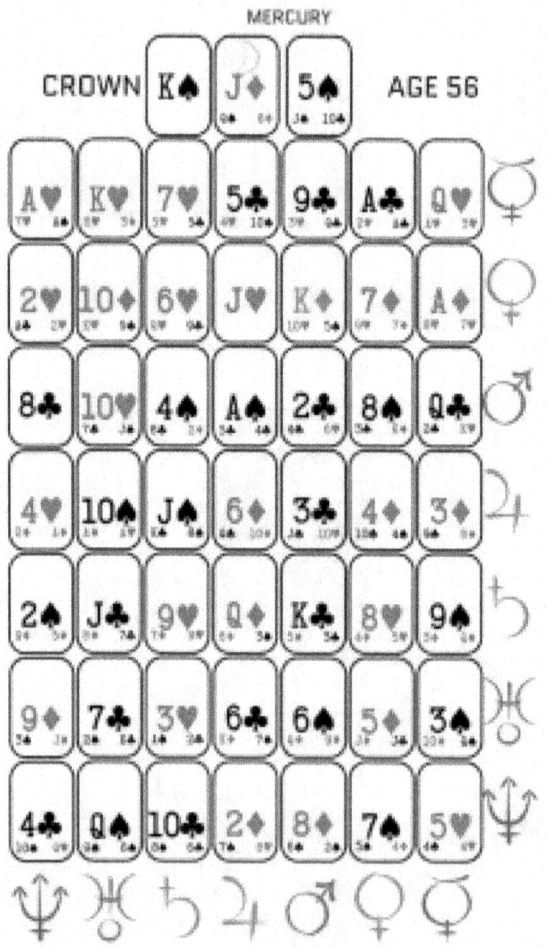

The Art of BEing HUman

Olusanya Bey

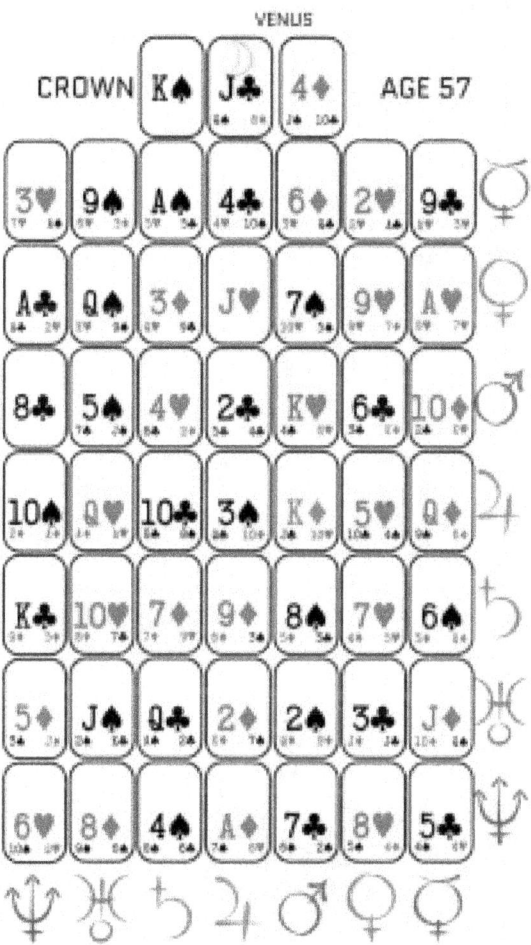

OlusanyaBey

The Art of BEing HUman

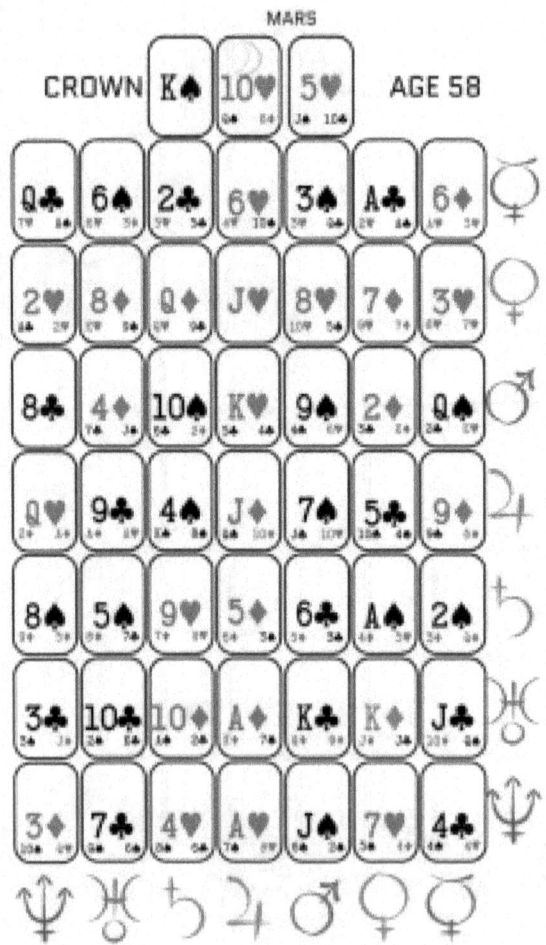

The Art of BEing HUman

Olusanya Bey

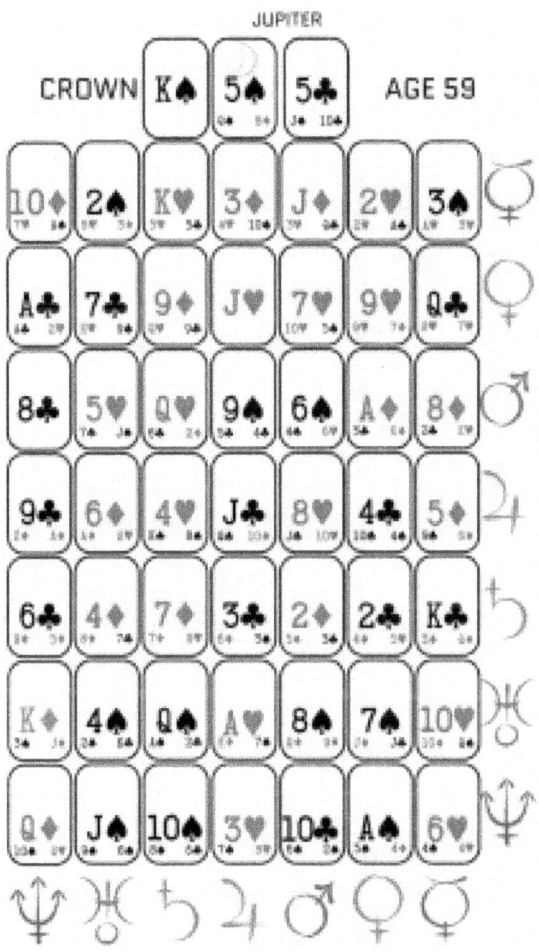

OlusanyaBey

The Art of BEing HUman

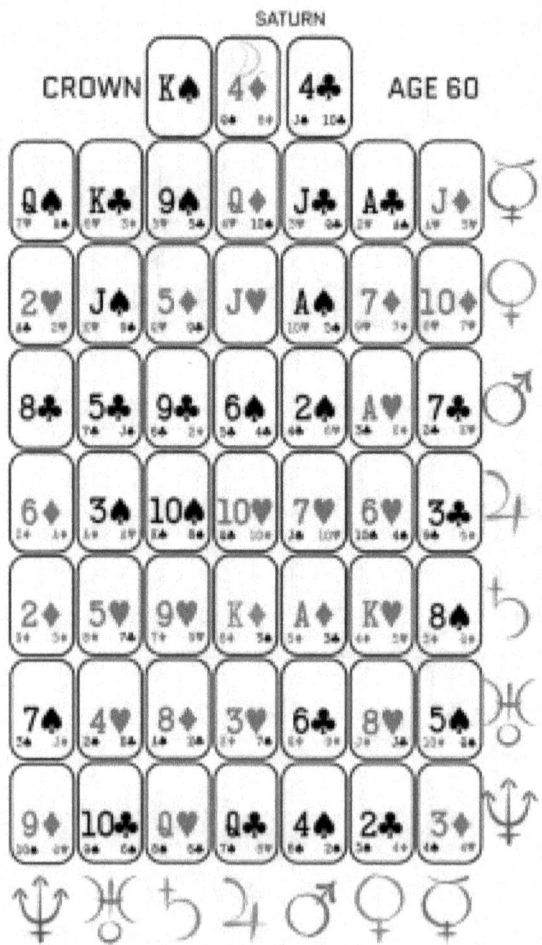

The Art of BEing HUman

Olusanya Bey

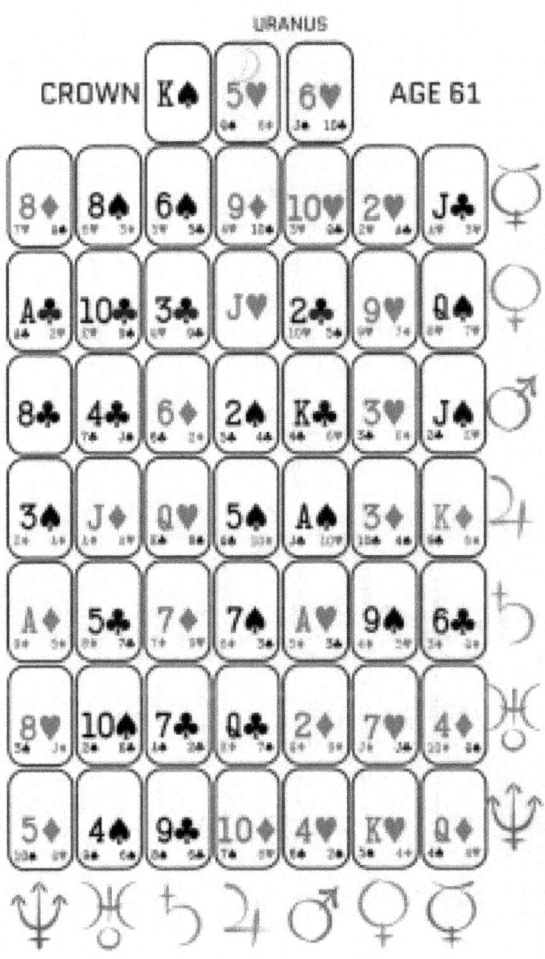

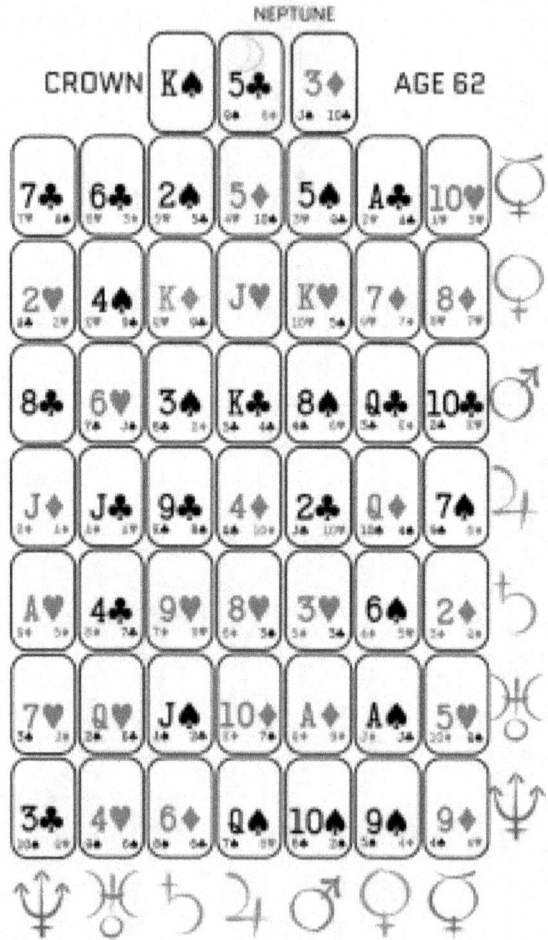

The Art of BEing HUman

Olusanya Bey

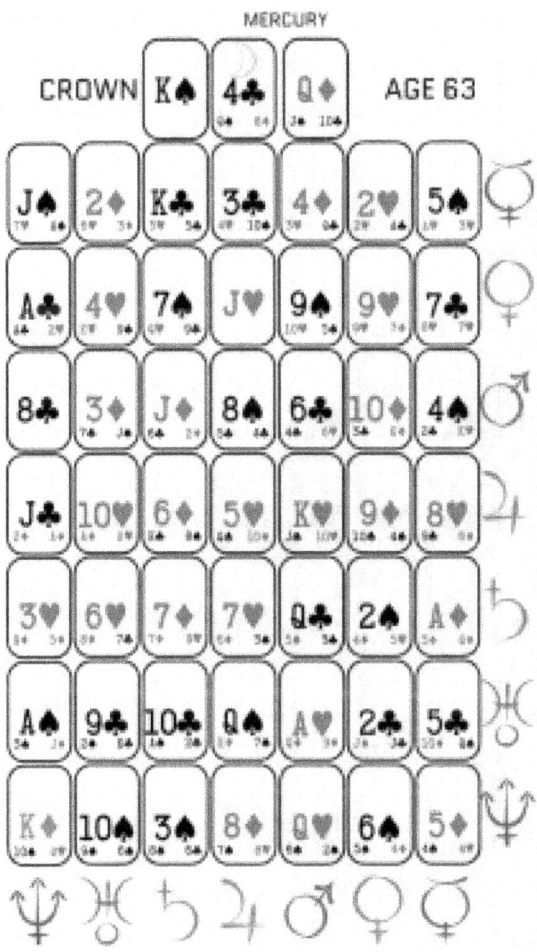

OlusanyaBey

The Art of BEing HUman

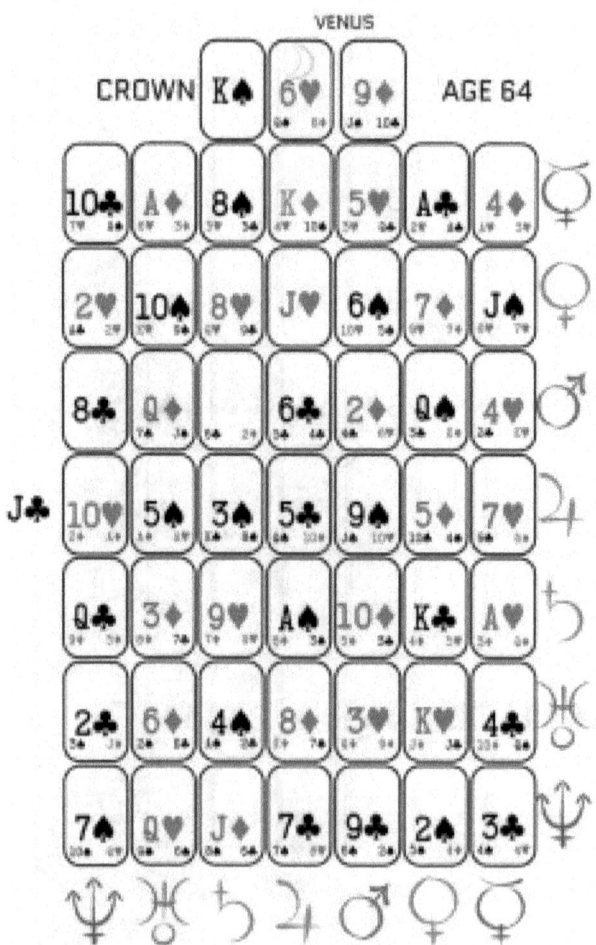

The Art of BEing HUman

Olusanya Bey

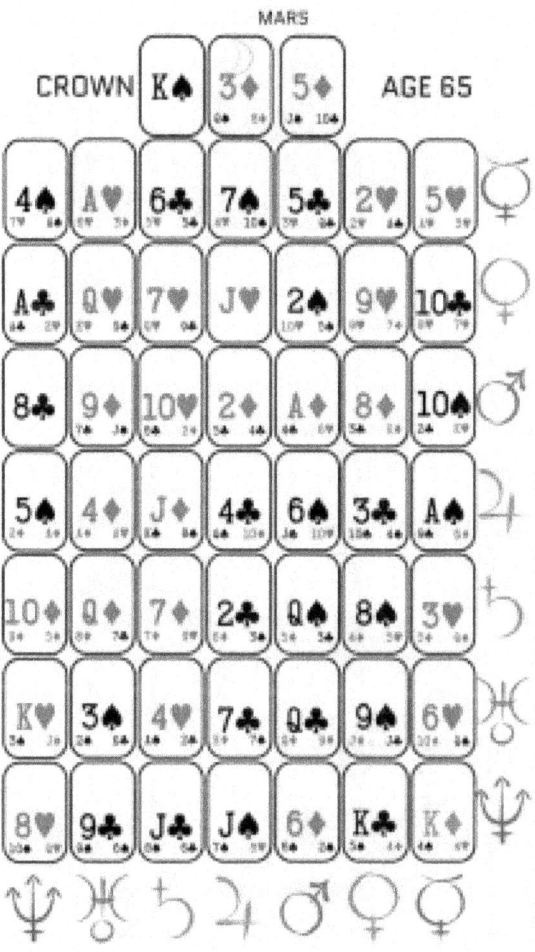

OlusanyaBey

The Art of BEing HUman

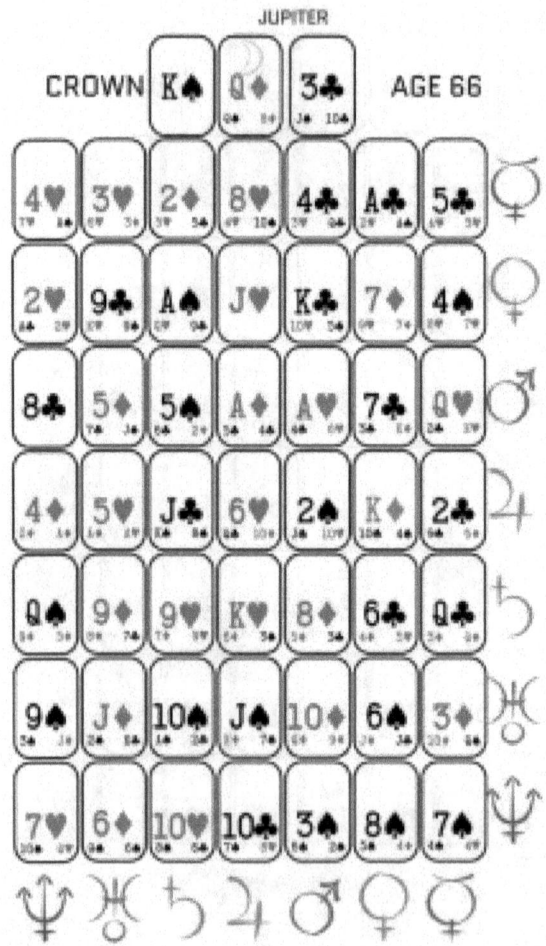

The Art of BEing HUman

Olusanya Bey

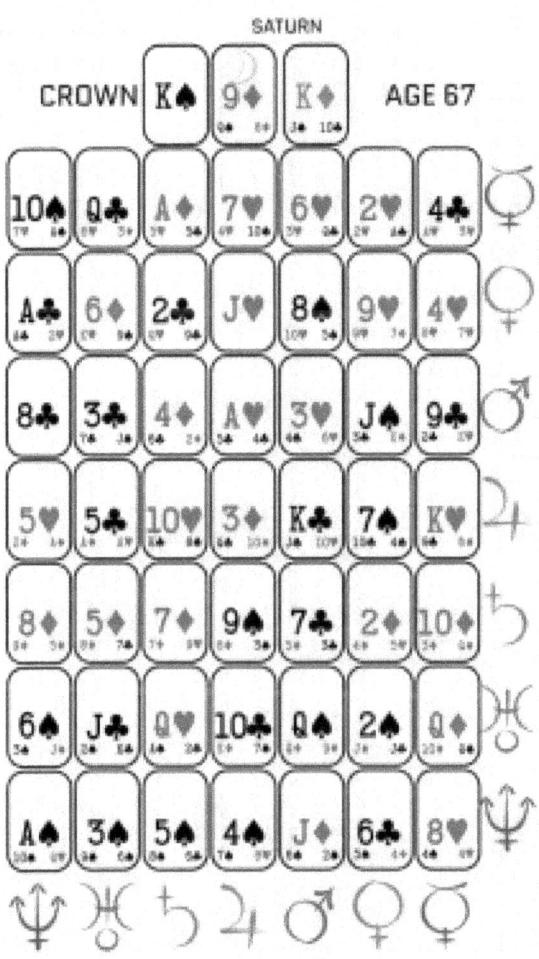

OlusanyaBey

The Art of BEing HUman

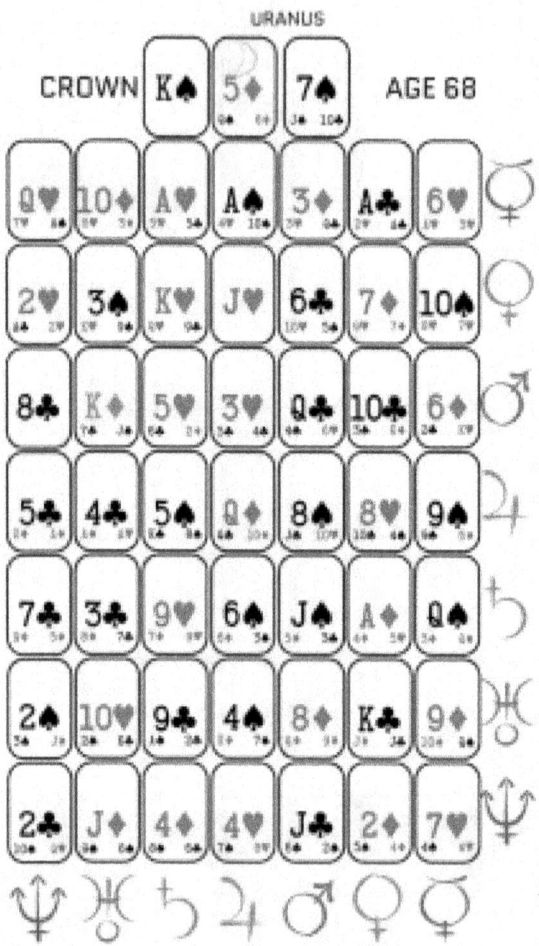

The Art of BEing HUman

Olusanya Bey

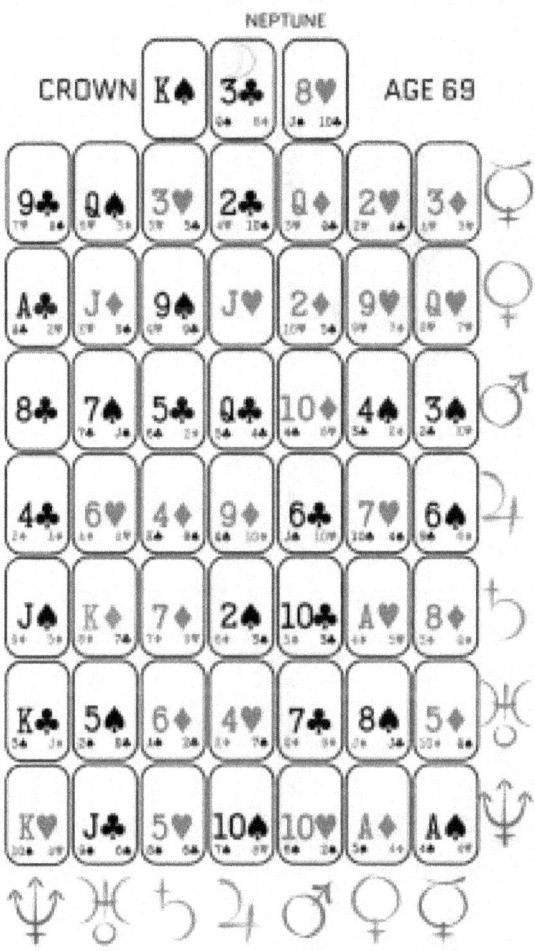

OlusanyaBey

The Art of BEing HUman

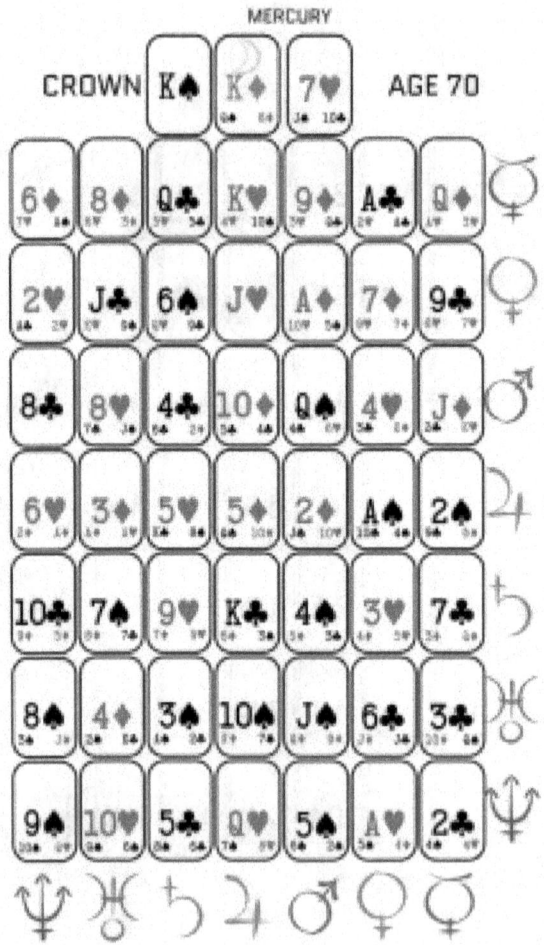

The Art of BEing HUman

Olusanya Bey

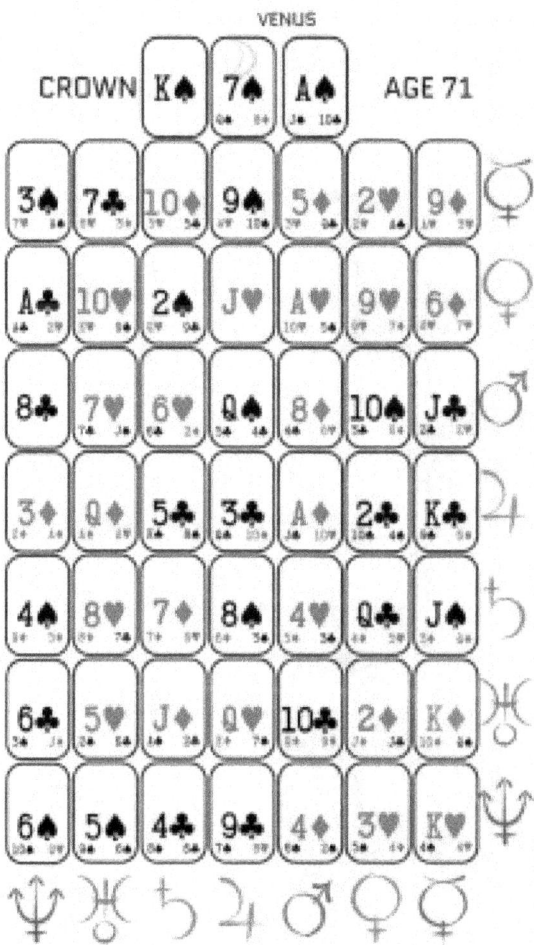

OlusanyaBey

The Art of BEing HUman

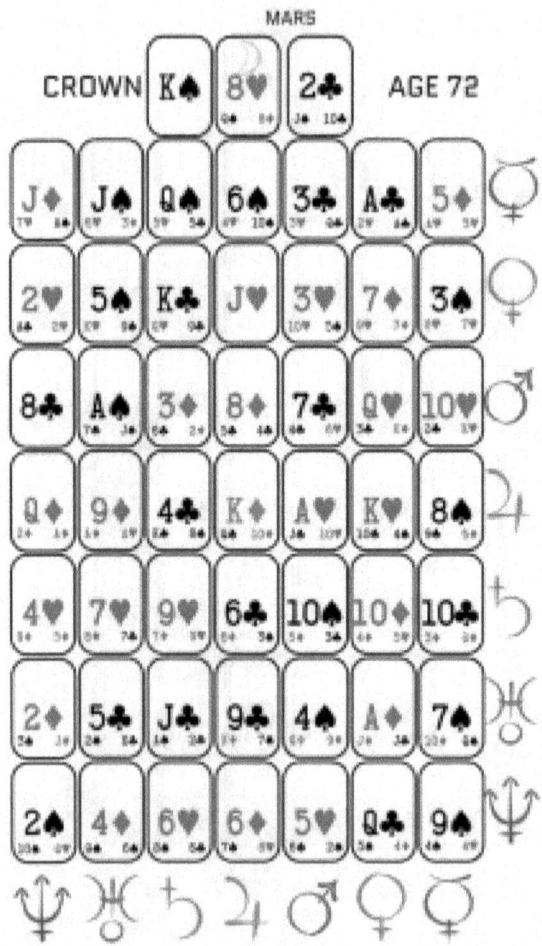

The Art of BEing HUman

Olusanya Bey

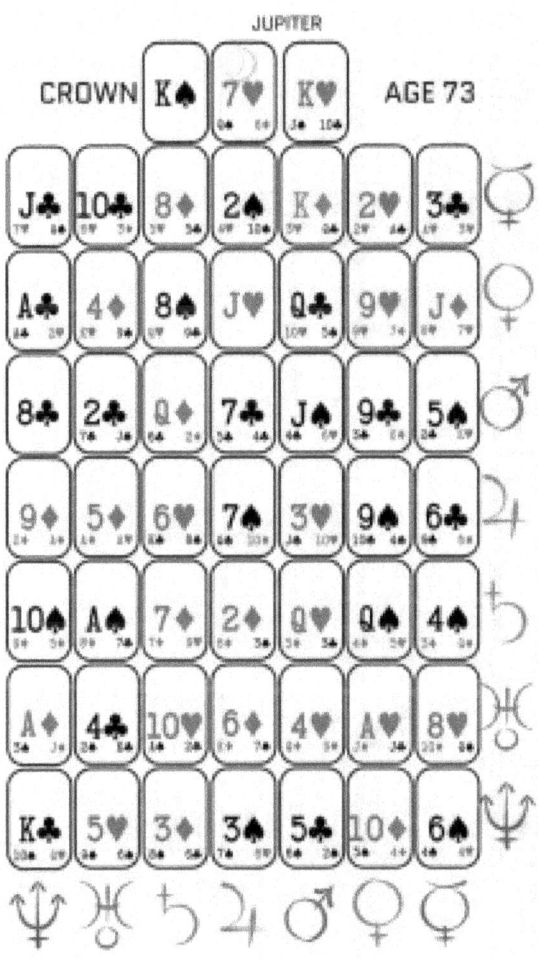

OlusanyaBey

The Art of BEing HUman

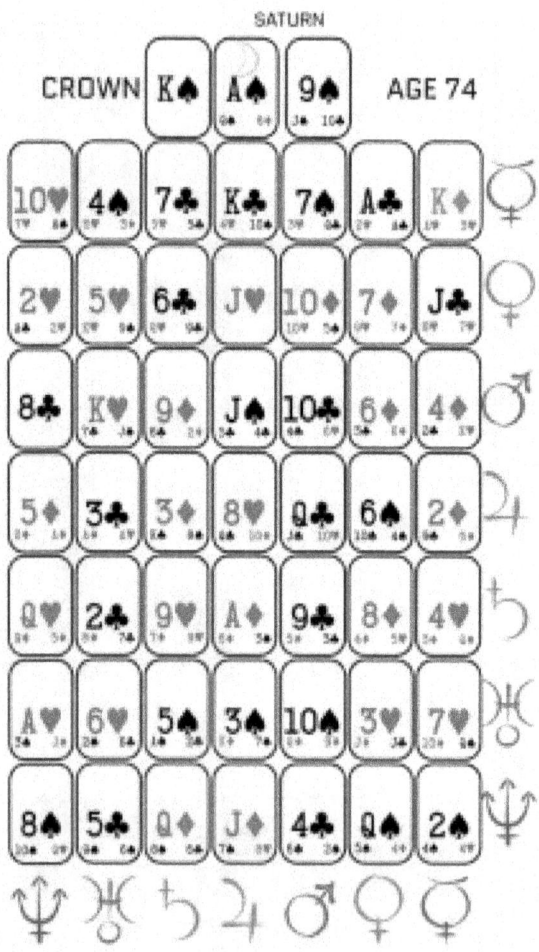

The Art of BEing HUman

Olusanya Bey

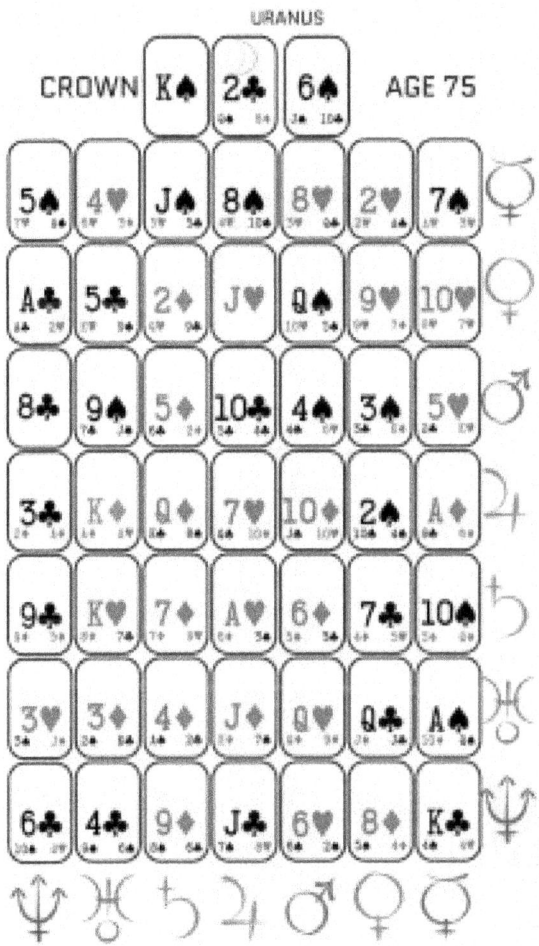

OlusanyaBey

The Art of BEing HUman

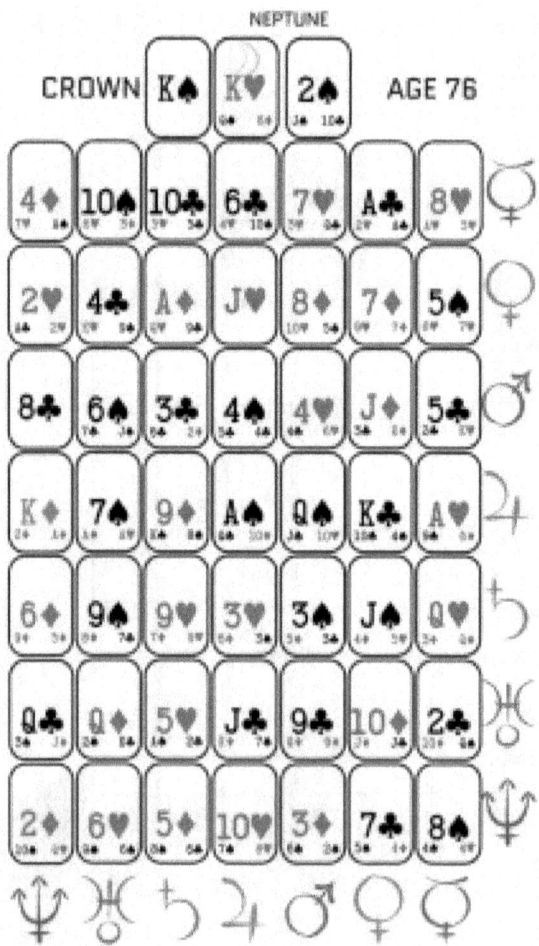

The Art of BEing HUman

Olusanya Bey

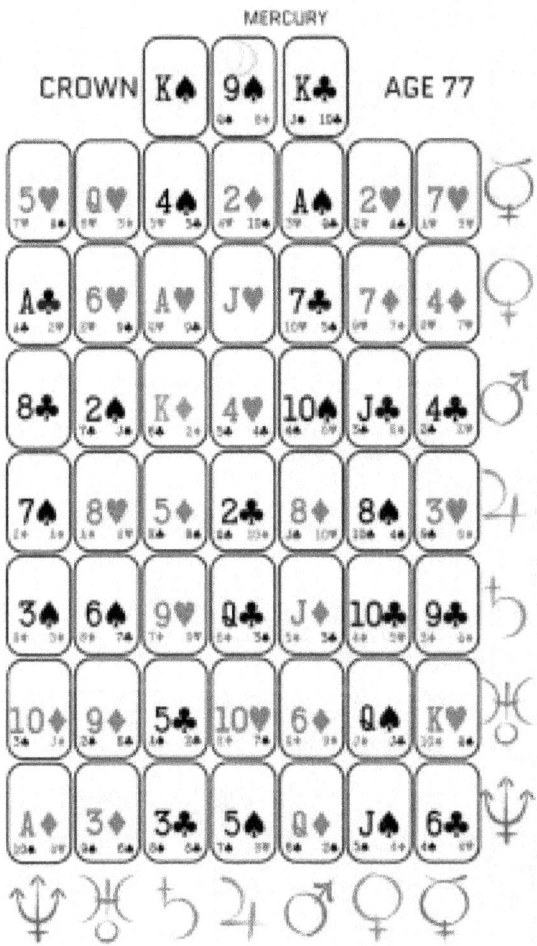

OlusanyaBey

The Art of BEing HUman

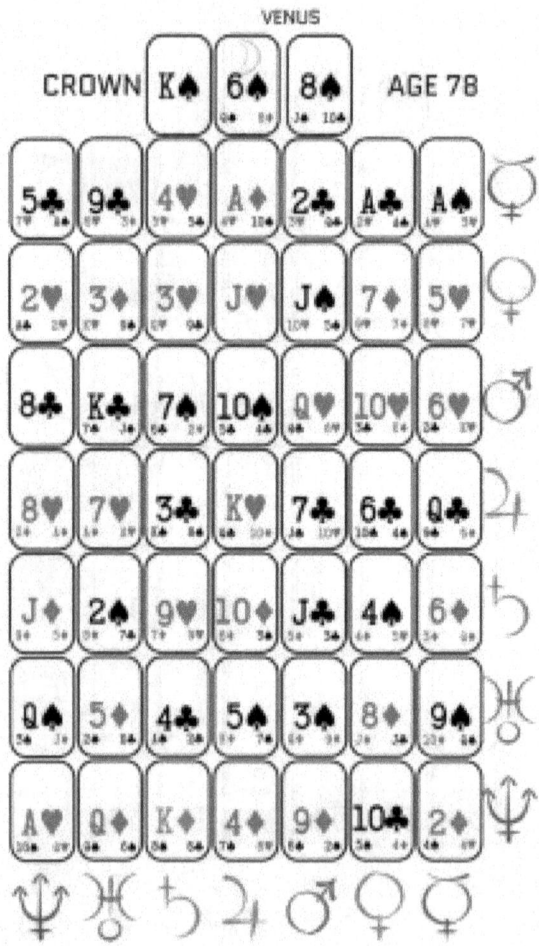

The Art of BEing HUman

Olusanya Bey

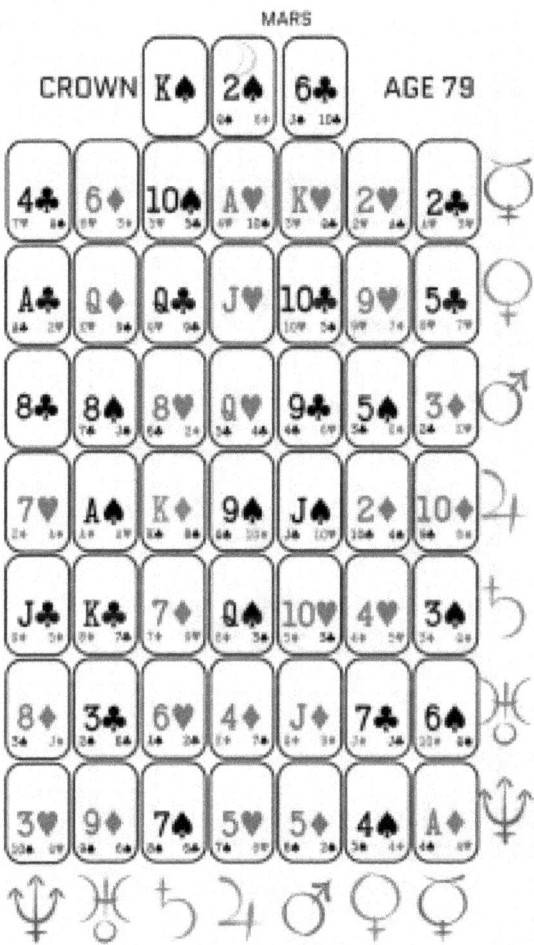

OlusanyaBey

The Art of BEing HUman

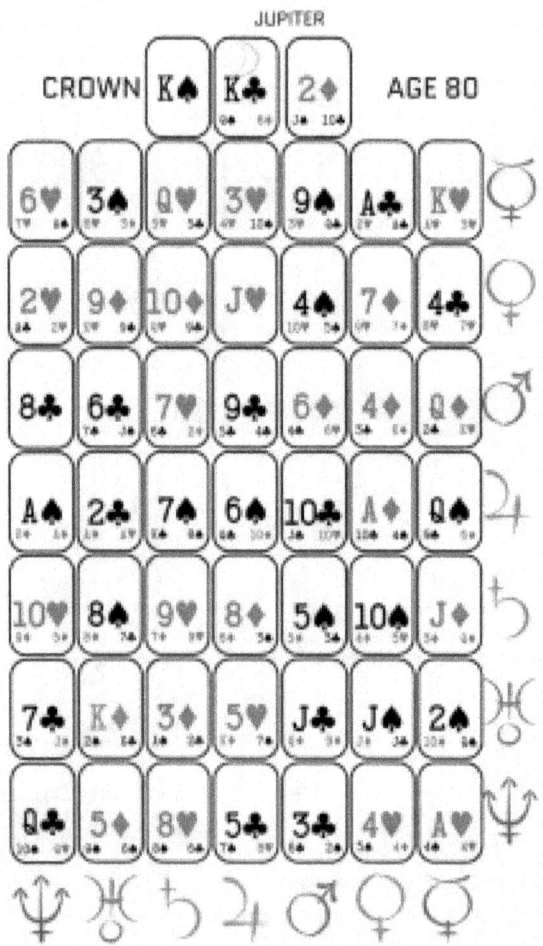

The Art of BEing HUman

Olusanya Bey

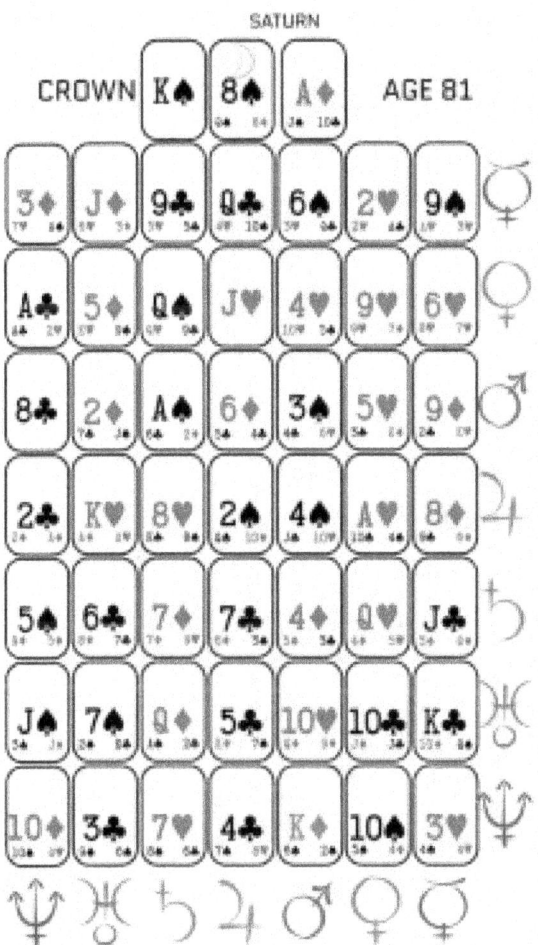

OlusanyaBey

The Art of BEing HUman

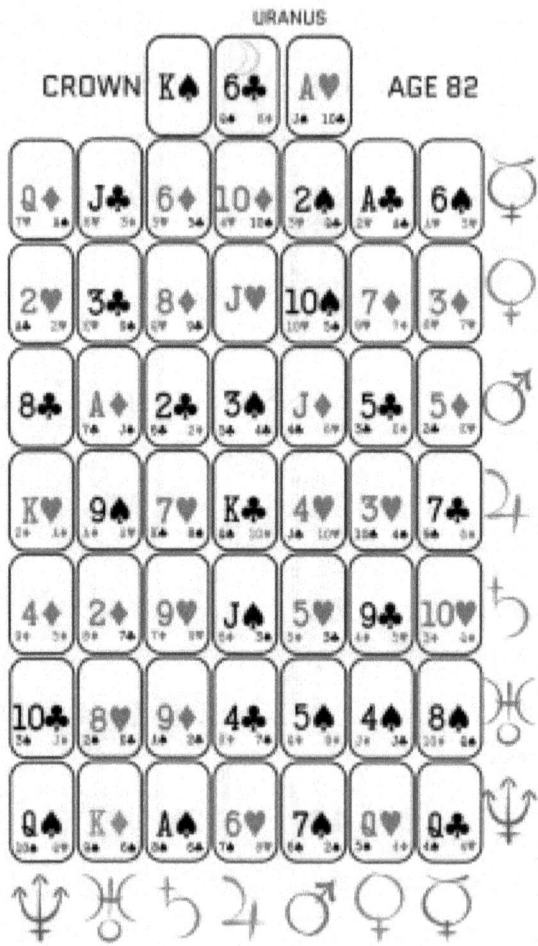

The Art of BEing HUman

Olusanya Bey

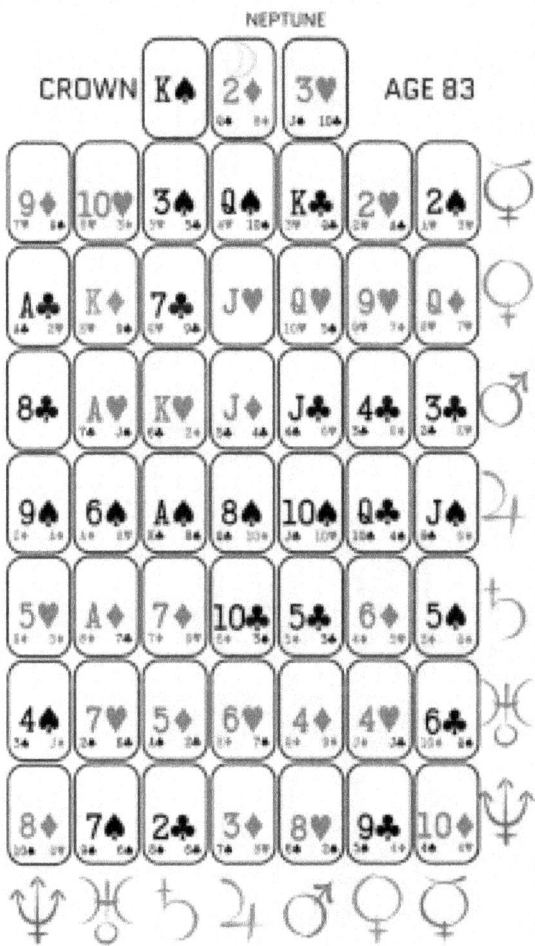

OlusanyaBey

The Art of BEing HUman

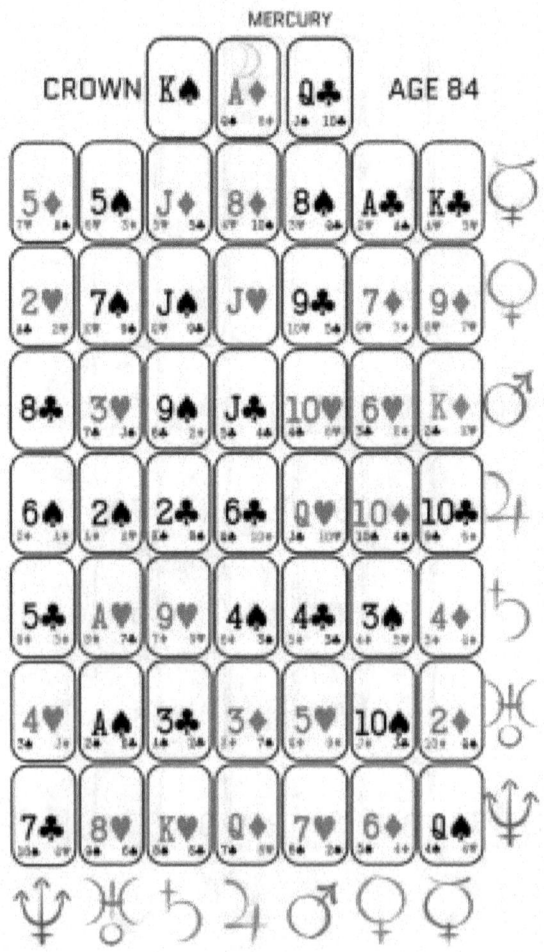

The Art of BEing HUman

Olusanya Bey

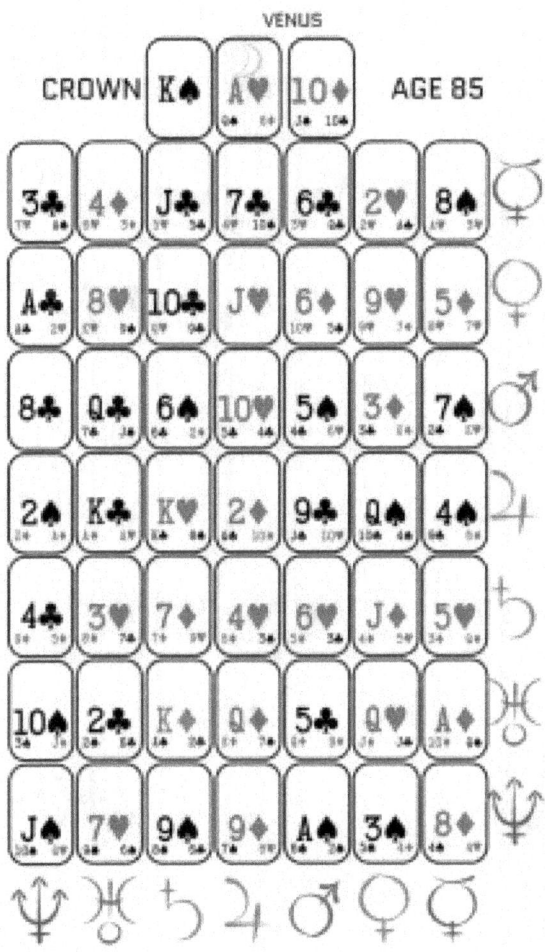

The Art of BEing HUman

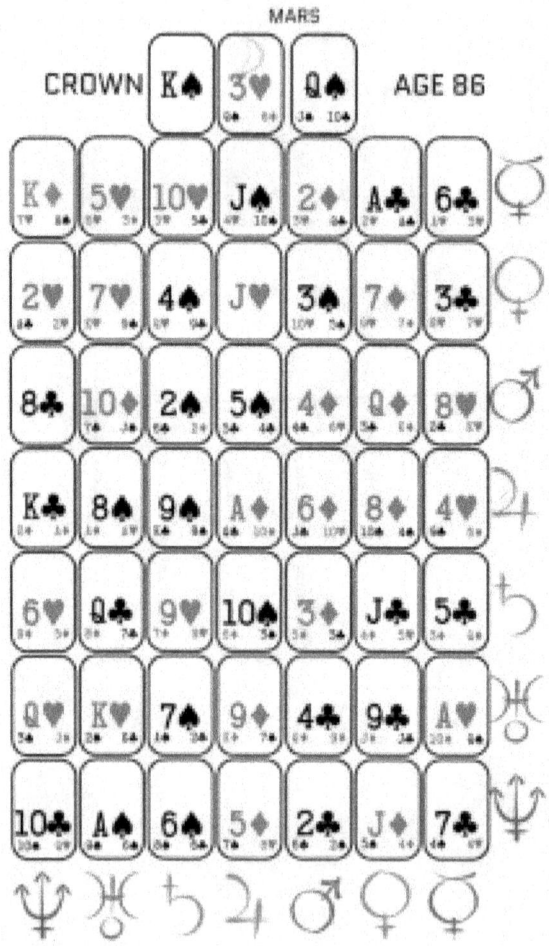

The Art of BEing HUman

Olusanya Bey

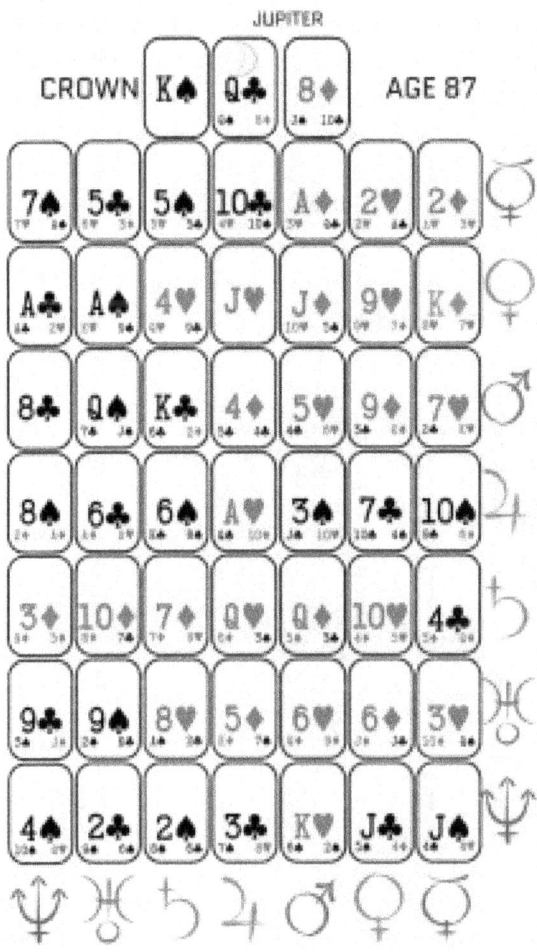

OlusanyaBey

The Art of BEing HUman

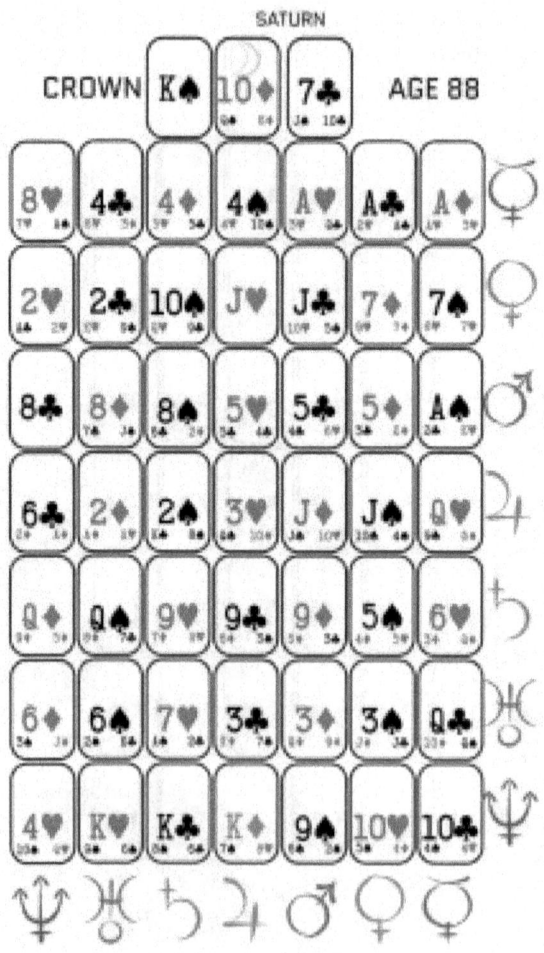

The Art of BEing HUman

Olusanya Bey

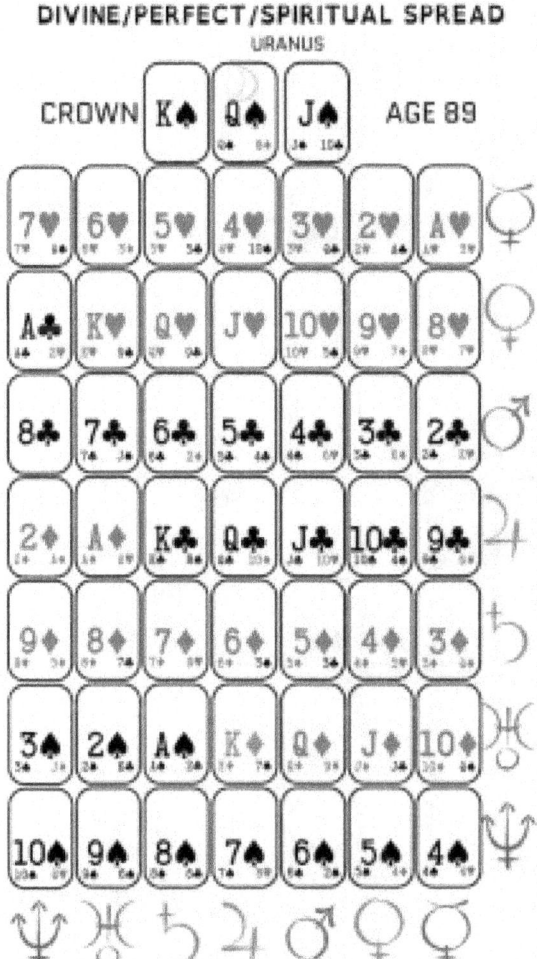

OlusanyaBey

The Art of BEing HUman

MUNDANE/EARTHLY/MATERIAL SPREAD
NEPTUNE

CROWN K♠ 8♦ 10♣ AGE 90

A♠	3♦	5♣	10♠	Q♣	A♣	3♥	☿
2♥	9♠	9♣	J♥	5♠	7♦	7♥	♀
8♣	J♠	2♦	4♣	6♥	K♦	K♥	♂
A♦	A♥	8♠	10♦	10♥	4♠	6♦	♃
5♦	7♣	9♥	3♠	3♣	5♥	Q♦	♄
J♦	K♣	2♣	7♠	9♦	J♣	Q♠	♅
Q♥	6♠	6♣	8♥	2♠	4♦	4♥	♆

♆ ♅ ♄ ♃ ♂ ♀ ☿

The Art of BEing HUman

Olusanya Bey

FINDING YOUR DAILY CARDS

For the purpose of these instructions we are going to find the 7-Day/Weekly cards spread for a 4♦ with an August 9ᵗʰ birthdate.

1. To begin, locate the birthday in question on the 7 Day Chart, this is your starting point.
2. Next, within the same column, locate the current date. Today's date is 10/28. Looking at our table we can see that 10/28 falls between the weeks 10/25 and 11/1, so we will use 10/25 as the start of our week.
3. -the current week you are in. In this case that is 10/25, there are 12 weeks between 8/9 and 10/25. Make a note of this number.
4. Now go to the 7 Day Progressions Chart and locate the Plate/Quadrate number associated with the age of the person in question. In this case the individual is 36 years old. Looking at our chart we see that the Plate for a person age 36 is 72.
5. Take your 12 from step 3 add it to 72 and subtract 1 (12 + 72 - 1 = 83).
6. Go to your Solar Spreads/Quadrates and find Quadrate 83. Locate the birth card for this example. The 4♦ is positioned on the Uranus line, in the Saturn column. Now we can determine our 13 direct cards, as well as our vertical support cards.

The 7 daily cards, their vertical support cards and week-long influence cards for the 4♦ are as follows:

The Art of BEing HUman

Day 1	10/25 ☿	6♥	VS	5♣
Day 2	10/26 ♀	5♦	VS	10♥
Day 3	10/27 ♂	7♥	VS	J♣
Day 4	10/28 ♃	4♣	VS	Q♥
Day 5	10/29 ♄	10♦	VS	K♣
Day 6	10/30 ♅	9♣	VS	3♥
Day 7	10/31 ♆	8♥	VS	3♦

Along with our Planetary Day cards we also have our week-long influence cards, these cards give us further insight about our coming week:

♇ (Pluto)   3♦
♇ᵣ (TransPluto)   2♣
Cosmic Lesson   7♦
Cosmic Result   8♦
Cosmic Transformation 3♥
☽ (Moon)   4♥

We can also apply this procedure to our Planetary Ruling and Planetary Number Card. At this point, I want to clarify that while some individuals may read the Vertical Support cards of all 13 cards in a spread, I do not do this in my personal practice. It is my experience that our 7 planetary time-period cards will tell us the overall story of our week and we can fine-tune the details of this story with our week-long influence cards.

The Art of BEing HUman

Olusanya Bey

7 Day Chart

1	2	3	4	5	6	7
1-1	1-2	1-3	1-4	1-5	1-6	1-7
1-8	1-9	1-10	1-11	1-12	1-13	1-14
1-15	1-16	1-17	1-18	1-19	1-20	1-21
1-22	1-23	1-24	1-25	1-26	1-27	1-28
1-29	1-30	1-31	2-1	2-2	2-3	2-4
2-5	2-6	2-7	2-8	2-9	2-10	2-11
2-12	2-13	2-14	2-15	2-16	2-17	2-18
2-19	2-20	2-21	2-22	2-23	2-24	2-25
2-26	2-26	2-26	2-26	2-26	2-26	3-4
3-5	3-5	3-5	3-5	3-5	3-5	3-11
3-12	3-12	3-12	3-12	3-12	3-12	3-18
3-19	3-19	3-19	3-19	3-19	3-19	3-25
3-26	3-26	3-26	3-26	3-26	3-26	4-1
4-2	4-2	4-2	4-2	4-2	4-2	4-8
4-9	4-9	4-9	4-9	4-9	4-9	4-15
4-16	4-16	4-16	4-16	4-16	4-16	4-22
4-23	4-23	4-23	4-23	4-23	4-23	4-29
4-30	4-30	4-30	4-30	4-30	4-30	5-6
5-7	5-7	5-7	5-7	5-7	5-7	5-13
5-14	5-14	5-14	5-14	5-14	5-14	5-20
5-21	5-21	5-21	5-21	5-21	5-21	5-27
5-28	5-28	5-28	5-28	5-28	5-28	6-3
6-4	6-5	6-6	6-7	6-8	6-9	6-10
6-11	6-12	6-13	6-14	6-15	6-16	6-17
6-18	6-19	6-20	6-21	6-22	6-23	6-24
6-25	6-26	6-27	6-28	6-29	6-30	7-1
7-2	7-3	7-4	7-5	7-6	7-7	7-8
7-9	7-10	7-11	7-12	7-13	7-14	7-15
7-16	7-17	7-18	7-19	7-20	7-21	7-22
7-23	7-24	7-25	7-26	7-27	7-28	7-29
7-30	7-31	8-1	8-2	8-3	8-4	8-5
8-6	8-7	8-8	8-9	8-10	8-11	8-12
8-13	8-14	8-15	8-16	8-17	8-18	8-19
8-20	8-21	8-22	8-23	8-24	8-25	8-26
8-27	8-28	8-29	8-30	8-31	9-1	9-2
9-3	9-4	9-5	9-6	9-7	9-8	9-9
9-10	9-11	9-12	9-13	9-14	9-15	9-16
9-17	9-18	9-19	9-20	9-21	9-22	9-23
9-24	9-25	9-26	9-27	9-28	9-29	9-30
10-1	10-2	10-3	10-4	10-5	10-6	10-7
10-8	10-9	10-10	10-11	10-12	10-13	10-14
10-15	10-16	10-17	10-18	10-19	10-20	10-21
10-22	10-23	10-24	10-25	10-26	10-27	10-28
10-29	10-30	10-31	11-1	11-2	11-3	11-4
11-5	11-6	11-7	11-8	11-9	11-10	11-11
11-12	11-13	11-14	11-15	11-16	11-17	11-18
11-19	11-20	11-21	11-22	11-23	11-24	11-25
11-26	11-27	11-28	11-29	11-30	12-1	12-2
12-3	12-4	12-5	12-6	12-7	12-8	12-9
12-10	12-11	12-12	12-13	12-14	12-15	8-19
12-17	12-18	12-19	12-20	12-21	12-22	8-26
12-24	12-25	12-26	12-27	12-28	12-29	12-30
				PAWAH	TUUN	12-31

Catalog

7 Day Progressions

DAYS OF THE WEEK

Sheik Ibn al-'Arabi (known as the Greatest of Sufi Sheiks) tells us, that for every day there is a prophet from among the prophets, from whom descends a secret upon the heart of the verifying witness, a secret in which you take delight during your day and by which you know something of that which requires to be known. This only happens to those who possess a heart.

In my personal practice I use the following information to align myself with the daily energies of the week. For instance, regardless of which planet may be playing my card for any particular day, I also take into account the natural planetary owner of each day (ie. Today is Friday- Venus, I have Neptune playing the 9♣" How will Neptune function under the influence of Venus, how will this effect my expression of the 9♣?

I will also use the following information to choose a Divine Name/Neteru/Orisha to chant, be mindful of during the course of the day, so that I can attune myself to its energy and vibration. I will do this almost daily depending on my level of self-discipline, and always celebrate my incarnation day chanting the Divine Name for that day, aswell as my own name, praising and giving thanks to my Fultah, and praying and giving thanks to my Ancestors. This information comes from the Sufi tradition, but many cultures have similar correspondences to the days of the week, the reader may choose to use a system of correspondences from their own spiritual tradition.

As in all things spiritual... tap into your Indwelling Divinity (your Rabb) and submit/surrender to its guidance.

Sunday. Prophet Idris

Day 1: Sunday

If your day is Sunday, then Idrîs (Enoch) is your companion, so bother not with anyone! On the first day, i.e. Sunday, it is Idris who addresses you with a secret revealing to you the causes of things before the existence of their effects.

SUNDAY:

Arabic: Al-Ahad
Divine attribute: Hearing
Prophet: Idrîs
Planet (Arabic): Ash-Shams
Planet: Sun
Creating divine name: An-Nûr
Prayer: Imam
Constellation (Arabic): Simâk
Constellation: Arcturus
Heaven: Fourth
Earthly region: Fourth Arabic

letter: ن (Nun)

Commentary:

Each day of the week is ruled by a specific divine name. The Sun and its heavenly orb were created on Sunday. The Sun is the heart of the world and the heart of the seven heavens. God made it a place for the Pole of human spirits, Idrîs. Idrîs is the centre and he has been placed at the heart or the centre, because the Sun is the central, fourth heaven, out of seven heavens. This fourth heaven was created by the self-disclosure of the divine name an-Nûr, the Light. It has been called a high place by God (see Qur'an 19:57) because it is a heart, although the heaven above it, is higher in physical space. But God meant the highness of status. God created it in as-simâk, which is the central, 14th station of the 28 stations or 'mansions' of the Moon, and created its planet, the Sun, and its orb, and created the letter nûn out of it.

There are seven substitutes (abdâl) who are each responsible for one of the seven earthly regions. Every affair of knowledge in the First Day is from the matter of Idrîs. And every higher celestial effect on that day in the elements of air and fire is from the orbiting of the Sun and its supervision, which is entrusted to it by God.

As for what comes from the effect on the elements of water and earth on that day, it is from the motion of the fourth orb containing the Sun. The earthly place of the substitute (badal) who upholds that influence among the seven climes is in the fourth clime.

Why Idrîs? The model for the Sufis is the night journey (isra) where he went from the near temple (Mecca) to the far temple (Jerusalem) and then was taken upward through the planetary spheres and beyond -- to "within two bow lengths or nearer to Allah." In the planetary spheres, Muhammad met earlier prophets -- traditionally Adam (Moon), Jesus (Mercury), Joseph (Venus), Idrîs (Enoch/Elias) in the Sun, Aaron (Mars), Moses (Jupiter), Abraham (Saturn).

Monday. Prophet Adam
Day 2: Monday

If your day is Monday, then Adam is your companion in the interval of the two worlds. On Monday it is Adam who addresses you with a secret by which you come to know the reasons why the stations wax or wane.

MONDAY:

The Art of BEing HUman

Arabic: al-ithnayn
Divine attribute: Living
Prophet: Adam
Planet (Arabic): al-qamar
Planet: Moon
Creating divine name: al-Mubîn
Prayer: Ma'mûm
Constellation (Arabic): Iklîl
Constellation: Corona
Heaven: First
Earthly region: Seventh

Arabic letter: د *(Dal)*

Commentary:

The motion of Monday was created from the divine attribute of the Living One (al-Hayy) and through it life was in the world, so everything in the world start to become living on Monday. The Moon is in the first celestial sphere above the Earth. The divine name the Clarifying One, al-Mubîn, was intent on bringing into existence this lowest heaven and its planet, the Moon, on the second day of creation in the lunar mansion of Iklîl, the Crown, which is the 17th station of the 28 lunar stations, and the letter dâl is from the motion of this orb.

The Moon is the fastest moving planet in the heavens, moving to a lunar mansion every day, so it goes through all 28 lunar mansions in its "day", which equals 28 Earth days. From this motion the 28 letters of the alphabet are created, regardless of how they are written or spoken in different languages.

God made this first heaven the place for the first prophet Adam, since he is the first manifestation of the perfect human being.

The Art of BEing HUman

Olusanya Bey

Tuesday. Prophet Aaron
Day 3: Tuesday

If your day is Tuesday, then Aaron is your companion, so adhere to right guidance and John, the Baptist, will be your intimate, so cleave to purity and contentment. On Tuesday it is either Aaron or John who addresses you with a secret by which he comes to know what is beneficial or harmful about the influences that come upon you from the world of the unseen.

TUESDAY:

Arabic: al-thulâthâ'
Divine attribute: Seeing
Prophet: Aaron
Planet (Arabic): al-marrikh
Planet: Mars
Creating divine name: al-Qâhir
Prayer: 'Ishâ
Constellation (Arabic): 'Awwa
Constellation: Bootes Heaven:
Fifth
Earthly region: Third

Arabic letter: ل (Lam)

Commentary:

The motion of Tuesday was created from the divine attribute Seeing (basar), so there is no part of the world but that it is witnessing its Creator, i.e. in relation to its own individual essence, not the Essence of the Creator, because the Essence of God, the Creator, may not be seen. He may be seen only through the manifestation of His attributes throughout the creation.

The divine name the All-Prevailing (al-Qâhir) was intent on bringing into being the third heaven (the fifth from the Earth), so

He caused its distinctive spiritual reality to appear, along with its planet Mars, al-marrîkh, and its sphere and he made it the dwelling for Aaron. The existence of this planet and the motion of its sphere were in the lunar mansion 'Awwa, which is the 13th station of the 28 Moon stations on Tuesday. From the motion of this sphere appeared the letter lâm.

Wednesday. Prophet Jesus

Day 4: Wednesday

If your day is Wednesday, Jesus is your companion, so hold fast to holy life and persevere in the desert. On Wednesday it is Jesus who addresses you with a secret by which you come to know the completion of the stations, how they are sealed and by whom.

> WEDNESDAY:
>
> Arabic: al-arba'â'
> Divine attribute: Willing
> Prophet: Jesus
> Planet (Arabic): al-kâtib Planet: Mercury
> Creating divine name: al-Muhsî
> Prayer: 'Asr
> Constellation (Arabic): Zabana
> Constellation: Librae
> Heaven: Second
> Earthly region: Sixth
>
> Arabic letter: ت *(Ta)*

Commentary:

The motion of the forth day, i.e. Wednesday, came into existence from the divine attribute of Willing, al-irâda, so there is no part of the world but that it is seeking to glorify the One Who gave it existence.

Mercury is in the sixth sphere from the Earth and this heaven was created through the self-disclosure of the divine name the Enumerator, al-Muhsî. God created this heaven, its planet Mercury, the fourth day, i.e. Wednesday, and the letter tâ in the lunar mansion of the constellation Zabana. This is the 16th station of the 28 Moon mansions and He caused Jesus to dwell there.

The fourth day, Wednesday, is the centre of the week, just as the Sun occupies the central fourth. Thus it is the day of Light, Nûr. As Wednesday is the day of Jesus, it also alludes to his central position in time, as the seal of universal sainthood.

Thursday. Prophet Moses
Day 5: Thursday

If your day is Thursday, then Moses is your companion: for the covering is quite lifted away and you are addressed in the manner of an unveiling, not by any man or fire; and indeed the angel rejoiced while the devil withdrew.

On Thursday it is Moses who addresses you with a secret by which you come to know the religious prescriptions and the mysteries of intimate conversations.

THURSDAY:

Arabic: al-khamîs
Divine attribute: Power
Prophet: Moses
Planet (Arabic): al-mushtari
Planet: Jupiter

The Art of BEing HUman

Creating divine name: al-'Alîm
Prayer: Zuhr
Constellation (Arabic): Sirfa
Constellation: Virginis
Heaven: Sixth
Earthly region: Second

Arabic letter: ض *(Dad)*

Commentary:

The motion of Thursday came into existence from the divine attribute of power, i.e al-qudra, so there is no part of existence, but that it has been enabled to praise the One Who gave it existence.

Jupiter, al-mushtarî, is in the sixth heaven from the Earth and it and its sphere were brought into existence through the self-disclosure of the divine name the All-Knowing, al-'Alîm. God created this heaven, its planet, the fifth day and the letter dâd in the lunar manson of the constellation Sirfa, which is the 12th station of the 28 Moon stations. He made it a place for the prophet Moses.

Friday. Prophet Joseph

Day 6: Friday

If your day is Friday, then Joseph, possessor of the qualities of the passionate beloved, is your companion. On Friday it is Joseph who addresses you with a secret by which you come to know the mysteries of constant ascension through the stations, the divine decree and where it is established.

FRIDAY

Arabic: al-juma
Divine attribute: Knowing Prophet: Joseph
Planet (Arabic): al-zuhara
| Planet: Venus
Creating divine name: al-Musawwir
Prayer: Maghrib (sunset)
Constellation (Arabic): Ghafr
Constellation: Cover
Heaven: Third
Earthly region: Fifth

Arabic letter: ر (Ra)

Commentary:

Friday is a special day. Our souls received its secrets from our Lord on this day. The motion of Friday came into being through the divine attribute of knowledge, so there is no part of the world but that it knows the One Who gave it existence.

Venus is the second sphere of the heavens from the Earth and this heaven was brought into existence by the self-disclosure of the divine name al-Musawwir, the Designer. God created this heaven, its planet Venus, the Day of Gathering (Friday) and the letter râ' in the lunar mansion of the constellation Ghafr, which is the 15th station out of the 28 stations of the Moon and He made it a place for the prophet Joseph.

Saturday. Prophet Abraham
Day 7: Saturday

If your day is Saturday, then it is Abraham, so hasten to the honouring of your guest before he vanishes. On Saturday it is Abraham who addresses you with a secret whereby you come to know how to deal with enemies and when they are to be fought against, and this is the presence of the substitutes (abdâl).

SATURDAY

Arabic: as-sabt
Divine attribute: Speaking (kalâm)
Prophet: Abraham
Planet (Arabic): kaywân
Planet: Saturn
Creating divine name: ar-Rabb
Prayer: Maghrib (sunset)
Constellation (Arabic): Khirtân
Constellation: Mane
Heaven: Seventh
Earthly region: First

Arabic letter: ي (Ya)

Commentary:

The motion of Saturday was created from the divine attribute of speaking (kalâm), so everything in the existence glorifies in thanks of its Creator, but we don't understand their glorification.

Saturn (kaywân) is in the 7th sphere from the earth, and this heaven was created by the self-disclosure of the divine name ar-Rabb, the Lord. God created this heaven, its planet and the 'Day of Rest' (as-sabt), i.e. Saturday, in the lunar mansion of the constellation khirtân (also called az-Zabra) and it is in the 11th mansion of the 28 Moon mansions. He made it a dwelling place for the prophet Abraham.

Olusanya Bey

POESIS

WARNING! THIS LOVE POEM IS TWISTED

i been thinking 'bout words like...
love & silence cuz
i wreck silence every time i say it,
i place limitations on love every time i
seek to define your divinity
i wreck silence every time i say it "so
what is the point of a word?"
you say a ha!
i'm pointing at your full moon...
stop staring at my finger!
i place limitations on love
in every attempt to form words
capable of giving... a measure
to your formlessness
i am a poet, this poem has no time,
signature. to play,
music with words.
every time?
i seek to define your divinity
the words are not the point,
its where they're pointing
that is the center of this cipher...
the words circle the love i seek to circumscribe
i am forever,
looking for ways to say, "i love you!"
even though what that means to me...
cannot be put into words.
i mean... siriusly!
i just want to kiss your sacred flower
come... here... woman

OlusanyaBey

The Art of BEing HUman

stop staring at my finger!

The Art of BEing HUman

Olusanya Bey

SILENCE IS...

from golden silence
speak...
in silver tongues
bhija...
seed syllables
simple sighs of breath
words all grown up
become earth prayers
wild and sacred
worship...
before loyalty for ideas and
dogma.
once... we called it love
beautiful children
beautiful souls
your scripture resembles poetry
your poetry...
is beginning to resemble propaganda!
wRites of passage?
earth children are supposed to inherit
the... sun and wind
not hatred...
or a heritage of... hot air.
our love to... hate
will transform us into our own worst enemy
so let's give them... LOVE!
to talk about.
poetry or propaganda?
poet or pundit?
healing words or...
salt on the wounds?
Kua ba dati [NOW... is the time!]
make a decision.

OlusanyaBey

The Art of BEing HUman

word... sound... power...
our poetry...
will not change the world if it doesn't even change...
US!
speak...
in silver tongues
or let your silence...
be golden.

The Art of BEing HUman

Olusanya Bey

RISE!

I saw a picture...
within a photograph,
behind a picture painted by a woman...
become a love poem,
then transpose itself into a love song...
that no one could sing!
a love song that could not be   phrased...
because it's words touched souls so tenderly
it would be interpreted as gospel or...
scripture,
giving birth to new beliefs, new dogmas...
whole new religions,
and the unholy wars they bring.
that's what happens when
Angels fall... in love,
mimicking humans in their behavior.

an asura...
perhaps pan
plays a tune on his lyre,
slightly off key... in tones that tell tales of a
tainted loves redemption,
that only the mindful and
momentary enlightened can hear.
listen... to love's musical savior!
love is a dream with a...
haunting melody.
listen!
when your heart speaks in silence,
and love roars like a...
hungry lion.
lay down little lamb,
don't be afraid, trust...

The Art of BEing HUman

there is no pain when you are being devoured...
by love,
BE... devoured... you must...
like...

starving artists...
consumed by an appetite for creativity,
as the flames of their passions rise...
efforts... perspiring,
the flames... aspiring...
eating away at all illusions of separateness,
as loneliness senses it's... demise.
so... she
summons images from blank canvas,
in silence...
as I...
paint pictures with colorful words, and we...
watch as thee...
art of love creates...
from a pallete of feminine and masculine energies,
it renders... a perfect picture of creative spirits...
calling across space and time,
embodying human vessels, so... that...
IT... may take form.
see... love uses humans, like...
humans use art...
there's no Creator and creation,
just two sides of Attractive energy, that...
touches every heart,
and demonstrates...
[as HE craves... HER]
just how powerful love IS...
when we aspire,
following our creative passions fire... and
RISE...
towards love!

The Art of BEing HUman

Olusanya Bey

mimicking the Angels...
in OUR behavior!

The Art of BEing HUman

NO ORDINARY LOVE

A full moon appearing at night:
my view of her face amidst the pitch black of her hair.
My perception gives birth to thoughts of sadness:
tears fall upon my face;
this black narcissus shedding tears for a rose.
The quality of her aesthetic... is truly overwhelming:
even beauty becomes silent!
Her wonder; fleeting,
constantly escapes the pursuit of my thinking,
her nature... beyond the spectrum of my sight.
I seek to quiet my mind, so I do not tarnish her subtle essence
[my thoughts lack the finesse to fully perceive her].
This BEing true... how can I expect to see her correctly
with this clumsy organ called an eye?
Poetry's thief: whenever I seek to describe or explain her,
she... defeats me!
At every attempt I find myself at a loss for words;
they sprout wings and take flight.
Knowing that I am trying to define what has no definition....
they... want no part of this madness!
There are those who would lower their aspirations
[settle for an experience of... "ordinary love"]... —
sometimes, even I wish I could, but...
I can't.
THIS... IS! ...
no Ordinary Love.

The I.R.S., [k]nee-grows... and 10 40's

I remain a fugitive...
a fugee... a refugee...
from the I.R.S...
[Ignorance Related Slavery]
and the taxing of our...
gold minds.

see...
federal reserve notes...
be like...
washington and jefferson's I.O.U's...
promises that... afRakan chattle...
converted into 14th amendment citizens...
[its freedumb time!]
will still cover the national debt...

and the Ancestors...
blood... sweat... and tears...

at this rate... will keep new orleans so wet...
maafa bones that have been buried fathoms deep...
will creep... into our collective consciousness...
revealing ALL of our fears...
like...

what if our freedom can't be found in a book... or a buck?
what if our problem is... not enuff of us...
give a F@*#?

brothas and sistas dying in the congo mines...
and still the hip hop nation promotes bling bling...
[savages in the mind-less pursuit of... good times?]
while an american sista said, "that nigga don't luv U...
where's the diamond ring?"

OlusanyaBey

The Art of BEing HUman

that shit makes about as much sense as...
down payments on... fake hair!
is it just me... or have we lost our sense?

and why do we keep... giving away our cents?

we can't keep track of our senses...
while they track us in their census...

baa baa black sheep... have you any wool?
well massa... I had a nickel bag full...
but it went up in smoke like...
all of my... american dreams.
but thats whats cracking... right?

so middle-class Kneegrows [named Jones] submit 1040's, and...
lower-class Kneegrows [who forgot their names] sip 10 forties
[but not b4 they pour some out for the brothas/sistas in
lockdown]...

[meanwhile... 4 blocks from the whitehouse...
another low-income project gets... knocked down], and...
check it...
the I.R.S. has you thinking the only sure things in life are...
yeah... that's right... DEATH... and TAXES.
What about the suffering of the masses?

isn't it a bit ironic?
free individuals dont necessarily have to pay income tax... but they do,
to be free... individuals have to think... but they dont...

aint that some shit!

The Art of BEing HUman

Olusanya Bey

Why I... Smile

to exist as a... thought...
in a fertile mind... such as yours...
gives birth to a single smile...
folded upon itself a thousand times...
ten thousand times... so many times that...
it's energy becomes the collapsed light of a...
UNIverse unfolding... where...
I become your world... at the same time...
U become mine... and everything under the sum of...
these suns... is a child of... ONE!
thought... ONE!
aim... ONE! destiny.
deep... penetrating... thoughts...
shared... thru U and Me...
they're like... sex in the morning...
hugs before bedtime, and...
kisses while U dream. in other words... awake or asleep...
U are on my mind.
do I have to tell U...
it is the experience of U that makes me happy...or...
can U see it when I smile?
so... i'm going down...
to southern hemispheres where...
soul food abounds, flesh covered mounds...
nourish luv-starved spirits...
passion plays...
songs of desire for all who...
strive to live it, not just... hear it.
how have u come to hear my soul so well?
opening spaces in my heart where...
SHE!
can be and... dwell... in an infinite bliss...
and thrill me endlessly like a... third-eye kiss.
this... luv for the world is... rooted in u!

OlusanyaBey

The Art of BEing HUman

so i_ drink your_ morning dew and_ spit!
luv poems in_ all of their faces_ your river runs_
deep within, filling_ all empty spaces_
i'm so glad_ u have come_ home.

BIBLIOGRAPHY

Works Cited

Amen, Ra Un Nefer. I Ching Praxis: 40 Years of Practical Insights Into the I Ching. Khamit Media TransVisions, 2014.

---. MAAT: The 11 Laws of God. Khamit Publications, 2003.

---. Men Ab: Kamitic Behavioral Transcendence Meditation. Khamit Media TransVisions, 2014.

---. Metu Neter: The Great Oracle of Tehuti and the Egyptian System of Spiritual Cultivation. Khamit Corpopration, 1990.

Ashby, Muata. The Kemetic Tree of Life Ancient Egyptian Metaphysics and Cosmology for Higher Consciousness. Sema Institute, 2008.

Bertschinger, Richard. Yijing, Shamanic Oracle of China. Singing Dragon, 2011, www.singingdragon.com.

Blavatsky, H. P. Isis Unveiled. Quest Books, 2015.

Butler, Octavia E. Parable of the Sower. Grand Central Publishing, 2023.

Camp, Robert Lee. Cards of Your Destiny. Sourcebooks, Inc., 2014.

---. Cartas Espiritus. Seven Thunders Publishing, 2017.

---. Exploring the Little Book of the Seven Thunders. Seven Thunders Publishing, 2012.

---. The Advanced Oracle Workbook. Seven Thunders Publishing, 1993.

Chandler, Wayne B. Ancient Future. Black Classic Press, 2000.

Crawford, Saffi, and Geraldine Sullivan. The Power of Playing Cards. Simon and Schuster, 2008.

Dunlop, Alexander. Play Your Cards Right. Life Elevated Publishing, 2017.

Gadalla, Moustafa. Egyptian Cosmology. Moustafa Gadalla, 2016.

---. Sacred Geometry And Numerology. Tehuti Research Foundation, 2016.

---. The Enduring Ancient Egyptian Musical System: Theory and Practice. Tehuti Research Foundation, 2017.

Heath, Richard. Precessional Time and the Evolution of Consciousness. Simon and Schuster, 2011.

---. Sacred Number and the Lords of Time. Simon and Schuster, 2014.

---. Sacred Number and the Origins of Civilization. Simon and Schuster, 2006.

---. The Harmonic Origins of the World. Simon and Schuster, 2018.

Hulusi, Ahmed. Decoding the Quran (a Unique Sufi Interpretation). Ahmed Hulusi, 2013.

---. Read! (The Reality Behind Muhammad's First Revelation). Allah, 2014.

Jones, Gina. Face Value. CreateSpace Independent Publishing, 2014.

Lein, Arne. What's Your Card? META-CARD, 1978.

Lubicz, R. A. Schwaller. A Study of Numbers. Simon and Schuster, 1986.

McLaren-Owens, Iain. The Primary Stages Explained: Suits, Numbers, Planets, The "Key" & Life Spreads. Astro-Cards Enterprises, 2020.

---. Universal Spread: The Ruling Cards of Time. Astro-Cards Enterprises, 1997.

Morrell, Thomas. The Ancient Book of Time, The Lost Mayan Time Codes. Awakening Visions, 2011.

---. The God Clock. Awakening Visions, 2015.

Muhammad, Ajaw Amaru Nama Taga Xi-Ali. Aboriginal Cosmology Instruction Manual Book 1, A Guide for the Book of the Ancestors Volume 1. International Indigenous Society, 2012.

---. Book of The Ancestors Volume 1 Introduction. International Indigenous Society, 2012.

Onstott, Scott. Taking Measure. CreateSpace, 2012.

Pottenger, Milton Alberto. Symbolism: A Treatise on the Soul of Things; How the Natural World Is but a Symbol of the Real World; the Modern Church, with Its Spire and Cross, and the Bible Account of Noah's Ark Symbols of the Phalic Religion. Symbol Publishing Company, 1905.

Randall, Edith, and Florence Evylinn Campbell. Sacred Symbols of the Ancients. DeVorss, 2018.

Richmond, Olney H. THE MYSTIC TEST BOOK or The Magic of The Cards. The Temple Publishing Company, 1893.

Schmalz, John Barnes. Nuggets From King Solomon's Mine (Classic Reprint). Forgotten Books, 2015.

Wen, Benebell. Holistic Tarot. North Atlantic Books, 2015.

---. I Ching, the Oracle. North Atlantic Books, 2023.

www.ingramcontent.com/pod-product-compliance
Lightning Source LLC
Chambersburg PA
CBHW062006180426
43198CB00037B/2441